ONE OF THE BEST BOOKS OF THE YEAR

The New York Times

USA Today

Time

Los Angeles Times

San Francisco Chronicle

· Essence

O: The Oprah Magazine

The Week

Kirkus Reviews

FINALIST

PEN/Jean Stein Book Award

Los Angeles Times Book Prize

Dayton Literary Peace Prize

"Indispensable . . . bracing . . . compelling . . .
A new book from Coates is not merely a literary
event. It's a launch from Cape Canaveral."

—JENNIFER SENIOR,
THE NEW YORK TIMES

'Eloquently unfurls blunt truths . . . Such a voice, in such a moment, is a ray of light." — *USA TODAY*

"There is a fresh clarity to [Coates's] voice—urgent, outraged, electric—that's never felt more necessary." —*Entertainment Weekly*

"It is a look at the history of race in America. It is an unapologetic laying out of facts. More than anything, *We Were Eight Years in Power* settles an argument: If, by chance, we ever came together to draft someone to pen the story of being black in America, there is no doubt that Ta-Nehisi Coates should be the consensus first-round pick. . . . The compilation of essays . . . examines every detail of the first black presidency in microscopic, high-definition detail. . . . *We Were Eight Years in Power* is a detailed examination of Obama's America, but its findings are, in truth, Coates's historically informed diagnosis of America itself. It is an annotated, full-throated analysis of the historical disease of white supremacy, often euphemized as "American greatness," and how it led to the terminal condition of Trumpism. That is why, with the first pick of 2017, black America, for its unequivocal, unabashed truth, selects Ta-Nehisi Coates's *We Were Eight Years in Power*." —*The Root*

"A new book from Coates is not merely a literary event. It's a launch from Cape Canaveral. There's a lot of awe, heat, resistance. . . . *We Were Eight Years in Power* is . . . a selection of Coates's most influential pieces [but] the book is actually far more than that. . . . [Coates is] the pre-eminent black public intellectual of his generation."
—Jennifer Senior, *The New York Times*

"Coates has become one of the most vital and respected voices in the cultural and political conversation. This newest collection pairs some of his most widely-shared *Atlantic* pieces . . . with new work exploring Coates's personal thoughts on Obama's tenure in the White House. Part memoir, part historical journalism, *We Were Eight Years in Power* is an essential text to help us understand the America we're living in today." —*W* magazine

"Raw and hard to read. You'll never forget his point of view, nor should you."   —*Glamour*

"*We Were Eight Years in Power* is more than a "loose memoir"; it's Coates giving himself a deep read, and inviting us to join him in this look at his intellectual journey. And by showcasing a range of essays . . . he asks his readers to consider him as a writer, nothing more and nothing less."   —*Slate*

"Coates . . . eloquently unfurls blunt truths in his latest book. . . . There is no sugarcoating, no effort to cloak the nation's underbelly in order to soothe those who do not want to believe it exists. Some may find Coates's words validating. Others may pronounce them a bleak sermon or even a eulogy for the dashed possibilities imagined by some when Obama was first elected. But however you see this collection, there is no disputing that Coates writes what he means and speaks what he feels. To have such a voice, in such a moment, is a ray of light."   —*USA Today*

"As [Coates] explains throughout these pages, black Americans struggle out of fear for their and their children's lives; they struggle to avoid their feelings. . . . Coates's writing emerges from this struggle while articulating a way of holding this madness at bay aesthetically and intellectually. . . . Across his oeuvre, Coates's prose style and literary prowess are hip-hop sharpened: he believes in the art of dexterous reference, potent, lyrical critique and political storytelling. . . . Coates couches his analyses in a synthesis of investigative and reported journalism, African American studies, political science, sociology, literary criticism and American history. Coates fronts each piece with context-shaping, prefatory narratives. In total, the personal writing develops a portrait of the artist. . . . Reading American life through Coates' lens these last eight years has forced his many readers (myself included) to improve their own habits of reasoning and skills for argumentation.

As the best critics do, Coates draws us into conversation, into argument, rather than closing off discourse with canned proclamations or static resolutions. . . . By the end of *We Were Eight Years in Power* we can hear the Jim Crow South echoing loudly in the Trump administration."
—Baltimore *Sun*

"A collection of the major magazine essays [Coates] wrote throughout the Obama years . . . But Coates adds an unexpected element that renders *We Were Eight Years in Power* both new and revealing. Interspersed among the essays are introductory personal reflections. . . . Together, these introspections are the inside story of a writer at work, with all the fears, insecurities, influences, insights and blind spots that the craft demands. . . . I would have continued reading Coates during a Hillary Clinton administration, hoping in particular that he'd finally write the great Civil War history already scattered throughout his work. Yet reading him now feels more urgent, with the bar set higher."
—Carlos Lozada, *The Washington Post*

"Coates's collection of his essays from the past decade examines the recurrence of certain themes in the black community. . . . As he charts social changes, Coates also offers a fascinating look at his own transformation as a black man and a writer. . . . Coates is a crucial voice in the public discussion of race and equality, and readers will be eager for his take on where we stand now and why."
—*Booklist* (starred review)

"Though the essays are about a particular period, Coates's themes reflect broader social and political phenomena. It's this timeless timeliness—reminiscent of the work of George Orwell and James Baldwin—that makes Coates worth reading again and again."
—*Publishers Weekly* (starred review)

"Biting cultural and political analysis from the award-winning journalist . . . [Coates] reflects on race, Barack Obama's presidency and its jarring aftermath, and his own evolution as a writer in eight stunningly incisive essays. . . . [He] contextualizes each piece with candid personal revelations, making the volume a melding of memoir and critique. . . . His conclusions are disquieting, his writing passionate, his tenor often angry. . . . Although Coates subtitles the book 'An American Tragedy,' he allows a ray of hope for 'a resistance intolerant of self-exoneration, set against blinding itself to evil.' Emotionally charged, deftly crafted, and urgently relevant essays." —*Kirkus Reviews* (starred review)

WE WERE EIGHT YEARS IN POWER

—

WE WERE
EIGHT YEARS
IN POWER

An
AMERICAN TRAGEDY

TA-NEHISI
COATES

—

ONE WORLD
NEW YORK

2018 One World Trade Paperback Edition

Copyright © 2017 by BCP Literary, Inc.

Published in the United States by One World, an imprint of Random House,
a division of Penguin Random House LLC, New York.

ONE WORLD and its colophon are registratered trademarks
of Penguin Random House LLC.

Originally published in hardcover in the United States by
One World, an imprint of Random House, a division of
Penguin Random House LLC, in 2017.

Grateful acknowledgment is made to *The Atlantic* for permission to reprint the
following articles by Ta-Nehisi Coates originally published in *The Atlantic:*
"This Is How We Lost to the White Man" and "American Girl," copyright © 2009
by Ta-Nehisi Coates; "The Legacy of Malcolm X," copyright © 2011 by Ta-Nehisi Coates;
"Why Do So Few Blacks Study the Civil War?" and "Fear of a Black President,"
copyright © 2012 by Ta-Nehisi Coates; "The Case for Reparations,"
copyright © 2014 by Ta-Nehisi Coates; "The Black Family in the Age of
Mass Incarceration," copyright © 2015 by Ta-Nehisi Coates; "My President Was Black,"
copyright © 2016 by Ta-Nehisi Coates. Reprinted by permission of *The Atlantic.*

LIBRARY OF CONGRESS CATALOGING-IN-PUBLICATION DATA
Names: Coates, Ta-Nehisi, author.
TITLE: We were eight years in power : an American tragedy / by Ta-Nehisi Coates.
DESCRIPTION: First edition. | New York : One World, 2017.
IDENTIFIERS: LCCN 2017039343 | ISBN 9780399590573 | ISBN 9780399590580 (ebook)
SUBJECTS: LCSH: United States—Race relations—21st century. | African Americans—
Social conditions—21st century. | United States—Politics and government—2009-2017. |
Coates, Ta-Nehisi—Political and social views. | Obama, Barack—Influence.
CLASSIFICATION: LCC E185.615 .C6336 2017 | DDC 305.896/0730905—dc23
LC record available at lccn.loc.gov/2017039343
International edition ISBN 978-0-525-51028-4

Printed in the United States of America on acid-free paper

oneworldlit.com
randomhousebooks.com

468975

Book design by Barbara M.Bachman

To Kenyatta, Tom, Nikola and Amelie,
who went with me into the deep,
and saw me back to shore

"We don't just shine, we illuminate the whole show."

—JAY-Z

CONTENTS

INTRODUCTION

REGARDING GOOD NEGRO GOVERNMENT

IN 1895, TWO DECADES AFTER HIS STATE MOVED FROM THE egalitarian innovations of Reconstruction to an oppressive "Redemption," South Carolina congressman Thomas Miller appealed to the state's constitutional convention:

> We were eight years in power. We had built schoolhouses, established charitable institutions, built and maintained the penitentiary system, provided for the education of the deaf and dumb, rebuilt the ferries. In short, we had reconstructed the State and placed it upon the road to prosperity.

By the 1890s, Reconstruction had been painted as a fundamentally corrupt era of "Negro Rule." It was said that South Carolina stood under threat of being "Africanized" and dragged into barbarism and iniquity. Miller hoped that by highlighting black achievement in governance and marshaling a credible defense of black morality, he might convince the doubtlessly fair-minded people of South

Carolina to preserve the citizenship rights of African Americans. His plea went unheeded. The 1895 constitution added both literacy tests and property requirements as qualifications for enfranchisement. When those measures proved insufficient to enforcing white supremacy, black citizens were shot, tortured, beaten, and maimed.

Assessing Miller's rebuttal and the 1895 convention, W.E.B. Du Bois made a sobering observation. From Du Bois's perspective, the 1895 constitutional convention was not an exercise in moral reform, or an effort to purge the state of corruption. This was simply cover for the convention's true aim—the restoration of a despotic white supremacy. The problem was not that South Carolina's Reconstruction-era government had been consumed by unprecedented graft. Indeed, it was the exact opposite. The very successes Miller highlighted, the actual record of Reconstruction in South Carolina, undermined white supremacy. To redeem white supremacy, that record was twisted, mocked, and caricatured into something that better resembled the prejudices of white South Carolina. "If there was one thing that South Carolina feared more than bad Negro government," wrote Du Bois, "it was good Negro government."

The fear had precedent. Toward the end of the Civil War, having witnessed the effectiveness of the Union's "colored troops," a flailing Confederacy began considering an attempt to recruit blacks into its army. But in the nineteenth century, the idea of the soldier was heavily entwined with the notion of masculinity and citizenship. How could an army constituted to defend slavery, with all of its assumptions about black inferiority, turn around and declare that blacks were worthy of being invited into Confederate ranks? As it happened, they could not. "The day you make a soldier of them is the beginning of the end of our revolution," observed Georgia politician Howell Cobb. "And if slaves seem good soldiers, then our whole theory of slavery is wrong." There could be no win for white supremacy here. If blacks proved to be the cowards that "the whole theory of slavery" painted them as, the battle would literally be lost. But much worse, should they fight effectively—and prove themselves capable of "good Negro government"—then the larger war could never be won.

The central thread of this book is eight articles written during the eight years of the first black presidency—a period of Good Negro Government. Obama was elected amid widespread panic and, in his eight years, emerged as a caretaker and measured architect. He established the framework of a national healthcare system from a conservative model. He prevented an economic collapse and neglected to prosecute those largely responsible for that collapse. He ended state-sanctioned torture but continued the generational war in the Middle East. His family—the charming and beautiful wife, the lovely daughters, the dogs—seemed pulled from the Brooks Brothers catalogue. He was not a revolutionary. He steered clear of major scandal, corruption, and bribery. He was deliberate to a fault, saw himself as the keeper of his country's sacred legacy, and if he was bothered by his country's sins, he ultimately believed it to be a force for good in the world. In short, Obama, his family, and his administration were a walking advertisement for the ease with which black people could be fully integrated into the unthreatening mainstream of American culture, politics, and myth.

And that was always the problem.

One strain of African American thought holds that it is a violent black recklessness—the black gangster, the black rioter—that strikes the ultimate terror in white America. Perhaps it does, in the most individual sense. But in the collective sense, what this country really fears is black respectability, Good Negro Government. It applauds, even celebrates, Good Negro Government in the unthreatening abstract—*The Cosby Show,* for instance. But when it becomes clear that Good Negro Government might, in any way, empower actual Negroes over actual whites, then the fear sets in, the affirmative-action charges begin, and birtherism emerges. And this is because, at its core, those American myths have never been colorless. They cannot be extricated from the "whole theory of slavery," which holds that an entire class of people carry peonage in their blood. That peon class provided the foundation on which all those myths and conceptions were built. And as much as we can theoretically imagine a seamless black integration into the American myth, the white part of this country remembers the myth as it was conceived.

I think the old fear of Good Negro Government has much explanatory power for what might seem a shocking turn—the election of Donald Trump. It has been said that the first black presidency was mostly "symbolic," a dismissal that deeply underestimates the power of symbols. Symbols don't just represent reality but can become tools to change it. The symbolic power of Barack Obama's presidency—that whiteness was no longer strong enough to prevent peons from taking up residence in the castle—assaulted the most deeply rooted notions of white supremacy and instilled fear in its adherents and beneficiaries. And it was that fear that gave the symbols Donald Trump deployed—the symbols of racism—enough potency to make him president, and thus put him in position to injure the world.

There is a basic assumption in this country, one black people are not immune to, which holds that if blacks comport themselves in a way that accords with middle-class values, if they are polite, educated, and virtuous, then all the fruits of America will be open to them. In its most vulgar form, this theory of personal Good Negro Government denies the existence of racism and white supremacy as meaningful forces in American life. In its more nuanced and reputable form, the theory pitches itself as an equal complement to antiracism. But the argument made in much of this book is that Good Negro Government—personal and political—often augments the very white supremacy it seeks to combat. That is what happened to Thomas Miller and his colleagues in 1895. It is what happened to black people all through South Carolina during Redemption. It is what happened to black people on the South Side of Chicago during the postwar implementation of the New Deal. And it is what, I contend, is right now happening to the legacy of the country's first black president.

Each of the essays in the book takes up some aspect of an ongoing argument, mostly in my own head, about the utility and place of Good Negro Government. They are me in motion, thinking matters through, a process that continues even as I write this introduction. I do not doubt, for instance, that, say, wearing a suit and tie affects how some sectors of people react to one another. I'm just not sure that lack of a suit and tie is the real problem. (In terms of Good Negro Government, Barack Obama was the best of us. And when he left office, a majority of the opposition party did not believe he was a citizen.) Before each of these essays there is a kind of extended blog post, one that attempts to capture why I was writing and where I was in my life at the time. Taken together they form a loose memoir, one that I hope enhances the main pieces. At the end of the book, there is an epilogue that attempts to assess the post-Obama age in which we now find ourselves.

I wanted these articles—all eight of them originally published in *The Atlantic*—collected in a single volume. But I also had an urge to try to make something new of them. This book is made in this way because I enjoyed the challenge of doing so. If I can communicate half of that joy to you, then I will have done my job.

WE WERE EIGHT YEARS IN POWER

I.

NOTES FROM
THE
FIRST YEAR

———

THIS STORY BEGAN, AS ALL WRITING MUST, IN FAILURE. IT WAS
February 2007. I was seated in a state office building on 125th Street,
not far from the Jamaican patty joint, not far from the fried fish
spot, both of which I put to so much injudicious use in those days
of conspicuous failure. I was thirty-one years old. I was living in
Harlem with my partner, Kenyatta, and our son, Samori, both
named for African anti-colonialists, of consecutive centuries. The
names reflected a household ostensibly committed to the dream of
pan-Africa, to the notion that black people here and now are united
with black people there and then in a grand operatic struggle. This
idea was the deep subtext of our lives. It had to be. The visible text
was survivalist.

I had just lost my third job in seven years and so I'd come to that
state office building for a brief seminar on work, responsibility, and
the need to stay off the dole. "The dole" was small, time-limited,
and humiliating to access. How anyone could enjoy or accustom
themselves to it was beyond me. But the ghost of welfare reform
past was strong and haunted the halls of unemployment offices ev-

erywhere. There in a classroom, amid a cohort of presumed losers and layabouts, I took my lessons in the great sin of idleness. The venue at least felt appropriate; the classroom had always been the site of my most indelible failures and losses. In the classrooms of my youth, I was forever a "conduct" problem, forever in need of "improvement," forever failing to "work up to potential." I wondered then if something was wrong with me, if there was some sort of brain damage that compelled me to color outside the lines. I'd felt like a failure all of my life—stumbling out of middle school, kicked out of high school, dropping out of college. I had learned to tread in this always troubled water. But now I felt myself drowning, and now I knew I would not drown alone.

Kenyatta and I had been together for nine years, and during that time I had never been able to consistently contribute a significant income. I was a writer and felt myself part of a tradition stretching back to a time when reading and writing were, for black people, the marks of rebellion. I believed, somewhat absurdly, that they still were. And so I derived great meaning from the work of writing. But I could not pay rent with "great meaning." I could not buy groceries with "great meaning." With "great meaning" I overdrew accounts. With "great meaning" I burned through credit cards and summoned the IRS. Wild and unlikely schemes often appeared before me. Maybe I should go to culinary school. Maybe I should be a bartender. I'd considered driving a cab. Kenyatta had a more linear solution: "I think you should spend more time writing."

At that moment, in that classroom, going through all the mandated motions, I could not see it. I could not see anything. And like almost every other lesson administered to me in a classroom, I don't remember a single thing said that day. And as with all the other buried traumas accumulated in the classrooms, I did not allow myself to feel the ache of that failure. Instead, I fell back on the old habits and logic of the street, where it was so often necessary to deny humiliation and transmute pain into rage. So I took the agony of that era like a collection notice and hid it away in the upper dresser of the mind, resolved to return to it when I had means to pay. I think now, today, I have settled almost all of those old accounts. But the ache and aftershock of failure remain long after the drawer is bare.

I can somehow remember all that I did not allow myself to feel walking away from the unemployment office and through the Harlem streets that day, just as I remember all that I did not let myself feel in those young years trapped between the schools and the street. And I know that there are black boys and black girls out there lost in a Bermuda triangle of the mind or stranded in the doldrums of America, some of them treading and some of them drowning, never feeling and never forgetting. The most precious thing I had then is the most precious thing I have now—my own curiosity. That is the thing I knew, even in the classroom, they could not take from me. That is the thing that buoyed me and eventually plucked me from the sea.

Like any myth of self-generated success, there is some truth here. But the greater truth is that the wind around me awakened and shifted to blow my small vessel back to civilization. My curiosity had long been focused on the color line, a phenomenon that, in those mid-aughts, seemed in an odd flux. National energies had shifted in the wake of 9/11. The most crucial questions of justice during the Bush years revolved around spying and torture. The old civil rights generation was aging out, and there was a general fatigue, even among black activists, with the paratrooper model of leadership represented by Jesse Jackson and Al Sharpton. The choreography had gotten repetitive. Some outrage would be perpetrated. A march would be held. Predictable positions and platitudes exchanged. And the original offense would fade from memory. The outrage was, most often, crucial and very real—the killing of Sean Bell by the NYPD, for instance. But the lack of any substantive action, and, more, the fact that the tactics seemed to not have changed in some forty years, made many of us feel that we were not witnessing movement politics so much as a kind of cathartic performance. Outside of the activist community, a different idea was ascendant, the notion that we needed to, somehow, "get past" the "distraction" of racism. There were books lamenting the deployment of the so-called race card and articles asserting the need to "look beyond" race in understanding the perils of the black community. No matter how sincere or disingenuous its expression, there was a palpable hunger for something new.

In the same season I found myself in that Harlem unemployment office recounting failures, Barack Obama launched his bid for the presidency.

I had never seen a black man like Barack Obama. He talked to white people in a new language—as though he actually trusted them and believed in them. It was not my language. It was not even a language I was much interested in, save to understand how he had come to speak it and its effect on those who heard it. More interesting to me was that he had somehow balanced that language with the language of the South Side. He referred to himself, unambiguously, as a black man. He had married a black woman. It is easy to forget how shocking this was, given the common belief at the time that there was a direct relationship between success and assimilation. The narrative held that successful black men took white wives and crossed over into that arid no-man's-land that was not black, though it could never be white. Blackness for such men was not a thing to root yourself in but something to evade and escape. Barack Obama found a third way—a means of communicating his affection for white America without fawning over it. White people were enchanted by him—and those who worked in newsrooms seemed most enchanted of all. This fact changed my life. It was the wind shifting, without which my curiosity would've stayed my own.

My contention is that Barack Obama is directly responsible for the rise of a crop of black writers and journalists who achieved prominence during his two terms. These writers were talented—

but talent is nothing without a field on which to display its gifts. Obama's presence opened a new field for writers, and what began as curiosity about the man himself eventually expanded into curiosity about the community he had so consciously made his home and all the old, fitfully slumbering questions he'd awakened about American identity. I was one of those writers. And though I could not see it then, making that doleful trek home from the unemployment office, back from the classroom, back across 125th Street, the wind was waking all around me.

I HAD, IN MY LAST JOB, taken an interest in Bill Cosby, who also, it seemed, felt the call for something new. He was then touring the country's inner cities, intent on convincing his people to stop "blaming the white man." The barnstorming began seemingly on impulse, initiated by the response to Cosby's infamous Pound Cake speech. In 2004, Cosby rose to the podium to speak, ostensibly to mark the fiftieth-anniversary commemoration of the *Brown v. Board of Education* Supreme Court decision that ended school segregation, at an event sponsored by the NAACP Legal Defense and Educational Fund. The NAACP LDF made its name by appealing to the courts to hold the country accountable for the myriad ways Jim Crow plundered black life. But when Cosby took the stage, he was set on holding not the plunderer but the plundered accountable. He inveighed against "the lower-economic and lower-middle-economic people" for not holding up their end of the civil rights bargain. He attacked black youth for obsessing over "$500 sneakers." He mocked black parents for giving their children names like "Shaniqua and Mohammed." He fumed at black women for loose morality.

I objected to this characterization and wrote about it in *The Village Voice*—another job I'd lose—shortly after he made the speech. But as it happened, some portion of "the lower-economic and lower-middle-economic people" actually agreed with Cosby. I know this because I saw Cosby take the message to them directly. He dubbed these sessions "call-outs." Typically, Cosby would assemble local officials—school principals, judges, parole officers, heads of community colleges—and put them onstage. He'd invite various "at-risk youth" to the event. The officials would then do their own version of the Pound Cake speech. The audience would cheer wildly. The spirit was one part Uncle Ruckus and one part Les Brown. It was flagellation. It was revival. But most of all it was nostalgia—a hunger for the uncomplicated time when all black men worked hard, all black women were virtuous, and all black parents, collectively, whipped each other's kids. I know now that all people hunger for a noble, unsullied past, that as sure as the black nationalist dreams of a sublime Africa before the white man's corruption, so did Thomas Jefferson dream of an idyllic Britain before the Normans, so do all of us dream of some other time when things were so simple. I know now that that hunger is a retreat from the knotty present into myth and that what ultimately awaits those who retreat into fairy tales, who seek refuge in the mad pursuit to be made great again, in the image of a greatness that never was, is tragedy.

Cosby's call-outs also engendered much cheering from white pundits. This was not surprising or interesting—the call-outs made no demands on the white conscience, so there was nothing shocking about white people cheering him on. But the hunger for a noble past, the current of black nostalgia, fascinated me because the black past was, to my mind, not even a useful mine for nostalgia; it was segregation and slavery. And my fascination extended to Cosby himself. He was not a conservative in our binary sense of electoral politics. If Cosby was mostly conflated with the affable "Dr. Huxtable" he played on *The Cosby Show,* the bourgeois façade of his most famous role obscured Cosby's sense of himself as a race man. He had supported the anti-apartheid struggle, donated to HBCUs, backed black leaders like Jesse Jackson and organizations like Trans-Africa. He seemed to be reviving a race-based black conservatism that had no real home in America's left-right politics but deep roots in the black community.

I thought I had a story to tell about all of this—a big one. I saw Cosby as emblematic of a strain of black thought that I disagreed with but wanted to understand. I wanted to draw this out with a mix of portraiture, opinion, and memoir. The essay that came from that—"This Is How We Lost to the White Man"—is an attempt to achieve that mix, if an ultimately unsuccessful one. But the attention it garnered and the relationship it began with *The Atlantic* marked the first period in my life where I was stable enough to make more attempts and thus fulfill my own dream of walking the same path as my heroes, as Baldwin, or Hurston. And like them, I sought with "This Is How We Lost" to find my own way to imagine black people as more than cartoons, as more than photo negatives or shadows.

The tradition of black writing is necessarily dyspeptic, necessarily resistant. That tradition was the house in which I wanted to live, and if my residency must be fixed to a certain point in time, I suppose fixing it here, with the publication of this piece, is as good as anywhere. I characterize this as an "attempt" because I felt myself trying to write a feeling, something dreamlike and intangible that lived in my head, and in my head is where at least half of it remained. And there were other challenges, more tangible, that were not met.

I don't know if Cosby's call-outs were a cover for the torrent of rape allegations that swirled around him even then. I knew about the allegations. They'd been written about by other journalists. I also know they deserved more than the one line they ultimately occupied in this piece. I had never actually written a story like "This Is How We Lost to the White Man." I had never written for such a prestigious national publication. I had my own fears of failure lingering. Better to tell a neater story, I reasoned, than attempt the messier one and have to contend with editors I did not then know. But the messier one was truer—indeed, the messier one might well have lent explanatory power to the simple story I chose to tell. And so it happened that in an attempt to analyze, in Cosby's movement, the lure of the simplistic, I myself fell prey to it.

And there was more to be said than even this that I did not say. There always is when you report and research, when you sit down to write and try to fit all the manifold sentiments you see, hear, and feel into some coherent arrangement of words. That was always the challenge in these years writing for *The Atlantic,* years that took me, ultimately, out of the unemployment office and into the Oval Office to bear witness to history. For all of that, in every piece in this book there is a story I told and many more I left untold, for better and worse. In the case of Bill Cosby, especially, it was for worse. That was my shame. That was my failure. And that was how this story began.

"THIS IS HOW WE LOST TO THE WHITE MAN"

THE AUDACITY OF BILL COSBY'S BLACK CONSERVATISM

LAST SUMMER, IN DETROIT'S ST. PAUL CHURCH OF GOD IN CHRIST, I watched Bill Cosby summon his inner Malcolm X. It was a hot July evening. Cosby was speaking to an audience of black men dressed in everything from Enyce T-shirts or polos to blazers and ties. Some were there with their sons. Some were there in wheelchairs. The audience was packed tight, rows of folding chairs extended beyond the wooden pews to capture the overflow. But the chairs were not enough, and late arrivals stood against the long shotgun walls, or out in the small lobby, where they hoped to catch a snatch of Cosby's oratory. Clutching a cordless mic, Cosby paced the front of the church, shifting between prepared remarks and comic ad-libs. A row of old black men, community elders, sat behind him, nodding and grunting throaty affirmations. The rest of the church was in full call-and-response mode, punctuating Cosby's punch lines with laughter, applause, or cries of "Teach, black man! Teach!"

He began with the story of a black girl who'd risen to become valedictorian of his old high school, despite having been abandoned by her father. "She spoke to the graduating class and her speech started like this," Cosby said. " 'I was five years old. It was Saturday and I stood looking out the window, waiting for him.' She never said what helped turn her around. She never mentioned her mother, grandmother, or great-grandmother."

"Understand me," Cosby said, his face contorted and clenched like a fist. "Men? Men? Men! Where are you, men?"

Audience: "Right here!"

Cosby had come to Detroit aiming to grab the city's black men by their collars and shake them out of the torpor that has left so many of them—like so many of their peers across the country— undereducated, over-incarcerated, and underrepresented in the ranks of active fathers. No women were in the audience. No reporters were allowed, for fear that their presence might frighten off fathers behind on their child-support payments. But I was there, trading on race, gender, and a promise not to interview any of the allegedly skittish participants.

"Men, if you want to win, we can win," Cosby said. "We are not a pitiful race of people. We are a bright race, who can move with the best. But we are in a new time, where people are behaving in abnormal ways and calling it normal. . . . When they used to come into our neighborhoods, we put the kids in the basement, grabbed a rifle, and said, 'By any means necessary.'

"I don't want to talk about hatred of these people," he continued. "I'm talking about a time when we protected our women and protected our children. Now I got people in wheelchairs, paralyzed. A little girl in Camden, jumping rope, shot through the mouth. Grandmother saw it out the window. And people are waiting around for Jesus to come, when Jesus is already within you."

Cosby was wearing his standard uniform—dark sunglasses, loafers, a sweat suit emblazoned with the seal of an institution of higher learning. That night it was the University of Massachusetts, where he'd gotten his doctorate in education thirty years ago. He was preaching from the book of black self-reliance, a gospel that he has spent the past four years carrying across the country in a series of events that he bills as "call-outs." "My problem," Cosby told the audience, "is I'm tired of losing to white people. When I say I don't care about white people, I mean let them say what they want to say. What can they say to me that's worse than what their grandfather said?"

From Birmingham to Cleveland and Baltimore, at churches and colleges, Cosby has been telling thousands of black Americans that racism in America is omnipresent but that it can't be an excuse to stop striving. As Cosby sees it, the antidote to racism is not rallies, protests, or pleas but strong families and communities. Instead of focusing on some abstract notion of equality, he argues, blacks need to cleanse their culture, embrace personal responsibility, and reclaim the traditions that fortified them in the past. Driving Cosby's tough talk about values and responsibility is a vision starkly different from Martin Luther King's gauzy, all-inclusive dream: It's an America of competing powers, and a black America that is no longer content to be the weakest of the lot.

It's heady stuff, especially coming from the man white America remembers as a sitcom star and affable pitchman for E. F. Hutton, Kodak, and Jell-O Pudding Pops. And Cosby's race-based crusade is particularly jarring now. Across the country, as black politics has become more professionalized, the rhetoric of race is giving way to the rhetoric of standards and results. Newark's young Ivy League–educated mayor, Cory Booker, ran for office promising competence and crime reduction, as did Washington's mayor, Adrian Fenty. Indeed, we are now enjoying a moment of national self-congratulation over racial progress, with a black man running for president as the very realization of King's dream. Barack Obama defied efforts by the Clinton campaign to pigeonhole him as a "black" candidate, casting himself instead as the symbol of a society that has moved beyond lazy categories of race.

Black America does not entirely share the euphoria, though. The civil rights generation is exiting the American stage—not in a haze of nostalgia but in a cloud of gloom, troubled by the persistence of racism, the apparent weaknesses of the generation following in its wake, and the seeming indifference of much of the country to black America's fate. In that climate, Cosby's gospel of discipline, moral reform, and self-reliance offers a way out—a promise that one need not cure America of its original sin in order to succeed. Racism may not be extinguished, but it can be beaten.

Has Dr. Huxtable, the head of one of America's most beloved television households, seen the truth: that the dream of integration should never supplant the pursuit of self-respect; that blacks should worry more about judging themselves and less about whether whites are judging them on the content of their character? Or has he lost his mind?

From the moment he registered in the American popular consciousness, as the Oxford-educated Alexander Scott in the NBC adventure series *I Spy,* Cosby proffered the idea of an America that transcended race. The series, which started in 1965, was the first weekly show to feature an African American in a lead role, but it rarely factored race into dialogue or plots. Race was also mostly inconspicuous in Cosby's performances as a hugely popular stand-up comedian. "I don't spend my hours worrying how to slip a social message into my act," Cosby told *Playboy* in 1969. He also said that he didn't "have time to sit around and worry whether all the black people of the world make it because of me. I have my own gig to worry about." His crowning artistic and commercial achievement—*The Cosby Show,* which ran from 1984 to 1992—was seemingly a monument to that understated sensibility.

In fact, blackness was never absent from the show or from Bill Cosby. Plots involved black artists like Stevie Wonder or Dizzy Gillespie. The Huxtables' home was decorated with the works of black artists like Annie Lee, and the show featured black theater veterans such as Roscoe Lee Browne and Moses Gunn. Behind the scenes, Cosby hired the Harvard psychiatrist Alvin Poussaint to make sure that the show never trafficked in stereotypes and that it depicted blacks in a dignified light. Picking up Cosby's fixation on education, Poussaint had writers insert references to black schools. "If the script mentioned Oberlin, Texas Tech, or Yale, we'd circle it and tell them to mention a black college," Poussaint told me in a phone interview last year. "I remember going to work the next day and white people saying, 'What's the school called Morehouse?'" In 1985, Cosby riled NBC by placing an anti-apartheid sign in his Huxtable son's bedroom. The network wanted no part of the debate. "There may be two sides to apartheid in Archie Bunker's house," the *Toronto Star* quoted Cosby as saying. "But it's impossible that the Huxtables would be on any side but one. That sign will stay on that door. And I've told NBC that if they still want it down, or if they try to edit it out, there will be no show." The sign stayed.

Offstage, Cosby's philanthropy won him support among the civil rights crowd. He made his biggest splash in 1988, when he and his wife gave $20 million to Spelman College, the largest individual donation ever given to a black college. "Two million would have been fantastic; 20 million, to use the language of the hip-hop generation, was off the chain," says Johnnetta Cole, who was then president of Spelman. Race again came to the fore in 1997, when Cosby's son was randomly shot and killed while fixing a flat on a Los Angeles freeway. His wife wrote an op-ed in *USA Today* arguing that white racism lay behind her son's death. "All African-Americans, regardless of their educational and economic accomplishments, have been and are at risk in America simply because of their skin colors," she wrote. "Most people know that facing the truth brings about healing and growth. When is America going to face its historical and current racial realities so it can be what it says it is?"

The column caused a minor row, but most of white America took little notice. To them, Cosby was still America's Dad. But those close to Cosby were not surprised. Cosby was an avowed race man, who, like much of his generation, had come to feel that black America had lost its way. The crisis of absentee fathers, the rise of black-on-black crime, and the spread of hip-hop all led Cosby to believe that, after the achievements of the 1960s, the black community was committing cultural suicide.

His anger and frustration erupted into public view during an NAACP awards ceremony in Washington in 2004 commemorating the fiftieth anniversary of *Brown v. Board of Education*. At that moment, the shades of mortality and irrelevance seemed to be drawing over the civil rights generation. Its matriarchs, Rosa Parks and Coretta Scott King, would be dead within two years. The NAACP's membership rolls had been shrinking; within months, its president, Kweisi Mfume, would resign (it was later revealed that he was under investigation by the NAACP for sexual harassment and nepotism— allegations that he denied). Other movement leaders were drifting into self-parody: Al Sharpton would soon be hosting a reality show and, a year later, would be doing ads for a predatory loan company; Sharpton and Jesse Jackson had recently asked MGM to issue an apology for the hit movie *Barbershop*.

That night, Cosby was one of the last honorees to take the podium. He began by noting that although civil rights activists had opened the door for black America, young people today, instead of stepping through, were stepping backward. "No longer is a person embarrassed because they're pregnant without a husband," he told the crowd. "No longer is a boy considered an embarrassment if he tries to run away from being the father of the unmarried child."

There was cheering as Cosby went on. Perhaps sensing that he had the crowd, he grew looser. "The lower-economic and lower-middle-economic people are not holding their end in this deal," he told the audience.

Cosby disparaged activists who charge the criminal-justice system with racism. "These are people going around stealing Coca-Cola. People getting shot in the back of the head over a piece of pound cake," Cosby said. "Then we all run out and are outraged: 'The cops shouldn't have shot him.' What the hell was he doing with the pound cake in his hand? I wanted a piece of pound cake just as bad as anybody else. And I looked at it and I had no money.

And something called parenting said, 'If you get caught with it, you're going to embarrass your mother.' "

Then he attacked African American naming traditions, and the style of dress among young blacks: "Ladies and gentlemen, listen to these people. They are showing you what's wrong. . . . What part of Africa did this come from? We are not Africans. Those people are not Africans. They don't know a damned thing about Africa— with names like Shaniqua, Shaligua, Mohammed, and all that crap, and all of them are in jail." About then, people began to walk out of the auditorium and cluster in the lobby. There was still cheering, but some guests milled around and wondered what had happened. Some thought old age had gotten the best of Cosby. The mood was one of shock.

After what has come to be known as "the Pound Cake speech"—it has its own Wikipedia entry—Cosby came under attack from various quarters of the black establishment. The playwright August Wilson commented, "A billionaire attacking poor people for being poor. Bill Cosby is a clown. What do you expect?" One of the gala's hosts, Ted Shaw, the director-counsel of the NAACP Legal Defense and Educational Fund, called his comments "a harsh attack on poor black people in particular." Dubbing Cosby an "Afristocrat in Winter," the Georgetown University professor Michael Eric Dyson came out with a book, *Is Bill Cosby Right? Or Has the Black Middle Class Lost Its Mind?*, that took issue with Cosby's bleak assessment of black progress and belittled his transformation from vanilla humorist to social critic and moral arbiter. "While Cosby took full advantage of the civil rights struggle," argued Dyson, "he resolutely denied it a seat at his artistic table."

But Cosby's rhetoric played well in black barbershops, churches, and backyard barbecues, where a unique brand of conservatism still runs strong. Outsiders may have heard haranguing in Cosby's language and tone. But much of black America heard instead the possibility of changing their communities without having to wait on the consciences and attention spans of policy makers who might not have their interests at heart. Shortly after Cosby took his Pound Cake message on the road, I wrote an article denouncing him as an elitist. When my father, a former Black Panther, read it, he upbraided me for attacking what he saw as a message of black empowerment. Cosby's argument has resonated with the black mainstream for just that reason.

The split between Cosby and critics such as Dyson mirrors not only America's broader conservative/liberal split but also black America's own historic intellectual divide. Cosby's most obvious antecedent is Booker T. Washington. At the turn of the twentieth century, Washington married a defense of the white South with a call for black self-reliance and became the most prominent black leader of his day. He argued that southern whites should be given time to adjust to emancipation; in the meantime, blacks should advance themselves not by voting and running for office but by working, and ultimately owning, the land.

W.E.B. Du Bois, the integrationist model for the Dysons of our day, saw Washington as an apologist for white racism and thought that his willingness to sacrifice the black vote was heretical. History ultimately rendered half of Washington's argument moot. His famous Atlanta Compromise—in which he endorsed segregation as a temporary means of making peace with southerners—was answered by lynchings, land theft, and general racial terrorism. But Washington's appeal to black self-sufficiency endured.

After Washington's death, in 1915, the black conservative tradition he had fathered found a permanent and natural home in the emerging ideology of Black Nationalism. Marcus Garvey, its patron saint, turned the Atlanta Compromise on its head, implicitly endorsing segregation not as an olive branch to whites but as a statement of black supremacy. Black Nationalists scorned the Du Boisian integrationists as stooges or traitors, content to beg for help from people who hated them.

Garvey argued that blacks had rendered themselves unworthy of the white man's respect. "The greatest stumbling block in the way of progress in the race has invariably come from within the race itself," wrote Garvey. "The monkey wrench of destruction as thrown into the cog of Negro Progress, is not thrown so much by the outsider as by the very fellow who is in our fold, and who should be the first to grease the wheel of progress rather than seeking to impede." Decades later, Malcolm X echoed that sentiment, faulting blacks for failing to take charge of their destinies. "The white man is too intelligent to let someone else come and gain control of the economy of his community," Malcolm said. "But you will let anybody come in and take control of the economy of your community, control the housing, control the education, control the jobs, control the businesses, under the pretext that you want to integrate. No, you're out of your mind."

Black conservatives like Malcolm X and Louis Farrakhan, the leader of the Nation of Islam, have at times allied themselves with black liberals. But in general, they have upheld a core of beliefs laid out by Garvey almost a century ago: a skepticism of (white) government as a mediating force in the "Negro problem," a strong belief in the singular will of black people, and a fixation on a supposedly glorious black past.

Those beliefs also animate *Come On People,* the manifesto that Cosby and Poussaint published last fall. Although it does not totally dismiss government programs, the book mostly advocates solutions from within as a cure for black America's dismal vital statistics. "Once we find our bearings," they write, "we can move forward, as we have always done, on the path from victims to victors." *Come On People* is heavy on black pride ("no group of people has had the impact on the culture of the whole world that African Americans have had, and much of that impact has been for the good"), and heavier on the idea of the Great Fall—the theory, in this case, that post–Jim Crow blacks have lost touch with the cultural traditions that enabled them to persevere through centuries of oppression.

"For all the woes of segregation, there were some good things to come out of it," Cosby and Poussaint write. "One was that it forced us to take care of ourselves. When restaurants, laundries, hotels, theaters, groceries, and clothing stores were segregated, black people opened and ran their own. Black life insurance companies and banks thrived, as well as black funeral homes. . . . Such successes provided jobs and strength to black economic well-being. They also gave black people that gratifying sense of an interdependent community." Although the authors take pains to put some distance between themselves and the Nation of Islam, they approvingly quote one of its ministers who spoke at a call-out in Compton, California: "I went to Koreatown today and I met with the Korean merchants," the minister told the crowd. "I love them. You know why? They got a place called what? Koreatown. When I left them, I went to Chinatown. They got a place called what? Chinatown. Where is your town?"

The notion of the Great Fall, and the attendant theory that segregation gave rise to some "good things," are the stock-in-trade of what Christopher Alan Bracey, a law professor at Washington University, calls (in his book *Saviors or Sellouts*) the "organic" black conservative tradition: conservatives who favor hard work and moral reform over protests and government intervention, but whose black-nationalist leanings make them anathema to the Heritage Foundation and Rush Limbaugh. When political strategists argue that the Republican Party is missing a huge chance to court the black community, they are thinking of this mostly male bloc—the old guy in the barbershop, the grizzled Pop Warner coach, the retired Vietnam vet, the drunk uncle at the family reunion. He votes Democratic, not out of any love for abortion rights or progressive taxation, but because he feels—in fact, he knows—that the modern-day GOP draws on the support of people who hate him. This is the audience that flocks to Cosby: culturally conservative black Americans who are convinced that integration, and to some extent the entire liberal dream, robbed them of their natural defenses.

"There are things that we did not see coming," Cosby told me over lunch in Manhattan last year. "Like, you could see the Klan, but because these things were not on a horse, because there was no white sheet, and the people doing the deed were not white, we saw things in the light of family and forgiveness. . . . We didn't pay attention to the dropout rate. We didn't pay attention to the fathers, to the self-esteem of our boys."

Given the state of black America, it is hard to quarrel with that analysis. Blacks are 13 percent of the population, yet black men account for 49 percent of America's murder victims and 41 percent of the prison population. The teen birth rate for blacks is 63 per 1,000, more than double the rate for whites. In 2005, black families had the lowest median income of any ethnic group measured by the census, making only 61 percent of the median income of white families.

Most troubling is a recent study released by the Pew Charitable Trusts, which concluded that the rate at which blacks born into the middle class in the 1960s backslid into poverty or near-poverty (45 percent) was three times that of whites—suggesting that the advances of even some of the most successful cohorts of black America remain tenuous at best. Another Pew survey, released last November, found that blacks were "less upbeat about the state of black progress now than at any time since 1983."

The rise of the organic black conservative tradition is also a response to America's retreat from its second attempt at Reconstruction. Blacks have watched as the courts have weakened affirmative action, arguably the country's greatest symbol of state-sponsored inclusion. They've seen a fraudulent war on drugs that, judging by the casualties, looks like a war on black people. They've seen themselves bandied about as playthings in the presidential campaigns of Ronald Reagan (with his 1980 invocation of "states' rights" in Mississippi), George Bush (Willie Horton), Bill Clinton (Sister Souljah), and George W. Bush (McCain's fabled black love child). They've seen the utter failures of school busing and housing desegregation, as well as the horrors of Katrina. The result is a broad distrust of government as the primary tool for black progress.

In May 2004, just one day before Cosby's Pound Cake speech, *The New York Times* visited Louisville, Kentucky, once ground zero in the fight to integrate schools. But the *Times* found that sides had switched, and that black parents were more interested in educational progress than in racial parity. "Integration? What was it good for?" one parent asked. "They were just setting up our babies to fail."

In response to these perceived failures, many black activists have turned their efforts inward. Geoffrey Canada's ambitious Harlem Children's Zone project pushes black students to change their study habits and improve their home life. In cities like Baltimore and New York, community groups are focusing on turning black men into active fathers. In Philadelphia last October, thousands of black men packed the Liacouras Center, pledging to patrol their neighborhoods and help combat the rising murder rate. When Cosby came to St. Paul Church in Detroit, one local judge got up and urged Cosby and other black celebrities to donate more money to advance the cause. "I didn't fly out here to write a check," Cosby retorted. "I'm not writing a check in Houston, Detroit, or Philadelphia. Leave these athletes alone. All you know is Oprah Winfrey and Michael Jackson. Forget about a check. . . . This is how we lost to the white man. 'Judge said Bill Cosby is gonna write a check, but until then . . .' "

Instead of waiting for handouts or outside help, Cosby argues, disadvantaged blacks should start by purging their own culture of noxious elements like gangsta rap, a favorite target. "What do record producers think when they churn out that gangsta rap with antisocial, women-hating messages?" Cosby and Poussaint ask in their book. "Do they think that black male youth won't act out what they have repeated since they were old enough to listen?" Cosby's rhetoric on culture echoes—and amplifies—a swelling strain of black opinion: Last November's Pew study reported that 71 percent of blacks feel that rap is a bad influence.

The strain of black conservatism that Cosby evokes has also

surfaced in the presidential campaign of Barack Obama. Early on, some commentators speculated that Obama's Cosby-esque appeals to personal responsibility would cost him black votes. But if his admonishments for black kids to turn off the PlayStation and for black fathers to do their jobs did him any damage, it was not reflected at the polls. In fact, this sort of rhetoric amounts to something of a racial double play, allowing Obama and Cosby to cater both to culturally conservative blacks and to whites who are convinced that black America is a bastion of decadence. (Curiously, Cosby is noncommittal verging on prickly when it comes to Obama. When Larry King asked him whether he supported Obama, he bristled: "Do you ask white people this question? . . . I want to know why this fellow especially is brought up in such a special way. How many Americans in the media really take him seriously, or do they look at him like some prize brown baby?" The exchange ended with Cosby professing admiration for Dennis Kucinich. Months later, he rebuffed my requests for his views on Obama's candidacy.)

The shift in focus from white racism to black culture is not as new as some social commentators make it out to be. Standing in St. Paul Church on that July evening listening to Cosby, I remembered the last time The Street felt like this: in the summer of 1994, after Louis Farrakhan announced the Million Man March. Farrakhan barnstormed the country holding "men only" meetings (but much larger). I saw him in my native Baltimore, while home from Howard University on vacation. The march itself was cathartic. I walked with four or five other black men, and all along the way black women stood on porches or out on the street, shouting, clapping, cheering. For us, Farrakhan's opinions on the Jews mostly seemed beside the point; what stuck was the chance to assert our humanity and our manhood by marching on the Mall, and not acting like we were all fresh out of San Quentin. We lived in the shadow of the '80s crack era. So many of us had been jailed or were on our way. So many of us were fathers in biology only. We believed ourselves disgraced and clung to the march as a public statement: The time had come to grow up.

Black conservatives have been dipping into this well of lost black honor since the turn of the twentieth century. On the one hand, vintage black nationalists have harked back to a golden age of black Africa, where mighty empires sprawled and everyone was a king. Meanwhile, populist black conservatives like Cosby point to pre-1968 black America as an era when blacks were united in the struggle: Men were men, and a girl who got pregnant without getting married would find herself bundled off to Grandpa's farm.

What both visions share is a sense that black culture in its present form is bastardized and pathological. What they also share is a foundation in myth. Black people are not the descendants of kings. We are—and I say this with big pride—the progeny of slaves. If there's any majesty in our struggle, it lies not in fairy tales but in those humble origins and the great distance we've traveled since. Ditto for the dreams of a separate but noble past. Cosby's, and much of black America's, conservative analysis flattens history and smooths over the wrinkles that have characterized black America since its inception.

Indeed, a century ago, the black brain trust was pushing the same rhetoric that Cosby is pushing today. It was concerned that slavery had essentially destroyed the black family and was obsessed with seemingly the same issues—crime, wanton sexuality, and general moral turpitude—that Cosby claims are recent developments. "The early effort of middle-class blacks to respond to segregation was, aside from a political agenda, focused on a social-reform agenda," says Khalil G. Muhammad, a professor of American history at Indiana University. "The National Association of Colored Women, Du Bois in *The Philadelphia Negro,* all shared a sense of anxiety that African Americans were not presenting their best selves to the world. There was the sense that they were committing crimes and needed to keep their sexuality in check." Adds William Jelani Cobb, a professor of American history at Spelman College: "The same kind of people who were advocating for social reform were denigrating people because they didn't play piano. They often saw themselves as reluctant caretakers of the less enlightened."

In particular, Cosby's argument—that much of what haunts young black men originates in post-segregation black culture—doesn't square with history. As early as the 1930s, sociologists were concerned that black men were falling behind black women. In his classic study, *The Negro Family in the United States,* published in 1939, E. Franklin Frazier argued that urbanization was undermining the ability of men to provide for their families. In 1965—at the height of the civil rights movement—Daniel Patrick Moynihan's milestone report, "The Negro Family: The Case for National Action," picked up the same theme.

At times, Cosby seems willfully blind to the parallels between his arguments and those made in the presumably glorious past. Consider his problems with rap. How could an avowed jazz fanatic be oblivious to the similar plaints once sparked by the music of his youth? "The tired longshoreman, the porter, the housemaid and the poor elevator boy in search of recreation, seeking in jazz the tonic for weary nerves and muscles," wrote the lay historian J. A. Rogers, "are only too apt to find the bootlegger, the gambler and the demi-monde who have come there for victims and to escape the eyes of the police."

Beyond the apocryphal notion that black culture was once a fount of virtue, there's still the charge that culture is indeed the problem. But to reach that conclusion, you'd have to stand on some rickety legs. The hip-hop argument, again, is particularly creaky. Ronald Ferguson, a Harvard social scientist, has highlighted that an increase in hip-hop's popularity during the early 1990s corresponded with a declining amount of time spent reading among black kids. But gangsta rap can be correlated with other phenomena, too—many of them positive. During the 1990s, as gangsta rap exploded, teen pregnancy and the murder rate among black men declined. Should we give the blue ribbon in citizenship to Dr. Dre?

"I don't know how to measure culture. I don't know how to test its effects, and I'm not sure anyone else does," says the Georgetown economist Harry Holzer. "There's a liberal story that limited opportunities, and barriers, lead to employment problems and criminal records, but then there's another story that has to do with norms, behaviors, and oppositional culture. You can't prove the latter statistically, but it still might be true." Holzer thinks that both arguments contain truth and that one doesn't preclude the other. Fair enough. Suffice it to say, though, that the evidence supporting structural inequality is compelling. In 2001, a researcher sent out black and white job applicants in Milwaukee, randomly assigning them a criminal record. The researcher concluded that a white man with a criminal record had about the same chance of getting a job as a black man without one. Three years later, researchers produced the same results in New York under more rigorous conditions.

The accepted wisdom is that such studies are a comfort to black people, allowing them to wallow in their misery. In fact, the opposite is true—the liberal notion that blacks are still, after a century of struggle, victims of pervasive discrimination is the ultimate collective buzzkill. It effectively means that African Americans must, on some level, accept that their children will be "less than" until some point in the future when white racism miraculously abates. That's not the sort of future that any black person eagerly awaits, nor does it make for particularly motivating talking points.

Last summer, I watched Cosby give a moving commencement speech to a group of Connecticut inmates who'd just received their GEDs. Before the speech, at eight in the morning, Cosby quizzed correctional officials on the conditions and characteristics of their inmate population. I wished, then, that my seven-year-old son could have seen Cosby there, to take in the same basic message that I endeavor to serve him every day—that manhood means more than virility and strut, that it calls for discipline and dutiful stewardship. That the ultimate fate of black people lies in their own hands, not in the hands of their antagonists. That as an African

American, he has a duty to his family, his community, and his ancestors.

If Cosby's call-outs simply ended at that—a personal and communal creed—there'd be little to oppose. But Cosby often pits the rhetoric of personal responsibility against the legitimate claims of American citizens for their rights. He chides activists for pushing to reform the criminal-justice system, despite solid evidence that the criminal-justice system needs reform. His historical amnesia—his assertion that many of the problems that pervade black America are of a recent vintage—is simply wrong, as is his contention that today's young African Americans are somehow weaker, that they've dropped the ball. And for all its positive energy, his language of uplift has its limitations. After the Million Man March, black men embraced a sense of hope and promise. We were supposed to return to our communities and families inspired by a new feeling of responsibility. Yet here we are again, almost fifteen years later, with seemingly little tangible change. I'd take my son to see Bill Cosby, to hear his message, to revel in its promise and optimism. But afterward, he and I would have a very long talk.

On the day last summer when Cosby met me for lunch in the West Village, it was raining, as it had been all week, and New York was experiencing a record-cold August. Cosby had just come from Max Roach's funeral and was dressed in a natty three-piece suit. Despite the weather, the occasion, and the oddly empty dining room, Cosby was energized. He had spent the previous day in Philadelphia, where he spoke to a group in a housing project, met with state health officials, and participated in a community march against crime. Grassroots black activists in his hometown were embracing his call. He planned, over the coming year, to continue his call-outs and release a hip-hop album. (He has also noted, however, that there won't be any profanity on it.)

Cosby was feeling warm and nostalgic. He asked why I had not brought my son, and I instantly regretted dropping him off at my partner's workplace for a couple of hours. He talked about breaking his shoulder playing school football, after his grandfather had tried to get him to quit. "Granddad Cosby got on the trolley and came over to the apartment," he recalled. "I was so embarrassed. I was laid out on the sofa. He was talking to my parents, and I was waiting for the moment when he would say, 'See, I told you, Junior.' He came back and reached in his pocket and gave me a quarter. He said, 'Go to the corner and get some ice cream. It has calcium in it.'"

Much pop psychology has been devoted to Cosby's transformation into such a high-octane, high-profile activist. His nemesis Dyson says that Cosby, in his later years, is following in the dishonorable tradition of upper-class African Americans who denounce their less fortunate brethren. Others have suggested more sinister motivations—that Cosby is covering for his own alleged transgressions. (In 2006, Cosby settled a civil lawsuit filed by a woman who claimed that he had sexually assaulted her; other women have come forward with similar allegations that have not gone to court.) But the depth of his commitment would seem to belie such suspicions, and in any case, they do not seem to have affected his hold on his audience: In the November Pew survey, 85 percent of all African American respondents considered him a "good influence" on the black community, above Obama (76 percent) and second only to Oprah Winfrey (87 percent).

Part of what drives Cosby's activism, and reinforces his message, is the rage that lives in all African Americans, a collective feeling of disgrace that borders on self-hatred. As the comedian Chris Rock put it in one of his infamous routines, "Everything white people don't like about black people, black people really don't like about black people. . . . It's like a civil war going on with black people, and it's two sides—there's black people and there's niggas, and niggas have got to go. . . . Boy, I wish they'd let me join the Ku Klux Klan. Shit, I'd do a drive-by from here to Brooklyn." (Rock stopped performing the routine when he noticed that his white fans were laughing a little too hard.) Liberalism, with its pat logic and focus on structural inequities, offers no balm for this sort of raw pain. Like the people he preaches to, Cosby has grown tired of hanging his head.

This disquiet spans generations, but it is most acute among those of the civil rights era. "I don't know a better term than *angst,*" says Johnnetta Cole. "I refuse to categorize every young African American with the same language, but there are some 'young'uns'—and some of us who are not 'young'uns'—who must turn around and look at where we are, because where we're headed isn't pretty." Like many of the stars of the civil rights movement, Cole has gifts that go beyond social activism. She rose out of the segregated South and went to college at age fifteen, eventually earning a bachelor's from Oberlin and a doctorate in anthropology from Northwestern. That same sort of dynamism exists today among many younger blacks, but what troubles the older generation is that their energy seems directed at other pursuits besides social uplift.

Cosby is fond of saying that sacrifices of the '60s weren't made so that rappers and young people could repeatedly use the word *nigger.* But that's exactly why they were made. After all, chief among all individual rights awarded Americans is the right to be mediocre, crass, and juvenile—in other words, the right to be human. But Cosby is aiming for something superhuman—twice as good, as the elders used to say—and his homily to a hazy black past seems like an effort to redeem something more than the present.

When people hear Bill Cosby's message, many assume that he is the product of the sort of family he's promoting—two caring parents, a stable home life, a working father. In fact, like many of the men he admonishes, Cosby was born into a troubled home. He was raised by his mother because his father, who joined the Navy, abandoned the family when Cosby was a child. Speaking to me of his youth, Cosby said, "People told me I was bright, but nobody stayed on me. My mother was too busy trying to feed and clothe us." He was smart enough to be admitted to Central High School, a magnet school in Philadelphia, but transferred and then dropped out in the tenth grade and followed his father into the service.

But the twists and turns of that reality seem secondary to the tidier, more appealing world that Cosby is trying to create. Toward the end of our lunch, in a long, rambling monologue, Cosby told me, "If you looked at me and said, 'Why is he doing this? Why right now?' you could probably say, 'He's having a resurgence of his childhood.' What do I need if I am a child today? I need people to guide me. I need the possibility of change. I need people to stop saying I can't pull myself up by my own bootstraps. They say that's a myth. But these other people have their mythical stories—why can't we have our own?"

2.

NOTES FROM
THE
SECOND YEAR

N THE SUMMER OF 2008, I ATTENDED THE ASPEN IDEAS FESTIVAL, a weeklong conference in the Colorado Rockies. The festival brings a slice of America's thinking class together to offer its analysis, recommendations, and ruminations to elite society. The temptation toward satire and sardonicism is powerful here. But satire wasn't within my grasp then; satire is itself a privilege—one that evidences a knowledge of its target. And there was so much I did not know then.

I was thirty-two years old. I had no passport. I had only recently realized why I might need one. Two years earlier Kenyatta had gone to France without me. I'd scoffed at her invitation. But when she returned, her stories rekindled something old in me. I remembered that once, as a child, I was filled with wonder, that I had marveled at tri-folded science projects, encyclopedias, and road atlases. I left much of that wonder somewhere back in Baltimore. Now I had the privilege of welcoming it back like a long-lost friend, though our reunion was laced with grief; I mourned over all the years that were lost. The mourning continues. Even today, from time to time, I find myself on beaches watching six-year-olds learn to surf, or at colleges listening to sophomores slip from English to Italian, or at cafés seeing young poets flip through "The Waste Land," or listening to the radio where economists explain economic things that I could've explored in my lost years, mourning, hoping that I and all my wonder, my long-lost friend, have not yet run out of time, though I know that we all run out of time, and some of us run out of it faster.

Kenyatta took the trip to Aspen with me. We walked the town together. We talked to people. At a dinner we met a couple who'd been together for decades. The husband was retired, and jokingly lamented that he could not get his wife to follow suit. He told us that that morning he'd taken his dog and driven out to the Continental Divide to watch the wildlife. I did not know what the Continental Divide was, and I did not ask. Later I felt bad about this. I knew, even then, that whenever I nodded along in ignorance, I lost an opportunity, betrayed the wonder in me by privileging the appearance of knowing over the work of finding out.

A huge mountain shadowed Aspen and a ski lift stretched up from the town to the peak. Kenyatta insisted we take the lift up. I am afraid of heights, but a mix of machismo and curiosity pushed me forth. I remember the sloping ground rising and falling beneath us, the lift swaying in the high wind, the town falling away from us, the fear tightening my arms, legs, throat, and then at the top, the clouds hanging over mountain ridges still, in June, speckled with white. I did not love it, but I loved it. The fear I felt then was not just the anguish in my gut but the price of seeing the world anew.

THAT SUMMER BARACK OBAMA closed out the Democratic primary and closed in on history. In Harlem, vendors hawked T-shirts emblazoned with his face and posters placing him in the black Valhalla where Martin, Malcolm, and Harriet were throned. It is hard to remember the excitement of that time, because I now know that the sense we had that summer, the sense that we were approaching an end-of-history moment, proved to be wrong. It is not so much that I logically reasoned out that Obama's election would author a post-racist age. But it now seemed possible that white supremacy, the scourge of American history, might well be banished in my lifetime. In those days I imagined racism as a tumor that could be isolated and removed from the body of America, not as a pervasive system both native and essential to that body. From that perspective, it seemed possible that the success of one man really could alter history, or even end it.

I also saw that those charged with analyzing the import of Obama's blackness were, in the main, working off an old script. Obama was dubbed "the new Tiger Woods of American politics," as a man who wasn't "exactly black." I understood the point— Obama was not "black" as these writers understood "black." It wasn't just that he wasn't a drug dealer, like most black men on the news, but that he did not hail from an inner city, he was not raised on chitterlings, his mother had not washed white people's floors. But this confusion was a reduction of racism's true breadth, premised on the need to fix black people in one corner of the universe so that white people may be secure in all the rest of it. So to understand Obama, analysts needed to give him a superpower that explained how this self-described black man escaped his assigned corner. That power was his mixed ancestry.

The precise ancestry of a black drug dealer or cop killer is irrelevant. His blackness predicts and explains his crime. He reinforces the racist presumption. It is only when that presumption is questioned that a fine analysis of ancestry is invoked. Frederick Douglass was an ordinary nigger while working the fields. But when he was a famed abolitionist, it was often said that his genius must derive from his white half. Ancestry isn't even really necessary. From age six, Kenyatta was the only black girl in her Tennessee gifted and talented classes. She could dance and double dutch with the best of them. Her white classmates did not care. "You're not really black," they would say. They meant it as a compliment. But what they really meant was to slander her neighbors and family, to reorder the world in such a way that confirmed their status among the master class. And if Obama, rooted in the world of slaves, could rise above the masters, all the while claiming the identity and traditions of slaves, was there any real meaning in being a master at all?

Denying Barack Obama his blackness served another purpose: It was a means of coping with having been wrong. Those of us who did not believe there could be a black president were challenged by the sudden prospect of one. It is easy to see how it all makes sense now—in every era there have been individual black people capable of defying the bonds of white supremacy, even as that same system held the great mass of us captive. I will speak for myself and say that before Obama's campaign began, the American presidency seemed out of reach. It existed so high in the firmament, and seemed so synonymous with the country's sense of itself, that I never gave the prospect of a black president much thought. By the summer of 2008, it was clear that I'd made an error. Two responses were possible: (1) Assess that error and reconsider the nature of the world in which I lived; or (2) refuse to accept the error and simply retrofit yesterday's reasoning to this new reality. The notion that Obama was a "different kind of black" allowed for that latter option and the comfort of being right. But some of us had not wanted to be right. And when we asserted that "America ain't never letting no nigger be president," we were not bragging. Instinct warned me against hope. But instinct had also warned me against Obama winning Iowa, and instinct was wrong. And if we had misjudged America's support for a black man running to occupy the White House, perhaps I had misjudged the nature of my country. Perhaps we were just now awakening from some awful nightmare, and if Barack Obama was not the catalyst of that awakening, he was at least the sign. And just like that, I was swept away, because I wanted desperately to be swept away, and taking the measure of my community, I saw that I was not alone.

There is a notion out there that black people enjoy the Sisyphean struggle against racism. In fact, most of us live for the day when we can struggle against anything else. But having been, by that very racism, pinned into ghettos, both metaphorical and real, our options for struggle are chosen long before we are born. And so we struggle out of fear for our children. We struggle out of fear for ourselves. We struggle to avoid our feelings, because to actually consider all that was taken, to understand that it was taken systemically, that the taking is essential to America and echoes down through the ages, could make you crazy. But after Iowa it seemed that perhaps there was another way. Perhaps we, as Americans, could elide the terrible history, elide the national crime. Maybe it was possible to fix the problems afflicting black people without focusing on race. Perhaps it was possible to think of black people as a community in disproportionate need, worthy of aid simply because they were Americans in need. Better schools could be built, better health care administered, better jobs made available, not because of anything specific in the black experience but precisely because there isn't. If you squinted for a moment, if you actually tried to believe, it made so much sense. All that was needed for this new theory was a champion—articulate, young, clean. And maybe this new champion had arrived.

TWO EVENTS OF CONSEQUENCE happened in Aspen. An editor at the magazine where Kenyatta worked called on our third day and announced that the entire operation was folding. This seemed catastrophic, and at first glance it appeared that this trip might well be our last hurrah at seeing something beyond our cloistered lives. But the fact was that she had long been plotting her way out. We were united in a desire for our lives to mean something, to devote ourselves to something more than simple survival, to engage in struggle. The axis I chose was race. The axis she chose was gender. She spent her spare hours volunteering for victims of domestic violence, escorting women seeking abortions, or hosting those coming from out of town in our home. She thought about this service all the time. It emerged from her own biography as the child of a young mother and as a young mother herself who'd almost died bringing our son to term. And it emerged out of her own denied dreams. She'd wanted to become a doctor as a young girl but was derailed from math and science in the way that young girls so often are. Maybe it was not yet too late. Kenyatta was thirty-one years old—still young enough to remake herself, young enough to marry the dream and mission. How this would be accomplished, we did not know. Like me, Kenyatta had dropped out of college. We had thought to proceed slowly—part-time in college, and then medical school. But when her job collapsed, we chose to take it as a cosmic sign.

And then the second thing happened—I got another assignment from *The Atlantic,* and I took this as proof that the magazine liked me and might one day like me enough to give me a steady job, and with that job I might support Kenyatta's marriage of mission and dream in the way she had, for so long, supported mine. This was not as altruistic as it sounds. All my life I had watched women support the dreams of men, hand over their own dreams to men, only to wonder, in the later years, whether it was all worth it. Whatever might be out there, I did not want it that way.

So there was love, and specifically the desire to give to someone who had given so much to me. But too there was a need to liberate myself from old models. I did not want a good woman behind me, beside me, in front of me, or proximate to me in any of the old and maudlin ways.

The magazine assignment was a profile of Michelle Obama. I was determined to see something different from the campaign narratives that had already become cliché, the wan comparison to the Huxtables. On the flight home, I was giddy at the possibility. I had been writing for a little over a decade. And now, at last, I was getting the chance to paint the big portraits I'd long dreamed of. But to paint a portrait the artist needs to see the subject, and in that business the Obama campaign was less than willing. The piece I pulled together was mostly taken from afar—comments from family and friends, my own tour of the South Side. This was less than ideal, but I didn't begrudge anyone for this. Journalists aren't entitled to anything, least of all cooperation. Sometimes I fear cooperation leads to the kind of allegiances no journalist should ever promise. I generally like the title of that piece—"American Girl"—more than I like the essay itself. I wanted a certain voice for the piece, a certain beat—again, I could hear it but I could not capture it. Now I know that this was part of the process, that this was part of the practice, and with every effort I drew closer to manifesting the music in my head. "American Girl" did not, in my mind, age well. However, it did mark a change that would make future efforts at capturing the mental music possible.

In January of 2008, six months before I took the trip to Aspen, I logged into BlogSpot and set up an account. I had so many ideas back then and nowhere to put them. At that time, outlets were still limited, and pitching was often laborious. I would post four or five times to the blog each day. They were loose threads that would sometimes come to nothing and other times become the basis for grander artistic pursuits. In the header I scrawled a couplet from the rapper MF Doom:

He wears the mask just to cover the raw flesh.
A rather ugly brother with flows that's gorgeous.

At first, only two people read this blog, and those two people were my dad and me. We'd come up with the idea together. He paid me a stipend—small in amount, huge in impact. It was steady money, which is to say a lifesaver for a family that turned "in over one's head" into a creed. More, it was an investment—the time spent on the blog was time to practice my craft in public while also garnering enough money for groceries. The blog offered limitless space to write, and then publish at whim. And slowly, with some links from other bloggers thrown my way, more and more people came to read it, until, by that summer, I had attracted a backing chorus—a steady group of commenters who read and offered their thoughts. The blog also drew the attention of *The Atlantic,* which offered to take it on and pay me a regular, less small salary.

This focus on money must seem strange, if you have never been without it, and it still must seem strange if you have been without it before, but think of the world of writing, as I once did, as some hallowed place beyond the reach of earthly difficulties. It is an easy mistake given that writing for a living, no matter how little, is still a relative privilege. It was hard for me to see that privilege through the infestations of bedbugs, through the booted car on the street, through the year we spent perpetually two months back on rent. And more, my chief identity, to my mind, was not *writer* but *college dropout,* which meant I had already forgone the one safety net my parents had urged me to secure. "College dropout" means something different when you're black. College is often thought of as the line between the power to secure yourself and your family and the power of someone else securing you in a prison or grave. I was, by then, seemingly well beyond the grasp of streets. But at night, I would see myself falling, not just into poverty but into shame. Samori would suffer and Kenyatta's investment in me would be betrayed. It was not vast sums of money I craved; I just feared burdening and betraying those I loved most. I can remember when that fear lifted, how it clarified my mind, how much easier it was to see and to think.

So I don't know how to discuss my journey through these eight years without talking about money and the great effect its absence, consistency, and abundancy had on our lives. We'd come to New York in 2001, in our midtwenties, with a young son, drawn by tales of limitless work for magazine writers. But the Internet bubble burst. 9/11 happened. And what we were left with was Kenyatta's $28,000-a-year job, and a one-year-old child. For six years we toiled, and now it seemed that the prospect of a black president had not just exerted its gravity on the country but on us particularly.

The fact of Barack Obama, of Michelle Obama, changed our lives. Their very existence opened a market. It is important to say this, to say it in this ugly, inelegant way. It is important to remember the inconsequence of one's talent and hard work and the incredible and unmatched sway of luck and fate. I knew it even as it was happening. I felt that I had not changed, but the world was changing around me. It was as if I had spent my years jiggling a key into the wrong lock. The lock was changed. The doors swung open, and we did not know how to act.

That fall we went out to California. I'd received a substantial fellowship requiring only that I spend a week with my hosts and pursue whatever writing I was working on. Can this be life? Yes. If only in the second year. We emptied our account to buy tickets and went out that October. I worked on "American Girl" during the plane ride. Our hosts greeted us with open arms and more, they greeted us with a check that, as luck would have it, was drawn on our bank. We drove to the bank and made the deposit. It was early evening. We felt incredible. California was beautiful. But not as beautiful as us—young and flush with cash. We drove to a fancy steak house and ordered every course from *aperitif* to *digestif,* and we did this in that magical time when we were still barbarians, still hood, still savage and proud to be savage, when we could still look at each other and toast, drunkenly, ridiculously, as if to simply say, "Nigga, we made it." That was what it was in the fall of 2008. That was how it felt to be black and, for the first time in our lives, proud of our country. Everything was bright. Everything was rising. Everything was a dream.

AMERICAN GIRL

T HE FIRST TIME I SAW MICHELLE OBAMA IN THE FLESH, I ALMOST took her for white. It was late July. Pundits were taking whispered bets on the fate of Hillary Clinton's female supporters. In part to heal the intraparty rift, and in part to raise some cash, Obama was presiding over a Chicago luncheon for Democratic women. They were an opulent, multiracial, mostly middle-aged bunch, in pantsuits and conservative dresses. Clinton-turned-Obama staffer Patti Solis Doyle waved from the floor when she was introduced. One of Clinton's longtime backers appealed for unity. Only a few weeks earlier, Obama had appeared on *The View* in a striking black-and-white floral dress. Now, throughout the room, some of the women were decked out in their best version of that number. Obama flashed her trademark sense of humor, her long arms cutting the air, as she made her points.

I'd flown into Midway that morning and driven up Lake Shore Drive, with William DeVaughn crooning "Be Thankful for What You Got" in the background. But even as I took in the stately beauty of Michigan Avenue, notions of Michelle Obama were spinning around in my head. I thought of an ecstatic phone call from my sister Kelley: "You have to ask her how she holds it down!" I thought of my Atlanta aunts, partisans of the Alpha Kappa Alpha pink and green, crowing over Obama's acceptance of an honorary membership that same month: "Tell her she made the right choice." I thought of a Chicago homeboy who'd summed her up for me: "Michelle is a six-foot black woman who says what she means."

And then I thought of an image from last February, when Michelle Obama, in a gray sweater and a non-smile, slipped into a box marked Angry Black Woman. "For the first time in my adult life," she had told a Milwaukee rally, "I am proud of my country, because it feels like hope is finally making a comeback." When I first saw that clip, I could almost hear the trapdoor opening. In that instant, Michelle Obama became a symbol of her husband's otherness. And for much of the rest of the campaign season, the opinion media obsessed over her love—or lack of love—of country.

Now, waiting in that cavernous downtown Hilton ballroom, I did not think I'd find Ida Wells or Stokely Carmichael. I did not expect to see Michelle Obama with her fist in the air, slinging bean pies, or hawking *The Final Call*. But still, I was unprepared for what I did encounter: Michelle Obama recounting her life as if she were an old stevedore hungering for the long-lost neighborhood of yore.

"I am always amazed at how different things are now for working women and families than when I was growing up," Obama told the crowd. "Things have changed just in that short period of time. See, when I was growing up, my father—as you know, a blue-collar worker—was able to go to work and earn enough money to support a family of four, while my mom stayed home with me and my brother. But today, living with one income, like we did, just doesn't cut it. People can't do it—particularly if it's a shift worker's salary like my father's."

In all my years of watching black public figures, I'd never heard one recall such an idyllic youth. Bill Cosby once said, "African Americans are the only people who do not have any good ol' days," and for years the rule was that all our bios must play on a dream deferred, must offer a nod to dilapidated public housing and mothers scrubbing white women's floors. But Obama waved off Richard Wright. Instead, the blues she sang was the ballad for the modern woman.

"I'm a working woman. I'm a daughter. I'm a sister. I'm a best friend. But the one role that I cherish the most that you've come to know is that role of mom," she told the audience. "On the campaign trail, in a fund-raiser, sitting in the back of a van somewhere, I am worried about how my girls are doing, about their well-being, about their stability."

Here was a black woman who minored in African American studies, whose home turf had been marked by the Blackstone Rangers and Gangster Disciples, casting her story not as an essay on the illusory nature of the American dream but as a rumination about our collective fall from motherhood, Chevrolet, and a chicken in every pot. I was waiting on slave narratives and oppression. I was looking for justice and the plight of the poor. Instead, I got homilies on the sainted place of women in American society. I got Michelle saluting and then ribbing her mother, who was seated in the audience. I left that ballroom thinking—as always—of the Du Boisian veil, the dark filter through which African Americans view their countrymen, and mulling the split perceptions of Michelle Obama. For all her spinning-out of a quintessential Horatio Alger tale, remixing black America into another ethnic group on the come-up, many Americans saw her largely through the prism of her belated, and wanting, expression of American pride.

There has been much chatter about Barack Obama as the answer to America's racial gap, as a biracial black man whose roots stretch from Hawaii to Kenya, with an Ivy League pedigree and the seal of the South Side. But he is not the only one entering the White House who has seen both sides, who intuitively grasps the heroic American narrative of work ethic and family, and how that narrative historically failed black people. He is not the only one who walks in both worlds. Indeed, if you're looking for a bridge, if you're looking for someone to connect the heart of black America with the heart of all of America, to allow us all to look at the American dream in the same way, if you're looking for common ground, then it's true, we should be talking about Obama. But we should make sure we're talking about the right one.

The essential Americanness of Michelle Obama is rooted in her home, the South Side of Chicago. What I originally knew of the South Side I had gleaned from my college years at Howard University. It was the mid-'90s, and all of us sported some measure of black pride—be it Afrocentric or ghettocentric. Often it was a mix of the two. But the South Side kids didn't boast about rep or whose 'hood was harder. They did not make a scene like the dudes from New York. Instead, they played the South Side rapper Common's *Resurrection* until the CD skipped, and walked around campus with their chins in the air, as if they knew something we didn't. The girls from Chicago were intoxicating—maybe it was the cadences of the South that still clung to their words, or their appreciation for Sam Cooke and Al Green. Ten years ago, I chose my partner from among that lot. Though she spurned her hometown, and the South Side particularly, as a cradle of bougie Negroes, her ties to that magical city still pulled me in.

A few weeks after I saw Obama in Chicago, I came back to town, pushing a white rental through the byways of the South Side. My guide was Timuel Black, ninety years old, who'd fought in World War II, helped bring Martin Luther King Jr. to the city, and, in his later years, turned to compiling an oral history of the Great Migration. A slight, energetic man with a gray mustache, he stepped into the car wearing a blue Obama/Biden hat, and we were off. For three hours, we followed the map of his memories across the South Side, down Cottage Grove, across Hyde Park Boulevard, down through Michelle's old neighborhood of South Shore. Black was seven when he saw Charles Lindbergh parading down Grand Boulevard, later rechristened Martin Luther King Jr. Drive. He pointed out Joe

Louis's home, and black Chicago's old commercial district, the Stroll, where he'd seen all the jazz acts.

The South Side's sheer mass and its shifting character astonished me. Bungalows would give way to mansions, mansions to burned-out lots, and at every gas station, panhandlers waited in search of change. I asked Black if he, or his brethren, thought of the South Side as a ghetto, and he shook his head, noting that it had always been filled with people like him and his parents, people who worked.

Like its New York counterparts—Harlem in Manhattan, Jamaica in Queens, and Bedford-Stuyvesant in Brooklyn—the South Side is a black island in a mostly white city. But if the South Side were an island, it would be huge. Unlike Harlem, the South Side isn't one neighborhood, but a collection of smaller neighborhoods covering 60 percent of the city. All told, the sprawling South Side is arguably the country's largest black enclave.

We stopped for lunch at Pearl's Place, a homey southern restaurant on South Michigan Avenue. We ate chicken, and Black broke down the South Side's place in black American lore with unabashed pride. "We were always entrepreneurial types," he explained. "We couldn't yell for taxis. They wouldn't come into the black community. So we created taxi companies. The concept of the jitney was created in Chicago. You couldn't afford to die, because white mortuaries wouldn't bury you. So we did it ourselves. We made places like this—places to eat. A single man could come up from the South and get good home cooking and companionship."

Black's memories of Chicago strivers draw from a deep well of myth and fact. The black power struggle in Chicago literally dates back to the city's founding by the eighteenth-century trader Jean Baptiste Point Du Sable, who, like the president-elect, was a biracial black man. The South Side has been home to the largest black insurance companies in the North, such as Supreme Liberty Life and Chicago Metropolitan Assurance. Ditto for black banks like Seaway National and Independence. Half of the first fourteen black CPAs came out of Chicago. The publications that defined black

Americans—*The Chicago Defender, Ebony,* and *Jet*—were also products of Chicago.

The first black congressmen elected in the twentieth century were South Siders Oscar De Priest and his successor Arthur Mitchell. For years, they were the only black congressmen. The only two serious African American presidential campaigns—those of Jesse Jackson and Barack Obama—came out of the South Side. Indeed, Barack Obama, Louis Farrakhan, and Jesse Jackson all lived or worked within a ten-minute drive of each other.

Chicago in the early twentieth century was racist and segregated, but whereas in the South black voters were violently suppressed, in the North they were encouraged—the better to feed Chicago's infamous machine. Moreover, Chicago's industry was booming, and the *Defender* painted the city to southerners in typical immigrant fashion—streets paved with gold, and jobs for all who wanted them. For years, the saying among Timuel Black's peers was a reverse of the old Frank Sinatra riff—"If you can't make it in Chicago," they'd say, "you can't make it anywhere."

That promise of a better life drew Michelle Obama's grandparents out of the South and into Chicago. Within Chicago's Black Belt—a network of neighborhoods kept segregated by Chicago's restrictive housing covenants—was the sort of oppressive poverty that spawned terms like *the underclass.* And yet, alongside this privation was a proto-middle-class group of blacks who held the community together. Obama's mother, Marian Robinson, came up among them.

"Most of the people were working government jobs, like the post office. My father was a decorator. There was a gentleman in our neighborhood who owned a grocery store," Robinson recalled. He "had to go to his farm to pick up his groceries. It was rough. There were plenty of reasons why people could not do. People who couldn't afford rent for a whole apartment, they would share."

But the hardship forged values in Robinson that she passed on to her kids. "That's where we got our understanding that it was going to be hard, but you just had to do whatever it takes," she said. "We all went to church. I was a Brownie. I was a Girl Scout. We all took piano lessons. We had drama classes. They took you to the museum, the Art Institute. They did all those things, but I don't know how. I grew up with a grandmother and an aunt. My aunt would do things my mother would not or could not."

In 1948, Chicago's method of segregating housing—restrictive covenants—was struck down in court, triggering white flight. The South Side suffered, but unlike in other neighborhoods in other cities, the black middle class in Chicago did not follow whites to the suburbs. The result is that while the South Side bears a disproportionate share of the city's poverty, it also has several steady working- to middle-class neighborhoods.

Michelle Obama's South Shore, for example, held on to its basic economic makeup. "When we moved over, [the neighborhood] was changing," Robinson said. "There were good schools, that's why people moved, and it was the reason *we* moved. I enjoyed living there. It was fine with me that it was changing. Some people felt the schools were too geared to whites. People were very conscious and wanted black artists in the schools. My point was just to go to school and learn what you have to learn."

Robinson and her husband also had the advantage of a few overlooked attributes of Chicago. The South Side was almost a black world unto itself, replete with the economic and cultural complexity of the greater city. There were debutantes and cotillions as well as gangs and drug addicts. Mostly, there were men like Fraser Robinson, black people working a job, trying to get by. The diversity and the demographics allowed the Robinsons to protect their kids from the street life, and also from direct, personal racism. And then there was family life. The Robinsons played board games on the weekends. Michelle loved *The Brady Bunch*.

"We had a very fortunate upbringing," says Obama's brother, Craig Robinson. "It was filled with good times. We were like every other family. We had love and discipline. We had caring parents. . . .

It wasn't unusual at all. It wasn't that everyone had both parents in the house, but it certainly wasn't like it is now, where you find single-parent families everywhere. Folks went to work, people were excited to get good grades. . . . People would laugh about folks finding out you were getting in trouble. People had mothers at home. So if someone broke a window, you always found out about it. You had a secondary line of defense."

This cocoon that surrounded Michelle Obama in her formative years helps explain some of the statements and actions that fanned controversy during the campaign. Obama's Princeton thesis on "Princeton-Educated Blacks and the Black Community," for example, has been interpreted as a budding Garveyite's call to arms. Exhibit A seems to be her banal citation of Stokely Carmichael to explain black separatism, and her observation that Princeton made her "more aware of [her] 'Blackness' than ever before."

A hostile reading of those words hinges on a misunderstanding of the complexities of segregation. In fact, for the legions of black people who grew up like Michelle Obama—in a functioning, self-contained African American world—racial identity recedes in the consciousness. You know you're black, but in much the same way that white people know they are white. Since everyone else around you looks like you, you just take it as the norm, the standard, the unremarkable. Objectively, you know you're in the minority, but that status hits home only when you walk out into the wider world and realize that, out there, you really are different.

I came up in segregated West Baltimore. I understood black as a culture—as Etta James, jumping the broom, the Electric Slide. I understood the history and the politics, the debilitating effects of racism. But I did not understand blackness as a minority until I was an "only," until I was a young man walking into rooms filled with people who did not look like me. In many ways, segregation protected me—to this day, I've never been called a nigger by a white person, and although I know that racism is part of why I define myself as black, I don't *feel* that way, any more than I feel that the two oceans define me as American. But in other ways, segregation left me unprepared for the discovery that my world was not *the* world. In her book *Michelle: A Biography*, Liza Mundy quotes another South Sider explaining the predicament:

> When you grow up in a black community with a warm black family, you are aware of the fact that you are black, but you don't feel it. . . . After a certain point you do just kind of think you're in your own world, and you become very comfortable in that world, and to this day there are African Americans who feel very uncomfortable when they step out of it. . . . This is a society that never lets you forget that you are black.

In her thesis, Michelle Obama grapples with her dawning sense of race as a divider, and with the idea that the world she knew as a child was very different from the one she was entering as a college student. In that light, her words in Wisconsin deserve another look. It's easy to be proud of America as a young black kid with a mother and a father, a solid community, and no direct exposure to racism. But Obama's statement was about her *adult* life. Post-1960s segregation shielded many of us from feeling different, but it could not save us from the weirdness of having white people touching our hair, from the awkwardness of not knowing whether Led Zeppelin was a man or a group, or, more viscerally, from the pain of witnessing the episodes involving Willie Horton, Sister Souljah, and Rodney King.

Standing behind that podium in Milwaukee, Obama was waxing nostalgic. That doesn't mean she was wrong. She was merely expressing the hope that the world could be as it was in South Shore, filled with people who get up, raise kids, and go to work, and never have to think about being "the other."

In most black people, there is a South Side, a sense of home, that never leaves, and yet to compete in the world, we have to go forth.

So we learn to code-switch and become bilingual. We save our Timberlands for the weekend, and our jokes for the cats in the mail room. Some of us give ourselves up completely and become the mask, while others overcompensate and turn every dustup into the Montgomery bus boycott.

But increasingly, as we move into the mainstream, black folks are taking a third road—being ourselves. Implicit in the notion of code-switching is a belief in the illegitimacy of blacks as Americans, as well as a disbelief in the ability of our white peers to understand us. But if you see black identity as you see southern identity, or Irish identity, or Italian identity—not as a separate trunk, but as a branch of the American tree, with roots in the broader experience—then you understand that the particulars of black culture are inseparable from the particulars of the country.

Pop culture has laid the groundwork for that recognition. Barack Obama's coalition—the young, the black, the urban, the hip—was originally assembled by hip-hop. Jay-Z and Nas may be problematic ambassadors, but their ilk are why those who thought Barack and Michelle were giving each other a "terrorist fist jab" were laughed off the stage. We are as physically segregated as ever, yet the changes in media have drawn black idiom into the broader American narrative.

In 2002, the rapper Ice Cube produced and starred in *Barbershop*. The movie was a surprise hit, spawning a sequel, a spin-off, and a short-lived TV series. Its success shocked industry-watchers, because it took place exclusively in a black community and seemingly focused on "black issues." But you could find the same characters in any other ethnic community. Think of Michelle Obama's sharp sense of humor and her insistence on viewing her husband as mortal, and how both traits were derided during the campaign as unfirst-ladylike and fed the caricature of her as an Angry Black Woman. In reality, her summation of her husband as "a gifted man, but in the end . . . just a man" could have come out of the mouth of any sitcom wife on TV.

When I saw Obama in Chicago and took her for white, it was not because of her cadences, mannerisms, or dress, but because of the radical proposition she put forth—a black community fully vested, no Du Boisian veil, in the country at large. A buddy of mine once remarked that Michelle "makes Barack black." But that understates things. She doesn't simply make Barack black—she makes him American.

"I keep saying this: Michelle, Barack, and my son are not abnormal," Marian Robinson said. "All my relatives, all my friends, all their friends, all their parents, almost all of them have the same story. It's just that their families aren't running for president. It bothers me that people see [Michelle and Barack] as so phenomenal, because there's so much of that in the black neighborhood. They went to the same schools we all did. They went through the same struggles."

The last time I saw Michelle Obama in person, in a small room at the Westin Tabor Center hotel in Denver, I was convinced that she could be taken for nothing but black. I had spent the past few weeks following her from set piece to set piece—Obama talks to military spouses in Virginia, Obama and her family make care packages for soldiers, Obama addresses the Hispanic caucus at the Democratic National Convention. But nothing I'd seen at those events outweighed the impressions of her character that I was forming from my encounters with the wide streets of the South Side, one of the few places in the country where African Americans could utter the mantra "black and proud" without a hint of irony.

Her day was almost finished, and she was tired. I was the last in a battery of interviews. Still, she smiled, shook my hand, and said, reaching for a vase of plastic flowers, "We got these for you. What, you don't believe we bought these for you?" I laughed, sat down, and asked her about her childhood.

"My mom and maybe a couple others were some of the few who were able to stay at home," she explained. "A lot of my friends, they weren't called latchkey kids, they were just kids whose parents worked. . . . We went to the public school right around the corner and we had lunch, and you could go home for lunch, and we had recess and there weren't closed campuses then. . . . They'd bring their bag lunch, they'd sit on the kitchen floor and talk to my mom. There was one other mother who we'd do that with."

There it was, that old neighborhood nostalgia and pride, woven into the larger American quilt. Obama's recollections offer no nods to the disproportionate poverty that has always haunted black Chicago. But that was not her world, and it isn't her story. Since the days of Frederick Douglass—another biracial black man—black leaders have styled themselves as the social conscience of the country. As laudable—if at times opportunistic—as that approach may be, it has also marginalized the very people they were trying to help. The typical black political narrative of using one's humble beginnings to make the country true to itself flies against the dominant image of America as the "good guy." It's also a narrative that holds more truth for the activist, the professional scold, than for the rank and file. If Barack and Michelle Obama are to truly transcend the racial divide, it won't be through the narrative of justice, but through the mythology of the Great—and common—Cause.

On the night of his victory, Barack Obama talked about Ann Nixon Cooper, a black woman who, at the age of 106, had voted for him. But when Obama told her story, he presented her not just as someone who'd been born a generation after slavery and had seen segregation, but as a woman who'd seen the women's suffrage movement, the dawn of aviation and the automobile, the Depression and the Dust Bowl, and Pearl Harbor. He presented Nixon Cooper as an African American who was not doubly conscious, just conscious. That is the third road that black America is walking. It's not coincidental that two black people from the South Side are leading us on that road. If you're looking for the heralds of a "post-racial" America, if that adjective is ever to be more than a stupid, unlettered flourish, then look to those, like Michelle Obama, with a sense of security in who they are—those, black or white, who hold blackness as more than the losing end of racism.

These heralds offer a deeper understanding of African American life, a greater appreciation of the bourgeois ordinariness of our experience. "People have never met a Michelle Obama," the soon-to-be first lady said toward the end of our interview. "But what they'll come to learn is that there are thousands and thousands of Michelle and Barack Obamas across America. You just don't live next door to them, or there isn't a TV show about them."

There is now.

3·

NOTES FROM
THE
THIRD YEAR

I HAVE OFTEN WONDERED HOW I MISSED THE COMING TRAGedy. It is not so much that I should have predicted that Americans would elect Donald Trump. It's just that I shouldn't have put it past us. It was tough to keep track of the currents of politics and pageantry swirling at once. All my life I had seen myself, and my people, backed into a corner. Had I been wrong? Watching the crowds at county fairs cheer for Michelle Obama, or flipping through the enchanting photo spreads of this glamorous incoming administration, it was easy to believe that I had been. It was hard to not reassess yourself at, say, the sight of John Patterson, the man who'd "outniggered" George Wallace to become governor of Alabama in 1959, endorsing Obama. It was hard to not feel that you had been wrong about your country when the very men who'd tangled with Patterson and Wallace seemed to believe that something had changed too. "We seem to be evolving," former SNCC leader Bob Moses told a reporter. "The country is trying to reach for the best part of itself." And it was more than symbolic. Obama's victory meant not just a black president but also that Democrats, the party supported by most black people, enjoyed majorities in Congress. Prominent intellectuals were predicting that modern conservatism—a movement steeped in white resentment—was at its end and that a demographic wave of Asians, Latinos, and blacks would sink the Republican Party.

That was one way of thinking about things. Here was another. "Son," my father said of Obama, "you know the country got to be messed up for them folks to give him the job." The economy was on the brink. The blood of untold numbers of Iraqis was on our hands. Katrina had shamed the society. From this other angle, postracialism and good feeling were taken up not so much out of elevation in consciousness but out of desperation. It all makes so much sense now. The pageantry, the math, the magazines, the essays heralded an end to the old country with all its divisions. We forgot that there were those who loved that old country as it was, who did not lament the divisions but drew power from them.

And so we saw postcards with watermelons on the White House lawn. We saw simian caricatures of the First Family, the invocation of a "food-stamp president" and his anticolonial, Islamist agenda. These were the fetishes that gathered the tribe of white supremacy, that rallied them to the age-old banner, and if there was one mistake, one reason why I did not see the coming tragedy, why I did not account for its possibilities, it was because I had not yet truly considered that banner's fearsome power.

The opportunity for that consideration came by coincidence. The eight years of Barack Obama bracketed the 150th anniversary of the Civil War—America's preeminent existential crisis. In 1861, believing themselves immersed in a short war, the forces of union thought white supremacy was still affordable. So even in the North the cause of abolition was denounced, and blacks were forbidden from fighting in the army. But the war dragged on, and wallowing in white supremacy amidst the increase of dead was like wallowing in pearls amidst a famine. Emancipation was embraced. Blacks were recruited and sent into battle. Later they were enfranchised and sent to serve in the halls of government, national and statewide. But in 1876, the hot war now passed, the need for black soldiers gone, the country returned to its supremacist roots. "A revolution has taken place by force of arms and a race are disenfranchised," wrote Mississippi's Reconstruction-era governor, Adelbert Ames.

> They are to be returned to a condition of serfdom—an era of second slavery. . . . The nation should have acted but it was "tired of the annual autumnal outbreaks in the South." . . . The political death of the negro will forever release the nation from the weariness from such "political outbreaks." You may think I exaggerate. Time will show you how accurate my statements are.

So there was nothing new in the suddenly transracial spirit that saw the country, in 2008, reaching "for the best part of itself." It had done so before—and then promptly retrenched in the worst part of itself. To see this connection, to see Obama's election as part of a familiar cycle, you would have had to understand how central the brand of white supremacy was to the country. I did not. I could remember, as a child, the nationalists claiming the country was built by slaves. But this claim was rarely evidenced and mostly struck me as an applause line or rhetorical point. I understood slavery as bad and I had a vague sense that it had once been integral to the country and that the dispute over it had, somehow, contributed to the Civil War. But even that partial sense ran contrary to the way the Civil War was presented in the popular culture, as a violent misunderstanding, an honorable duel between wayward brothers, instead of what it was—a spectacular chapter in a long war that was declared when the first Africans were brought chained to American shores.

When it comes to the Civil War, all of our popular understanding, our popular history and culture, our great films, the subtext of our arguments are in defiance of its painful truths. It is not a mistake that *Gone with the Wind* is one of the most read works of American literature or that *The Birth of a Nation* is the most revered touchstone of all American film. Both emerge from a need for palliatives and painkillers, an escape from the truth of those five short years in which 750,000 American soldiers were killed, more than all American soldiers killed in all other American wars combined, in a war declared for the cause of expanding "African slavery." That war was inaugurated not reluctantly, but lustily, by men who believed property in humans to be the cornerstone of civilization, to be an edict of God, and so delivered their own children to his maw. And when that war was done, the now-defeated God lived on, honored through the human sacrifice of lynching and racist pogroms. The history breaks the myth. And so the history is ignored, and fictions are weaved into our art and politics that dress villainy in martyrdom and transform banditry into chivalry, and so strong are these fictions that their emblem, the stars and bars, darkens front porches and state capitol buildings across the land to this day.

The implications of the true story are existential and corrosive to our larger national myth. To understand that the most costly war in this country's history was launched in direct opposition to everything the country claims to be, to understand that this war was the product of centuries of enslavement, which is to see an even longer, more total war, is to alter the accepted conception of America as a beacon of freedom. How does one face this truth or forge a national identity out of it?

For now the country holds to the common theory that emancipation and civil rights were redemptive, a fraught and still-incomplete resolution of the accidental hypocrisy of a nation founded by slaveholders extolling a gospel of freedom. This common theory dominates much of American discourse, from left to right. Conveniently, it holds the possibility of ultimate resolution, for if right-thinking individuals can dedicate themselves to finishing the work of ensuring freedom for all, then perhaps the ghosts of history can be escaped. It was the common theory—through its promise of a progressive American history, where the country improves itself inexorably and necessarily—that allowed for Obama's rise. And it was that rise that offered me that chance to see that theory for the illusion that it was.

I began fitfully, unintentionally, blindly almost. My blog at *The Atlantic* was my tool, one that my editors circumscribed neither in length, nor style, nor topic. And so at first I blogged about everything I loved—Biggie Smalls, Jim Shooter, Robert Hayden, E. L. Doctorow—and everything I wanted to understand. But the desire to comprehend eventually overpowered the desire to be a fan or evangelist. The blog had an open feel to it, but not too open. I moderated the commenters and banned people. I had to. I wanted to maximize the number of commenters who could tell me things, and for that I had to build something beyond the profane cynicism that inevitably overruns any unregulated space. Between all the posts about Rakim and Spider-Man, I would write about my attempts to conquer *Leviathan* or my reconsiderations of Howard Zinn, and the commenters would offer their responses. We would engage, sometimes argue, and I would learn. Grad students would show up under anonymous handles, offering contexts, objections, and clarifications. A kind of seminar evolved in which scholars dead and present—Beryl Satter, Rebecca Scott, Primo Levi, John Locke—became my virtual professors. The process began to feed itself—commenters would recommend other books, and I would read those and we would engage again. The great Ishmael Reed says writing is fighting, and I believed him. The blog was a gym, my commenters were my trainers. And the books were film reels offering up new angles, new combinations, and ultimately, new possibilities. It was not perfect. I think I could have been more charitable. I think, from time to time, I assumed malicious motives behind worthy objections. But these days, with the blog gone and thus my old community gone, with the gym shuttered and boarded up, I feel myself in constant danger—even as I write this—of allowing the power of my punch, the speed of my hands, to lapse.

But immersed in the reading and my electric seminar, it became clear to me that the common theory of providential progress, of the inevitable reconciliation between the sin of slavery and the democratic ideal, was myth. Marking the moment of awakening is like marking the moment one fell in love. If forced I would say I took my tumble with the dark vision of historian Edmund Morgan's *American Slavery, American Freedom*. Certainly slavery was contrary to America's stated democratic precepts, conceded Morgan, but in fact, it was slavery that allowed American democracy to exist in the first place. It was slavery that gifted much of the South with a working class that lived outside of all protections and could be driven, beaten, and traded into generational perpetuity. Profits pulled from these workers, repression of the normal angst of labor, and the ability to employ this labor on abundant land stolen from Native Americans formed a foundation for democratic equality among a people who came to see skin color and hair textures as defining features. Morgan showed the process in motion through the law—rights gradually awarded to the mass of European poor and oppressed, at precisely the same time they were being stripped from enslaved Africans and their descendants.

It was not just Edmund Morgan. It was James McPherson. It was Barbara Fields. It was David Blight. It was my commenters. Together they guided me through the history of slavery and its cataclysmic resolution. I became obsessed and insufferable. Civil War podcasts were always booming through the house. I'd drag Kenyatta and Samori to the sites of battles—Gettysburg, Petersburg, the Wilderness—audiobooks playing the whole way. I went to Tennessee. I saw Shiloh. I saw Fort Donelson. I saw Island Number 10. At every stop I was moved. The stories of suffering, limbs amputated, men burned alive, the bravery and gallantry, all of it seeped up out of the ground and enveloped me. But something else accompanied this hallowed feeling—a sense that the story, as it was told on these sites, as it was interpreted by visitors—most of them white—was incomplete, and this incompletion was not thoughtless but essential. The tactics of the war were always up for discussion, but the animating cause of those tactics, with but a few exceptions, went unsaid.

By then, I knew. The history books spoke where tourism could not. The four million enslaved bodies, at the start of the Civil War, represented an inconceivable financial interest—$75 billion in today's dollars—and the cotton that passed through their hands represented 60 percent of the country's exports. In 1860, the largest concentration of multimillionaires in the country could be found in the Mississippi River Valley, where the estates of large planters loomed.

White dependency on slavery extended from the economic to the social, and the rights of whites were largely seen as dependent on the degradation of blacks. "White men," wrote Mississippi senator and eventual president of the Confederacy Jefferson Davis, "have an equality resulting from a presence of a lower caste, which cannot exist were white men to fill the position here occupied by the servile race." Antebellum Georgia governor Joseph E. Brown made the same point:

> Among us the poor white laborer is respected as an equal. His family is treated with kindness, consideration and respect. He does not belong to the menial class. The negro is in no sense of the term his equal. He feels and knows this. He belongs to the only true aristocracy, the race of *white* men. He blacks no masters boots, and bows the knee to no one save God alone. He receives higher wages for his labor, than does the laborer of any other portion of the world, and he raises up his children, with the knowledge, that they belong to no inferior cast; but that the highest members of the society in which he lives, will, if their conduct is good, respect and treat them as equals.

Enslavement provided not merely the foundation of white economic prosperity but the foundation of white social equality and thus the foundation of American democracy. But that was 150 years ago. And the slave South lost the war, after all. Was it not the America of Frederick Douglass that had prevailed and the Confederacy of Jefferson Davis that had been banished? Were we not a new country exalting in Martin Luther King Jr.'s dream? I was never quite that far gone. But I had been wrong about the possibility of Barack Obama. And it seemed fair to consider that I might be wrong about a good deal more.

But the same year I began my exploration of the Civil War and the same summer I finished *American Slavery, American Freedom,* Harvard professor Henry Louis Gates was arrested. Gates was returning from a long trip. He was having trouble with the lock on his front door and so was attempting to force his way into his home. Someone saw this and called the police. They arrived and, after an exchange of words, Officer Michael Crowley arrested, charged, and jailed Gates for disorderly conduct. It caused a minor sensation. Commenting on the arrest, Obama asserted that anyone in Gates's situation would be "pretty angry" if they were arrested in their own home. Obama added that "the Cambridge police acted stupidly." He then cited the "long history" of "African Americans and Latinos being stopped by law enforcement disproportionately." I don't know why I expected this would go over well. I don't know why I thought this mild criticism from a new president in defense of one of the most respected academics at our country's most lauded university in a case of obvious but still bloodless injustice might be heard by the broader country and if not agreed with, at least grappled with.

In fact, there would be no grappling. Obama was denounced for having attacked the police, and the furor grew so great that it momentarily threatened to waylay his agenda. The president beat a hasty retreat. He apologized to the police officer, then invited Crowley and Gates to the White House for a beer. It was absurd. It was spectacle. But it cohered to the common theory, it appealed to the redemptive spirit and reduced the horror of being detained by an armed officer of the state, and all of the history of that horror, to something that could be resolved over a beer.

And now the lies of the Civil War and the lies of these post-racial years began to resonate with each other, and I could now see history, awful and undead, reaching out from the grave. America had a biography, and in that biography, the shackling of black people—slaves and free—featured prominently. I could not yet draw literal connections, though that would come. But what I sensed was a country trying to skip out on a bill, trying to stave off a terrible accounting. I did not yet fully comprehend the contents of the bill or its weight. Nor had I yet conceived of the incredible thing, the radical action it would take to set the account right.

WHY DO SO FEW BLACKS
STUDY THE CIVIL WAR?

———

IN MY SEVENTH-GRADE YEAR, MY SCHOOL TOOK A BUS TRIP from our native Baltimore to Gettysburg, Pennsylvania, the sanctified epicenter of American tragedy. It was the mid-'80s, when educators in our inner cities, confronted by the onslaught of crack, Saturday night specials, and teen pregnancy, were calling on all hands for help—even the hands of the departed.

Preposterous notions abounded. Black people talked openly of covert plots evidenced by skyrocketing murder rates and the plague of HIV. Conscious people were quick to glean, from the cascade of children murdered over Air Jordans, something still darker—the work of warlocks who would extinguish all hope for our race. The stratagem of these shadow forces was said to be amnesia: They would have us see no past greatness in ourselves, and thus no future glory. And so it was thought that a true history, populated by a sable nobility and punctuated by an ensemble of Negro "firsts," might be the curative for black youth who had no aspirations beyond the corner.

The attempt was gallant. It enlisted every field, from the arts (Phillis Wheatley) to the sciences (Charles Drew). Each February—known since 1976 as Black History Month—trivia contests rewarded those who could recall the inventions of Garrett A. Morgan, the words of Sojourner Truth, or the wizard hands of Daniel Hale Williams. At my middle school, classes were grouped into teams, each of them named for a hero (or a "shero," in the jargon of the time) of our long-suffering, yet magnificent, race. I was on the (Thurgood) Marshall team. Even our field trips felt invested with meaning—the favored destination was Baltimore's National Great Blacks in Wax Museum, where our pantheon was rendered lifelike by the disciples of Marie Tussaud.

Given this near-totemic reverence for black history, my trip to Gettysburg—the site of the ultimate battle in a failed war to protect and extend slavery—should cut like a lighthouse beam across the sea of memory. But when I look back on those years when black history was seen as tangible, as an antidote for the ills of the street, and when I think on my first visit to America's original hallowed ground, all is fog.

I remember riding in a beautiful coach bus, as opposed to the hated yellow cheese. I remember stopping at Hardee's for lunch, and savoring the respite from my vegetarian father's lima beans and tofu. I remember cannons, and a display of guns. But as for any connections to the very history I was regularly baptized in, there is nothing. In fact, when I recall all the attempts to inculcate my classmates with some sense of legacy and history, the gaping hole of Gettysburg opens into the chasm of the Civil War.

We knew, of course, about Frederick Douglass and Harriet Tubman. But our general sense of the war was that a horrible tragedy somehow had the magical effect of getting us free. Its legacy belonged not to us, but to those who reveled in the costume and technology of a time when we were property.

Our alienation was neither achieved in independence, nor stumbled upon by accident, but produced by American design. The belief that the Civil War wasn't for us was the result of the country's long search for a narrative that could reconcile white people with each other, one that avoided what professional historians now know to be true: that one group of Americans attempted to raise a country wholly premised on property in Negroes, and that another group of Americans, including many Negroes, stopped them. In the popular mind, that demonstrable truth has been evaded in favor of a more comforting story of tragedy, failed compromise, and individual gallantry. For that more ennobling narrative, as for so much of American history, the fact of black people is a problem.

In April 1865, the United States was faced with a discomfiting reality: It had seen 2 percent of its population destroyed because a section of its citizenry would countenance anything to protect, and expand, the right to own other people. The mass bloodletting shocked the senses. At the war's start, Senator James Chesnut Jr. of South Carolina, believing that casualties would be minimal, claimed he would drink all the blood shed in the coming disturbance. Five years later, 750,000 Americans were dead. But the fact that such carnage had been wreaked for a cause that Ulysses S. Grant called "one of the worst for which a people ever fought, and one for which there was the least excuse" invited the damnation of history. Honor is salvageable from a military defeat; much less so from an ideological defeat, and especially one so duly earned in defense of slavery in a country premised on liberty.

The fallen Confederacy's chroniclers grasped this historiographic challenge and, immediately after the war, began erasing all evidence of the crime—that is to say, they began erasing black people—from the written record. In his collection of historical essays *This Mighty Scourge,* James McPherson notes that before the war, Jefferson Davis defended secession, saying it was justified by Lincoln's alleged radicalism. Davis claimed that Lincoln's plan to limit slavery would make "property in slaves so insecure as to be comparatively worthless . . . thereby annihilating in effect property worth thousands of millions of dollars." Alexander Stephens renounced the notion that all men are created equal, claiming that the Confederacy was

> founded upon exactly the opposite idea . . . upon the great truth that the negro is not equal to the white man; that slavery, subordination to the superior race, is his natural and normal condition.

He called this ideology a "great physical, philosophical and moral truth."

But after the war, each man changed his interpretation. Davis referred to the "existence of African servitude" as "only an incident," not the cause of the war. Stephens asserted,

> Slavery, so called, was but the question on which these antagonistic principles . . . of Federation, on the one side, and Centralism . . . on the other . . . were finally brought into . . . collision.

Davis later wrote:

> Never was there happier dependence of labor and capital on each other. The tempter came, like the serpent of Eden, and decoyed them with the magic word of "freedom." . . . He put arms in their hands, and trained their humble but emotional natures to deeds of violence and bloodshed, and sent them out to devastate their benefactors.

In such revisions of history lay the roots of the noble Lost Cause—the belief that the South didn't lose, so much as it was simply overwhelmed by superior numbers; that General Robert E. Lee was a contemporary King Arthur; that slavery, to be sure a benevolent institution, was never central to the South's true designs. Historical lies aside, the Lost Cause presented to the North an attractive compromise. Having preserved the Union and saved white workers from competing with slave labor, the North could magnanimously acquiesce to such Confederate meretriciousness and the concomitant irrelevance of the country's blacks. That interpretation served the North too, for it elided uncomfortable questions about the profits reaped by the North from Southern cotton, as well as the North's long strategy of appeasement and compromise, stretching from the Fugitive Slave Act back to the Constitution itself.

By the time of the fiftieth-anniversary commemoration of Gettysburg, this new and comfortable history was on full display. Speakers at the ceremony pointedly eschewed any talk of the war's cause in hopes of pursuing what the historian David Blight calls "a mourning without politics." Woodrow Wilson, when he addressed the crowd, did not mention slavery but asserted that the war's meaning could be found in "the splendid valor, the manly devotion of the men then arrayed against one another, now grasping hands and smiling into each other's eyes." Wilson, born into the Confederacy and the first postbellum president to hail from the South, was at that very moment purging blacks from federal jobs and remanding them to separate washrooms. Thus Wilson executed a familiar act of theater—urging the country's white citizens away from their history, while continuing to act in the spirit of its darkest chapters. Wilson's ideas were not simply propaganda, but notions derived from some of the country's most celebrated historians. James McPherson notes that titans of American history like Charles Beard, Avery Craven, and James G. Randall minimized the role of slavery in the war; some blamed the violence on irreconcilable economic differences between a romantic pastoral South and a capitalistic manufacturing North, or on the hot rhetoric of radical abolitionists.

With a firm foothold in the public memory and in the academic history, the comfortable narrative found its most influential expression in the popular media. Films like *The Birth of a Nation* and *Gone with the Wind* revealed an establishment more interested in the alleged sins perpetrated upon Confederates than in the all-too-real sins perpetrated upon the enslaved people in their midst. That predilection continues. In 2010's *The Conspirator,* the director Robert Redford's Mary Surratt is the preferred victim of political persecution—never mind those whose very lives were persecution. The new AMC show *Hell on Wheels* deploys the trope of the blameless Confederate wife ravished and killed by Union marauders, as though Fort Pillow never happened.

The comfortable narrative haunts even the best mainstream presentations of the Civil War. Ken Burns's eponymous and epic documentary on the war falsely claims that the slaveholder Robert E. Lee was personally against slavery. True, Lee once asserted in a letter that slavery was a "moral & political evil." But in that same letter, he argued that there was no sense protesting the peculiar institution and that its demise should be left to "a wise Merciful Providence." In the meantime, Lee was happy to continue, in Lincoln's words, wringing his "bread from the sweat of other men's faces."

Burns also takes as his narrator Shelby Foote, who once called Lieutenant General Nathan Bedford Forrest, a slave-trader and Klansman, "one of the most attractive men who ever walked through the pages of history," and who presents the Civil War as a kind of big, tragic misunderstanding. "It was because we failed to do the thing we really have a genius for, which is compromise," said Foote, neglecting to mention the Missouri Compromise, the Fugitive Slave Act, the Kansas-Nebraska Act, and the fact that any further such compromise would have meant the continued enslavement of black people.

For that particular community, for my community, the message has long been clear: The Civil War is a story for white people—acted out by white people, on white people's terms—in which blacks feature strictly as stock characters and props. We are invited to listen, but never to truly join the narrative, for to speak as the slave would, to say that we are as happy for the Civil War as most Americans are for the Revolutionary War, is to rupture the narrative. Having been tendered such a conditional invitation, we have elected—as most sane people would—to decline.

In my study of African American history, the Civil War was always something of a sideshow. Just off center stage, it could be heard dimly behind the stories of Booker T. Washington, Ida B. Wells, and Martin Luther King Jr., a shadow on the fringe. But three years ago, I picked up James McPherson's *Battle Cry of Freedom* and found not a shadow, but the Big Bang that brought the ideas of the modern West to fruition. Our lofty notions of democracy, egalitarianism, and individual freedom were articulated by the founders, but they were consecrated by the thousands of slaves fleeing to Union lines, some of them later returning to the land of their birth as nurses and soldiers. The first generation of the South's postbellum black political leadership was largely supplied by this class.

Transfixed by the war's central role in making democracy real, I have now morphed into a Civil War buff, that peculiar specimen who pores over the books chronicling the battles, then walks the parks where the battles were fought by soldiers, then haunts the small towns from which the soldiers hailed, many never to return.

This journey—to Paris, Tennessee; to Petersburg, Virginia; to Fort Donelson; to the Wilderness—has been one of the most meaningful of my life, though at every stop I have felt myself ill dressed in another man's clothes. What echoes from nearly all the sites chronicling the war is a deep sense of tragedy. At Petersburg, the film in the visitor center mourns the city's fall and the impending doom of Richmond. At the Wilderness, the park ranger instructs you on the details of the men's grisly deaths. The celebrated Civil War historian Bruce Catton best sums up this sense when he refers to the war as "a consuming tragedy so costly that generations would pass before people could begin to say whether what it had bought was worth the price."

All of those "people" are white.

For African Americans, war commenced not in 1861, but in 1661, when the Virginia Colony began passing America's first black codes, the charter documents of a slave society that rendered blacks a permanent servile class and whites a mass aristocracy. They were also a declaration of war.

Over the next two centuries, the vast majority of the country's blacks were robbed of their labor and subjected to constant and capricious violence. They were raped and whipped at the pleasure of their owners. Their families lived under the threat of existential violence—in just the four decades before the Civil War, more than two million African American slaves were bought and sold. Slavery did not mean merely coerced labor, sexual assault, and torture, but the constant threat of having a portion, or the whole, of your family consigned to oblivion. In all regards, slavery was war on the black family.

African Americans understood they were at war, and reacted accordingly: running away, rebelling violently, fleeing to the British, murdering slave-catchers, and—less spectacularly, though more significantly—refusing to work, breaking tools, bending a Christian God to their own interpretation, stealing back the fruits of their labor, and, in covert corners of their world, committing themselves to the illegal act of learning to read. Southern whites also understood they were in a state of war, and subsequently turned the antebellum South into a police state. In 1860, the majority of people living in South Carolina and Mississippi, and a significant minority of those living in the entire South, needed passes to travel the roads, and regularly endured the hounding of slave patrols.

It is thus predictable that when you delve into the thoughts of black people of that time, the Civil War appears in a different light. In her memoir of the war, the abolitionist Mary Livermore recalls her prewar time with an Aunt Aggy, a house slave. Livermore saw Aggy's mixed-race daughter brutally attacked by the patriarch of the home. In a private moment, the woman warned Livermore that she could "hear the rumbling of the chariots" and that a day was coming when "white folks' blood is running on the ground like a river."

After the war had started, Livermore again met Aunt Aggy, who well recalled her prophecy and saw in the Civil War, not tragedy, but divine justice. "I always knowed it was coming," the woman told Livermore.

> I always heard the rumbling of the wheels. I always expected to see white folks heaped up dead. And the Lord, He's kept His promise and avenged His people, just as I knowed He would.

For blacks, it was not merely the idea of the war that had meaning, but the tangible violence, the actions of black people themselves as the killers and the killed, that mattered. Corporal Thomas Long, of the 33rd United States Colored Troops, told his fellow black soldiers,

> If we hadn't become soldiers, all might have gone back as it was before. . . . But now things can never go back, because we have shown our energy and our courage and our natural manhood.

Reflecting on the days leading to the Civil War, Frederick Douglass wrote:

> I confess to a feeling allied to satisfaction at the prospect of a conflict between the North and the South. Standing outside the pale of American humanity, denied citizenship, unable to call the land of my birth my country, and adjudged by the supreme court of the United States to have no rights which white men were bound to respect, and longing for the end of the bondage of my people, I was ready for any political upheaval which should bring about a change in the existing condition of things.

He went on to assert that the Civil War was an achievement that outstripped the American Revolution:

It was a great thing to achieve American independence when we numbered three millions. But it was a greater thing to save this country from dismemberment and ruin when it numbered thirty millions.

The twentieth century, with its struggles for equal rights, with the triumph of democracy as the ideal in Western thought, proved Douglass right. The Civil War marks the first great defense of democracy and the modern West. Its legacy lies in everything from women's suffrage to the revolutions now sweeping the Middle East. It was during the Civil War that the heady principles of the Enlightenment were first, and most spectacularly, called fully to account.

In our present time, to express the view of the enslaved—to say that the Civil War was a significant battle in the long war against bondage and for government by the people—is to compromise the comfortable narrative. It is to remind us that some of our own forefathers once explicitly rejected the republic to which they'd pledged themselves, and dreamed up another country, with slavery not merely as a bug, but as its very premise. It is to point out that at this late hour, the totems of the empire of slavery—chief among them, its flag—still enjoy an honored place in the homes, and public spaces, of self-professed patriots and vulgar lovers of "freedom." It is to understand what it means to live in a country that will never apologize for slavery, but will not stop apologizing for the Civil War.

In August, I returned to Gettysburg. My visits to battlefields are always unsettling. Repeatedly, I have dragged my family along, and upon arrival I generally wish that I hadn't. Nowhere, as a black person, do I feel myself more of a problem than at these places, premised, to varying degrees, on talking around me. But of all the Civil War battlefields I've visited, Gettysburg now seems the most honest and forward-looking. The film in the visitor center begins with slavery, putting it at the center of the conflict. And in recent years, the National Park Service has made an effort to recognize an understated historical element of the town—its community of free blacks.

The Confederate army, during its march into Pennsylvania, routinely kidnapped blacks and sold them south. By the time Lee's legions arrived in Gettysburg, virtually all of the town's free blacks had hidden or fled. On the morning of July 3, General George Pickett's division prepared for its legendary charge. Nearby, where the Union forces were gathered, lived Abraham Brian, a free black farmer who rented out a house on his property to Mag Palmer and her family. One evening before the war, two slave-catchers had fallen upon Palmer as she made her way home. (After the passage of the Fugitive Slave Act, slave-catchers patrolled the North, making little distinction between freeborn blacks and runaways.) They bound her hands, but with help from a passerby, she fought them off, biting off a thumb of one of the hunters.

Faulkner famously wrote of Pickett's Charge:

For every Southern boy fourteen years old, not once but whenever he wants it, there is the instant when it's still not yet two o'clock on that July afternoon in 1863 . . . and it's all in the balance, it hasn't happened yet, it hasn't even begun yet. . . . That moment doesn't need even a fourteen-year-old boy to think *This time.*

These "Southern boys," like Catton's "people," are all white. But I, standing on Brian's property, standing where Mag Palmer lived, saw Pickett's soldiers charging through history, in wild pursuit of their strange birthright—the license to beat and shackle women under the cover of night. That is all of what was "in the balance," the nostalgic moment's corrupt and unspeakable core.

FOR THE PORTION OF the country that still honors, or traces its ancestry to, the men who fired on Fort Sumter, and thus brought war, the truthful story of the Civil War tells of a defeat richly deserved, garnered in a pursuit now condemned. For the blameless

North, it throws up the failed legacy of appeasement of slaveholders, the craven willingness to bargain on the backs of black people, and the unwillingness, in the Reconstruction years, to finish what the war started.

For realists, the true story of the Civil War illuminates the problem of ostensibly sober-minded compromise with powerful, and intractable, evil. For radicals, the wave of white terrorism that followed the war offers lessons on the price of revolutionary change. White Americans finding easy comfort in nonviolence and the radical love of the civil rights movement must reckon with the unsettling fact that black people in this country achieved the rudiments of their freedom through the killing of whites.

And for black people, there is this—the burden of taking ownership of the Civil War as Our War. During my trips to battlefields, the near-total absence of African American visitors has been striking. Confronted with the realization that the Civil War is the genesis of modern America, in general, and of modern black America, in particular, we cannot just implore the Park Service and the custodians of history to do more outreach—we have to become custodians ourselves.

The Lost Cause was spread, not merely by academics and Hollywood executives, but by the descendants of Confederate soldiers. Now the country's battlefields are marked with the enduring evidence of their tireless efforts. But we have stories too, ones that do not hinge on erasing other people, or coloring over disrepute. For the Civil War to become Our War, it will not be enough to, yet again, organize opposition to the latest raising of the Confederate flag. The Civil War confers on us the most terrible burden of all—the burden of moving from protest to production, the burden of summoning our own departed hands, so that they, too, may leave a mark.

4.

NOTES FROM
THE
FOURTH YEAR

ANY FAIR CONSIDERATION OF THE DEPTH AND WIDTH OF enslavement tempts insanity. First conjure the crime—the generational destruction of human bodies—and all of its related offenses—domestic terrorism, poll taxes, mass incarceration. But then try to imagine being an individual born among the remnants of that crime, among the wronged, among the plundered, and feeling the gravity of that crime all around and seeing it in the sideways glances of the perpetrators of that crime and overhearing it in their whispers and watching these people, at best, denying their power to address the crime and, at worst, denying that any crime had occurred at all, even as their entire lives revolve around the fact of a robbery so large that it is written in our very names. This is not a thought experiment. America is literally unimaginable without plundered labor shackled to plundered land, without the organizing principle of whiteness as citizenship, without the culture crafted by the plundered, and without that culture itself being plundered.

To consider all of this, to empathize on any human level with the lynched and the raped, and then to watch all of the beneficiaries just going on with their heedless lives, could fill you with the most awful rage. I feel it myself, for example, walking through Washington, D.C., or Brooklyn, where gentrification has blown through like a storm. And I feel it not just because of the black people swept away but because I know that "gentrification" is but a more pleasing name for white supremacy, is the interest on enslavement, the interest on Jim Crow, the interest on redlining, compounding across the years, and these new urbanites living off of that interest are, all of them, exulting in a crime. To speak the word *gentrification* is to immediately lie. And I know, even in my anger, even as I write this, that I am no better. White people are, in some profound way, trapped; it took generations to make them white, and it will take more to unmake them. And in my gut, in the human part of me, I feel how hard that really must be. What people anywhere on this earth has ever, out of a strong moral feeling, ceded power? Can I say that I—we—are any different?

I understood the desire to avoid facing all of this. Some not insubstantial part of me preferred to not know the cost of history, the price of this great crime. But I was primed to know, just as sure as they were primed not to, by circumstance, primed by Baltimore, Park Heights, Woodbrook Avenue, Tioga Parkway, circa 1986, a corner of time-space where the rules of violence were branded upon the youth. While some dreamlike definition of childhood was made plain to us by the television, that medium of American aspiration, that life—big lawns, big garages, untrammeled adolescence—was alien to us. The television screen was a window into a party to which we would receive no invitation. Indeed, this exclusion was the entire basis of the party.

But we had parties too—ones rooted in all that was hard and known, jams more dynamic, more electric and alive than anything eligible for display in that American window. That is where I begin, as a writer: in hip-hop. It was the first music I ever really knew, which is to say the first literature I ever knew, which is to say the first place where I consciously developed a sense that words, strung together, could be—and really should be—beautiful. In 1985 I unfolded a steel chair next to my parents' stereo, popped in a tape, and then pulled out a pen and pad. For the next hour I played and rewound the first verse of LL Cool J's "I Can't Live without My Radio," recording each word on the pad. I was convinced there was something worth discovering in the lyrics, something extraordinary and arcane. I had to have it. I had to trap it on paper, consume it, make it mine:

> My radio, believe me, I like it loud
> I'm the man with the box that can rock the crowd

This was beyond music and poetry. This was incantation. I was ten and filled with all the ignorance and angst of any child at that age. There was so much I did not know, so much I could not control. Why did I live as I did? Why did my father force us to fast on Thanksgiving? Why could I never pay attention in Mrs. Boone's class? And what was that feeling, pushing out from the pit of me, drawing me toward certain brown-skinned girls in the same way I was drawn to cane syrup and molasses cookies? I felt ignorant and enfeebled before everything, a slave to my circumstance. And then I heard this MC, somewhere out there, in some distant land called Queens, who lived not among television dreams but as I did among the concrete playground alleys and Saturday night specials, out here in the real. Perhaps he'd once been like me—a slave. But then he grabbed the mic like a cudgel, raised it to the sky, lightning struck, and the cudgel was now a hammer, and the slave was transfigured into a god whose voice shivered the Earth. And that is the story hip-hop told me then. And for anyone who has felt, as I so often did, ignorant, enfeebled, enslaved to circumstance, this was myth and this was saga, awesome as any *Aeneid, Iliad,* or *Odyssey.*

From hip-hop, I drew my earliest sense of what writing should mean. Grammar was never the point. Grammar was for the schoolmen and their television dreams. Out here, in the concrete and real, sentences should be supernatural, words strung together until they compelled any listener to repeat them at odd hours, long after the bass line had died. And these sentences or bars, linked together into verses, should have a shading and mood that reflected their origins in slavery and struggle. The sentence might be magical, but the magic was never sentimental. It was born from the want of all that exceeded the slave's grasp and the exploration of all that divided that grasp from its desire.

That was what I felt in the summer of 1993. I spent the entire season studying Nas's "One Love" in hopes that I'd understand his technique. The song is a story, and the scene is this: Nas and a twelve-year-old drug dealer are sitting on a bench smoking marijuana:

> I sat back like The Mack, my army suit was black,
> We was chillin' on these benches where he pumped his
> loose cracks.

Nas attempts to advise the younger drug dealer, who routinely carries a gun, how to cope with the violence of the projects. His advice is beautiful, which is to say it is grounded in the concrete fact of slavery. That was how I wanted to write—with weight and clarity, without sanctimony and homily. I could not even articulate why. I guess if forced I would have mumbled something about "truth." What I know is that by then I had absorbed an essential message, an aesthetic, from Nas and from the hip-hop of that era. Art was not an after-school special. Art was not motivational speaking. Art was not sentimental. It had no responsibility to be hopeful or optimistic or make anyone feel better about the world. It must reflect the world in all its brutality and beauty, not in hopes of changing it but in the mean and selfish desire to not be enrolled in its lie, to not be coopted by the television dreams, to not ignore the great crimes all around us.

In the Obama years and in the time my work now afforded me

to sit back and study, I found a natural marriage between the blue aesthetic of hip-hop and the history I was then consuming.

I wanted to make writing that flowed like Nas, Raekwon, or Jay. In those early years at *The Atlantic,* I got my share of practice—the blog assured me of that. Even in those pieces that seemed to be casually tossed off, I was always searching for the right word, for the proper escape from the clichés that threatened every sentence, from truisms that threatened to steer me back into the sentimental dream. I was always trying to sharpen my language to become, as Ghostface put it, "the arsonist who burns with his pen, regardless."

This was the voice in my head I was constantly trying to unlock, to get out and onto the page. I wanted to produce writing that was not just correct on its merits but, through its form and flow, emotionally engaged the receiver, writing that was felt as much as it was understood. I could hear what that voice sounded like in my head. It was a blues with a beat dirtier than anything I had ever heard anywhere in the world. I did not know then that the music is unattainable, if only because it is imagined and unreal, its own dream. And the music—the music in one's head—is always changing.

And that music went beyond hip-hop. I saw it in all the reading I was doing—even now the sentences come back to me, haunting me as sure as any MC. I think of Ulysses S. Grant speaking of poor Southern whites—"They too needed emancipation"; Edith Wharton sighing at the naïveté of her hero—"Oh my dear—Where is that country?"; E. L. Doctorow expressing the motivating desires of his protagonist's occupation—"I report, that is my profession, I report as a loud noise testifies to a gun"; George Eliot on the storyteller's mission—"All the light I can command must be concentrated on this particular web"; C. V. Wedgwood's summary of the mercenary Ernst von Mansfeld—"The world was his oyster, and the sword the best tool to open it."

The first time I felt that I'd captured something close to that music on the page was in a book review I wrote of a biography of Malcolm X, which made sense in a way. Malcolm was a subject I knew well, and his analysis of America sprang from the same streets as hip-hop and was just as bleak. My descent into a more complicated analysis began around this time, and I thought often of Malcolm's deep skepticism of the country into which he was born but never claimed as his own. I needed to go back to him, because even then, even as I was falling into Edmund Morgan, even as the old voices of hip-hop, of the street, pointed me toward the likelihood of tragedy, I still wanted to believe in some other ending. Nothing is ever complete in me or, I think, in any person. A writer tries to convey all the shifting moods, emotions, and tides within, but like the music, the full complexity of this thinking lives beyond the narrative grasp. All I know is that even now, with outrages compiling daily, with the suicidal wish of whiteness on full display, with its impulse to burn down the country if the country can't dream itself white, I am hoping that I am wrong, that I am somehow unnecessarily bleak.

But it was in that fourth year that the full dimensions of a tragedy were starting to come into view for me, with the movement to cast Barack Obama as alien its first act. To give that movement a new name, to call the movement—which the country's first white president heartily embraced—"birtherism" is to, again, join in the lie, in the euphemistic game, which hides all the history undergirding the accusation. There was nothing new in this "birtherism," in this attempt to deny African Americans the rights entitled to other American citizens, and there was nothing new in that denial's power to organize a constituency. Large swaths of the Republican rank and file believed Obama to be Kenyan or "Muslim," which is to say an "other." Their politicians, in varying degrees, flirted with the theory, endorsed it, rallied around it. Obama was bemused. He stood before cameras and the assembled Washington press, having just released a copy of his birth certificate, laughed, and then noted that the country should be moving on to more important business. He did not believe this theory of illegitimacy posed any real threat to him, his agenda, or his legacy. I was not so sanguine. The threat sent me back to my native skepticism of the country's anti-racist possibilities and to Malcolm X's belief that this country, in fact, would not overcome.

The piece I ultimately wrote sounds better than it reads. That is to say it reflects the rhythm and voice I'd been working to achieve. But the Obama-Malcolm parallel is strained, and the praise of the book the piece ostensibly reviews—Manning Marable's biography, *Malcolm X: A Life of Reinvention*—has not held up. It was my enduring doubts about hope and change that sent me back to Malcolm X, the greatest twentieth-century skeptic of American democracy, even as I was still trying hard to believe in Obama's vision. You can see it in the approach to this piece, in the attempt to reconcile the import of two of the most dominant figures in black political life. I think, now, I was trying to reconcile something in me—the doubt that went back to my childhood, that went back to Malcolm, that I felt in my earliest flirtations with art, and the hope that the logical conclusions of that doubt, understandable as they may be, could ultimately be evaded. The answer was always there. The history told me. The streets told me. And so the music told me. I heard the tune. Soon I would hear the lyrics.

THE LEGACY OF
MALCOLM X

WHY HIS VISION LIVES ON
IN BARACK OBAMA

WHEN MY MOTHER WAS TWELVE, SHE WALKED FROM THE PROJ-
ects of West Baltimore to the beauty shop at North Avenue and
Druid Hill, and for the first time in her life, was relaxed. It was
1962. Black, bespectacled, skinny, and bucktoothed, Ma was also
considered to have the worst head of hair in her family. Her tales of
home cosmetology are surreal. They feature a hot metal comb, the
kitchen stove, my grandmother, much sizzling, the occasional ner-
vous flinch, and screaming and scabbing.

In the ongoing quest for the locks of Lena Horne, a chemical
relaxer was an agent of perfection. It held longer than hot combs,
and with more aggression—virtually every strand could be sub-
dued, and would remain so for weeks. Relying on chemistry instead of torque and heat, the relaxer seemed more worldly, more
civilized and refined.

That day, the hairdresser donned rubber gloves, applied petro-
leum jelly to protect Ma's scalp, stroked in a clump of lye, and told
my mother to hold on for as long as she could bear. Ma endured this
ritual every three to four weeks for the rest of her childhood. Some-

times, the beautician would grow careless with the jelly, and Ma's scalp would simmer for days. But on the long walk home, black boys would turn, gawk, and smile at my mother's hair made good.

Ma went off to college, leaving the house of my grandmother, a onetime domestic from Maryland's Eastern Shore who had studied nursing in night school and owned her own home. This was 1969. Martin Luther King Jr. was dead. Baltimore had exploded in riots. Ma hung a poster of Huey Newton in her dorm room. She donated clothes at the Baltimore office of the Black Panthers. There, she met my father, a dissident of strong opinions, modest pedigree, and ill repute. In the eyes of my grandmother, their entanglement was heretical, a rejection of the workhorse ethos of colored people, which had lifted my grandmother out of the projects and delivered her kids to college. The impiety was summed up in a final preposterous act that a decade earlier would have been inconceivable—my mother, at twenty, let her relaxer grow out, and cultivated her own natural, nappy hair.

The community of my youth was populated by women of similar ilk. They wore their hair in manifold ways—dreadlocks and Nubian twists, Afros as wide as planets or low and tapered from the temple. They braided it, invested it with beads and yarn, pulled the whole of it back into a crown, or wrapped it in yards of African fabric. But in a rejection aimed at something greater than follicles and roots, all of them repudiated straighteners.

The women belonged, as did I, to a particular tribe of America, one holding that we, as black people, were born to a country that hated us and that at all turns plotted our fall. A nation built on immigrants and a professed eclecticism made its views of us manifest through blackface, Little Sambo, and Tarzan of the Apes. Its historians held that Africa was a cannibal continent. Its pundits argued that we should be happy for our enslavement. Its uniformed thugs beat us in Selma and shot us down in northern streets. So potent was this hate that even we, the despised, were enlisted into its cause. So we bleached our skin, jobbed our noses, and relaxed our hair.

To reject hatred, to awaken to the ugly around us and the original beauty within, to be aware, to be "conscious," as we dubbed ourselves, was to reject the agents of deceit—their religion, their culture, their names. To be conscious was to celebrate the self, to cast blackness in all its manifestations as a blessing. Kinky hair and full lips were the height of beauty. Their bearers were the progeny, not of slaves, but of kidnapped kings of Africa, cradle of all humanity. Old customs were found, new ones pulled out of the air. *Kwanzaa* for "Christmas," *Kojo* for "Peter," and *jambo* for "hello." Conscious sects sprang up—some praising the creator sky god Damballah, some spouting Hebrew, and still others talking in Akan. Consciousness was inchoate and unorthodox—it made my father a vegetarian, but never moved him to wear dreadlocks or adopt an African name. What united us all was the hope of rebirth, of a serum to cure generational shame. What united us was our champion, who delivered us from self-hatred, who delivered my mother from burning lye, who was slaughtered high up in Harlem so that colored people could color themselves anew.

IN HIS LIFETIME, MALCOLM X covered so much ground that now, forty-six years after his murder, cross-sections of this country—well beyond the conscious advocates of my youth—still fight over his footprints. What shall we make of a man who went from thoughtless criminal to militant ascetic; from indignant racist to insurgent humanist; who could be dogmatically religious one moment, and then broadly open-minded the next; who in the last year of his life espoused capitalism and socialism, leaving both conservatives and communists struggling to lay their claims?

Gripping and inconsistent myths swirl about him. In one telling, Malcolm is a hate-filled bigot, who through religion came to see the kinship of all. In another he is the self-redeemer, a lowly pimp become an exemplar of black chivalry. In still another he is an avatar of collective revenge, a gangster whose greatest insight lay in changing not his ways, but his targets. The layers, the contradictions, the sheer profusion of Malcolm X's public pronouncements have been a gift to seemingly every contemporary black artist and intellectual from Kanye to Cornel West.

For virtually all of my sentient life, I have carried some talisman of Malcolm—key chain, audiotape, or T-shirt. I came of age not just among the black and conscious, but among that slice of the hip-hop generation that witnessed Malcolm X's revival in the late 1980s and early '90s, bracketed by the rapper KRS-One's appropriation of Malcolm's famous pose by the window and Spike Lee's sprawling biopic. For those who'd grown up in hardscrabble inner cities, Malcolm X offered the promise of transcending the street. For those who'd been the only black kids in their classes, Malcolm's early and troubled interactions with his own white classmates provided comfort. For me, he embodied the notion of an individual made anew through his greater commitment to a broad black collective. When I first lived alone, at the age of twenty, I purchased a giant black-and-white poster of Malcolm with the phrase NO SELL OUT scrawled at the top.

But my life grew in ways that did not adhere to slogans. Raised in de facto segregation, I was carried by my work into the mostly white world, and then to the blasphemies of having white friends and howling white music. In 2004, I moved to Malcolm's adopted home of Harlem, and though I occasionally marveled at Malcolm's old mosque at 116th and Lenox, or the YMCA where he roomed as an aspiring Harlem hustler, my years there passed without note. I declined to hang my giant Malcolm poster in my new digs, stuffing him and all my conscious days in the closet.

I spent Election Night 2008 with my partner and our son, at the home of two dear friends and their young son. That they were an interracial couple is both beside the point, and the point itself. By then, my friends were so varied in hue, and more varied still in their pairings, that I'd stopped thinking in ways I once took as elemental. I joined in the spectacle of America—a country that had incorporated the fact of African slavery into its Constitution—handing its standard to a black man of thin résumé and fantastical mien.

And the next day, I saw black people smiling. And some conscious part of me died with their smiles. I thought back on the debate running from Martin Delany and Frederick Douglass through Martin Luther King and Malcolm X, and I knew a final verdict had been reached. Who could look on a black family that had won the votes, if not the hearts, of Virginia, Colorado, and North Carolina, waving to their country and bounding for the White House, and seriously claim, as Malcolm once did, that blacks were not American?

The opportunity for crowing was not missed. Writing three weeks after the election in the New York *Daily News,* Stanley Crouch, the pugilist and contrarian who'd earlier argued that Obama was not black, dismissed Malcolm X as "one of the naysayers to American possibility whose vision was permanently crushed beneath the heel of Obama's victory on Nov. 4." Last year, offering up on *The New Republic*'s website a listicle of those whose impact on black people he wished he could erase, John McWhorter gave Malcolm X the top spot.

But from the shadows, still he looms. Bull Connor's world fell as the fortunes of Barack Obama rose. Yet its collapse was not assured until November of 2008. Now I see its amazing doom in ways both absurd and replete—Will Smith's conquest of cinema, his son as the new Karate Kid, the wild utterings of Michael Steele, the kids holding out for Lauryn Hill's mythical return. As surely as 2008 was made possible by black people's long fight to be publicly American, it was also made possible by those same Americans' long fight to be publicly black. That latter fight belongs especially to one man, as does the sight of a first family bearing an African name. Barack Obama is the president. But it's Malcolm X's America.

IN THE SPRING OF 1950, the *Springfield Union,* in Massachusetts, ran the following headline: "Local Criminals, in Prison, Claim

Moslem Faith Now: Grow Beards, Won't Eat Pork, Demand East-Facing Cells to Facilitate 'Prayers to Allah.'" The leader of the protest was an incarcerated and recently converted Malcolm X. Having converted several other prisoners, Malcolm began lobbying the warden for cells and food befitting his band's religious beliefs. He threatened to write the Egyptian consulate in protest. Prison cooks retaliated by serving Malcolm's food with utensils they'd used to prepare pork. Malcolm countered by spending his last two years in prison on a diet of bread and cheese.

The incident, as recounted in Manning Marable's new biography, *Malcolm X: A Life of Reinvention,* set the stage for Malcolm's political career, his split from the Nation of Islam, and ultimately the course of action that led to his death. The goal of his prison protest was to advance the kind of inner reform that first drew Malcolm to the Nation, with thousands to follow. But Malcolm's methods were protest and agitation, tools that the Nation rejected.

Unlike Bruce Perry's 1991 biography, *Malcolm,* which entertained the most outlandish stories in an attempt to present a comprehensive portrait, Marable's biography judiciously sifts fact from myth. Marable's Malcolm is trapped in an unhappy marriage, cuckolded by his wife and one of his lieutenants. His indignation at Elijah Muhammad's womanizing is fueled by his morals, and by his resentment that one of the women involved is an old flame. He can be impatient and petulant. And his behavior, in his last days, casts a shadow over his reputation as an ascetic. He is at times anti-Semitic, sexist, and, without the structure of the Nation, inefficient.

Still, the broad strokes of Malcolm's life—the family terrorized by white supremacists, the murdered father, the turn from criminal to race man—remain intact, and Marable's book is at its best in drawing out its subject's shifting politics. Marable reveals Malcolm to be, in many ways, an awkward fit for the Nation of Islam. Elijah Muhammad's Nation combined the black separatism of Marcus Garvey with Booker T. Washington's disdain for protest. In practice, its members were conservative, stressing moral reform, individual uplift, and entrepreneurship. Malcolm was equally devoted to reform, but he believed that true reform ultimately had radical implications.

Coming out of prison, Malcolm was shocked by the small membership of the Nation, which was seriously active only in Chicago and Detroit. He soon became the sect's most effective recruiter, organizing or reinvigorating mosques in Philadelphia, Boston, Atlanta, and New York. That dynamism was not confined to growing the Nation, but aimed to make it a force in the civil rights movement.

His energy left him with a sprawling web of ties, ranging from the deeply personal (Louis Farrakhan) to the deeply cynical (George Lincoln Rockwell). He allied with A. Philip Randolph and Fannie Lou Hamer, romanced the Saudi royal family, and effectively transformed himself into black America's ambassador to the developing world.

It is tempting to say that Malcolm's politics did not age particularly well. Even after rejecting black supremacy, Malcolm was deeply skeptical of white America and believed its intentions could best be divined from the actions of its zealots. Malcolm had little patience for the politicking of moderates and preferred stark choices. A Manichaean worldview extends from his days denouncing whites as devils up through his more nuanced speeches like "The Ballot or the Bullet."

But Marable complicates the case for firmly fixing Malcolm's ideology, by recounting how, as Malcolm tried to move away from Nation dogma, the sect made a concerted effort to rein him in. Officials demanded that Malcolm and the other ministers tape all their lectures and submit them for approval, to make sure they were pushing Nation ideology as opposed to political appeals on behalf of a broader black America. They repeatedly reprimanded him for going off-script, including, finally, when he seemed to revel in

John F. Kennedy's murder. Muhammad's subsequent response suspending Malcolm reveals much about the group's aims and politics: "The president of the country is our president too."

To Marable's credit, he does not judge Malcolm's significance by his seeming failure to forge a coherent philosophy. As Malcolm traveled to Africa and the Middle East, as he debated at Oxford and Harvard, he encountered a torrent of new ideas, new ways of thinking that batted him back and forth. He never fully gave up his cynical take on white Americans, but he did broaden his views, endorsing interracial marriage and ruing the personal coldness he'd shown toward whites. Yet Malcolm's political vision was never complete like that of Martin Luther King, who hewed faithfully to his central principle, the one he is known for today—his commitment to nonviolence.

For all of Malcolm's prodigious intellect, he was ultimately more an expression of black America's heart than of its brain. Malcolm was the voice of a black America whose parents had borne the slights of second-class citizenship, who had seen protesters beaten by cops and bitten by dogs, and children bombed in churches, and could only sit at home and stew. He preferred to illuminate the bitter calculus of oppression, one in which a people had been forced to hand over their right to self-defense, a right enshrined in Western law and morality and taken as essential to American citizenship, in return for the civil rights that they had been promised a century earlier. The fact and wisdom of nonviolence may be beyond dispute—the civil rights movement profoundly transformed the country. Yet the movement demanded of African Americans a superhuman capacity for forgiveness. Dick Gregory summed up the dilemma well. "I committed to nonviolence," Marable quotes him as saying. "But I'm sort of embarrassed by it."

BUT THE ENDURING APPEAL of Malcolm's message, the portion that reaches out from the Audubon Ballroom to the South Lawn, asserts the right of a people to protect and improve themselves by their own hand. In Malcolm's time, that message rejected the surrender of the right to secure your own body. But it also rejected black criminals' preying on black innocents. And, perhaps most significantly, it rejected the beauty standard of others and erected a new one. In a 1962 rally, Malcolm said:

> Who taught you to hate the texture of your hair? Who taught you to hate the color of your skin? Who taught you to hate the shape of your nose and the shape of your lips? Who taught you to hate yourself from the top of your head to the soles of your feet? Who taught you to hate your own kind?

The implicit jab was not at some specific white person, but at a systemic force that compelled black people toward self-loathing. To my mother, a poor black girl, Malcolm X said, "It's okay. And you're okay." To embrace Malcolm X was to be okay, it was to be relieved of the mythical curse of Ham, and reborn as a full human being.

Virtually all of black America has been, in some shape or form, touched by that rebirth. Before Malcolm X, the very handle we now embrace—*black*—was an insult. We were coloreds or Negroes, and to call someone *black* was to invite a fistfight. But Malcolm remade the menace inherent in that name into something mystical—*Black Power; Black Is Beautiful; It's a black thing, you wouldn't understand.*

Hip-hop, with its focus on the assertion of self, the freedom to be who you are, and entrepreneurship, is an obvious child of black consciousness. One of the most popular music forms today, it is also the first form of pop music truly to bear the imprint of post-'60s America, with a fan base that is young and integrated. Indeed, the coalition of youth that helped Barack Obama ride to the presidency was first assembled by hip-hop record execs. And the stars that the music has produced wear their hair however they please.

For all of Malcolm's invective, his most seductive notion was that of collective self-creation: the idea that black people could, through force of will, remake themselves. Toward the end of his book, Marable tells the story of Gerry Fulcher, a white police officer, who—almost against his will—fell under Malcolm's sway. Assigned to wiretap Malcolm's phone, Fulcher believed Malcolm to be "one of the bad guys," interested in killing cops and overthrowing the government. But his views changed. "What I heard was nothing like I expected," said Fulcher. "I remember saying to myself, 'Let's see, he's right about that. . . . He wants [blacks] to get jobs. He wants them to get education. He wants them to get into the system. What's wrong with that?'" For black people who were never given much of an opportunity to create themselves apart from a mass image of shufflers and mammies, that vision had compelling appeal.

What gave it added valence was Malcolm's own story, his incandescent transformation from an amoral wanderer to a hyper-moral zealot. "He had a brilliant mind. He was disciplined," Louis Farrakhan said in a speech in 1990, and went on:

I never saw Malcolm smoke. I never saw Malcolm take a drink. . . . He ate one meal a day. He got up at 5 o'clock in the morning to say his prayers. . . . I never heard Malcolm cuss. I never saw Malcolm wink at a woman. Malcolm was like a clock.

Farrakhan's sentiments are echoed by an FBI informant, one of many who, by the late 1950s, had infiltrated the Nation of Islam at the highest levels:

Brother Malcolm . . . is an expert organizer and an untiring worker. . . . He is fearless and cannot be intimidated. . . . He has most of the answers at his fingertips and should be carefully dealt with. He is not likely to violate any ordinances or laws. He neither smokes nor drinks and is of high moral character.

In fact, Marable details how Malcolm was, by the end of his life, perhaps evolving away from his hyper-moral persona. He drinks a rum and Coke and allows himself a second meal a day. Marable suspects he carried out an affair or two, one with an eighteen-year-old convert to the Nation. But in the public mind, Malcolm rebirthed himself as a paragon of righteousness, and even in Marable's retelling he is obsessed with the pursuit of self-creation. That pursuit ended when Malcolm was killed by the very Muslims from whom he once demanded fealty.

But the self-created, martially disciplined Malcolm is the man who lives on. The past forty years have presented black America through the distorting prism of crack, crime, unemployment, and skyrocketing rates of incarceration. Some of its most prominent public faces—Michael Jackson, Mike Tyson, Al Sharpton, Jesse Jackson, O. J. Simpson—have in varying degrees proved themselves all too human. Against that backdrop, there is Malcolm. Tall, gaunt, and handsome, clear and direct, Malcolm was who you wanted your son to be. Malcolm was, as Joe Biden would say, clean, and he took it as his solemn, unspoken duty never to embarrass you.

Among organic black conservatives, this moral leadership still gives Malcolm sway. It's his abiding advocacy for blackness, not as a reason for failure, but as a mandate for personal, and ultimately collective, improvement that makes him compelling. Always lurking among Malcolm's condemnations of white racism was a subtler, and more inspiring, notion—"You're better than you think you are," he seemed to say to us. "Now act like it."

Ossie Davis famously eulogized Malcolm X as "our living, black manhood" and "our own black shining prince." Only one man today could bear those twin honorifics: Barack Obama. Progressives who always enjoyed Malcolm's thundering denunciations more than his moral appeals are unimpressed by that message. But among blacks, Obama's moral appeals are warmly received, not because the listeners believe racism has been defeated, but because cutting off your son's PlayStation speaks to something deep and American in black people—a belief that, by their own hand, they can be made better, they can be made anew.

Like Malcolm, Obama was a wanderer who found himself in the politics of the black community, who was rooted in a nationalist church that he ultimately outgrew. Like Malcolm's, his speeches to black audiences are filled with exhortations to self-creation, and draw deeply from his own biography. In his memoir, Barack Obama cites Malcolm's influence on his own life:

> His repeated acts of self-creation spoke to me; the blunt poetry of his words, his unadorned insistence on respect, promised a new and uncompromising order, martial in its discipline, forged through sheer force of will. All the other stuff, the talk of blue-eyed devils and apocalypse, was incidental to that program, I decided, religious baggage that Malcolm himself seemed to have safely abandoned toward the end of his life.

Last summer, I moved from Harlem to Morningside Heights, a neighborhood around Columbia. It was the first neighborhood I'd ever lived in that was not majority-black, and one of the few that could not properly be termed a "hood." It has bars and restaurants on every corner, two different farmer's markets, and a supermarket that's open twenty-four hours and stays stocked with fresh vegetables. The neighborhood represents my new, fully cosmopolitan life.

I had spent the past two years in voracious reading about the Civil War. Repeatedly, I found myself confronting the kind of white Americans—Abraham Lincoln, Ulysses Grant, Adelbert Ames—that black consciousness, with some merit, would have dismissed. And yet I found myself admiring Lincoln, despite his diatribes against Negro equality; respecting Grant, despite his once owning a slave and his advocacy of shipping African Americans out of the country. If I could see the complexity in Grant or Lincoln, what could I see in Malcolm X?

And then I thought about the luxuries that I, and black people writ large, today enjoy. In his *Autobiography,* Malcolm harks back to his time in middle school, when he was one of the top students in his school and made the mistake of telling his teacher he wanted to be a lawyer. "That's no realistic goal for a nigger," Malcolm's teacher told him. Thinking back on that, Malcolm says,

> My greatest lack has been, I believe, that I don't have the kind of academic education I wish I had been able to get. . . . I do believe that I might have made a good lawyer.

What animated Malcolm's rage was that for all his intellect, and all his ability, and all his reinventions, as a black man in America, he found his ambitions ultimately capped. The right of self-creation had its limits then. But not anymore. Obama became a lawyer, and created himself as president, out of a single-parent home and illicit drug use.

And so it is for the more modest of us. I am, at my heart, a college dropout, twice kicked out of high school. Born out of wedlock, I, in turn, had my own son out of wedlock. But my parents do not find me blasphemous, and my mother is the first image of beauty I ever knew. Now no one questions my dark partner's right to her natural hair. No one questions our right to self-creation. It takes a particular arrogance to fail to honor that, and instead to hold, as his most pertinent feature, the prejudices of a man whose earliest memories were of being terrorized by white supremacists, whose ambitions were dashed by actual racists, who was called "nigger" as a child so often that he thought it was his name.

When I finished unpacking my new apartment, I made one immediate change. I took my old Malcolm X poster out of the bubble wrap and affixed it to my living room's western wall.

5.

NOTES FROM
THE
FIFTH YEAR

———

THERE WAS A TIME WHEN I BELIEVED IN AN ARC OF COSMIC justice, that good acts were rewarded and bad deeds punished, if not in my lifetime, then in the by-and-by. I acquired this belief in cosmic justice at the vague point in childhood when I began to cultivate, however rudely, a sense of right and wrong. Tragedy is an unnatural fit on me. My affinity angles toward bedtime stories, fairy tales, and preposterous romance. I would like to believe in God. I simply can't. The reasons are physical. When I was nine, some kid beat me up for amusement, and when I came home crying to my father, his answer—*Fight that boy or fight me*—was godless, because it told me that there was no justice in the world, save the justice we dish out with our own hands. When I was twelve, six boys jumped off the number 28 bus headed to Mondawmin Mall, threw me to the ground, and stomped on my head. But what struck me most that afternoon was not those boys but the godless, heathen adults walking by. Down there on the ground, my head literally being kicked in, I understood: No one, not my father, not the cops, and certainly not anyone's God, was coming to save me. The world was brutal—

and to eschew that brutality, to indulge all your boyish softness, was to advertise yourself as prey. The message was clear, even if I had trouble accepting it: Might really did make right, and he who swung first swung best, and if swinging was not enough, you stabbed, you shot, you did anything to make this whole heathen world understand that you were not the one.

Once I thought that there was something black in this, something about the streets. Then I learned that nations were atheists, which is to say they find their strength not in any God but in their guns. The code of the streets was the code of the world. The chrome .38 was a nuclear warhead—falsifying security, eroding humanity, and threatening all civilized existence.

Nothing in the record of human history argues for divine morality, and a great deal argues against it. What we know is that good people very often suffer terribly, while the perpetrators of horrific evil backstroke through all the pleasures of the world. There is no evidence that the score is ever evened in this life or any after. The barbarian Andrew Jackson rejoiced in mass murder, regaled in enslavement, and died a national hero. For three decades, J. Edgar Hoover incited murder and perfected blackmail against citizens who only sought some equal pursuit of liberty and happiness. Today his name is affixed to a building that we are told was erected in the pursuit of justice. Hitler pushed an entire people to the brink of extinction, escaped human censure, and now finds acolytes among some of the very states he conquered. The warlords of history are still kicking our heads in, and no one, not our fathers, not our Gods, is coming to save us.

Ideas like cosmic justice, collective hope, and national redemption had no meaning for me. The truth was in the everything that came after atheism, after the amorality of the universe is taken not as a problem but as a given. It was then that I was freed from considering my own morality away from the cosmic and the abstract. Life was short, and death undefeated. So I loved hard, since I would not love for long. So I loved directly and fixed myself to solid things—my wife, my child, my family, health, work, friends.

I found, in this fixed and godless love, something cosmic and spiritual nonetheless. The fixed things gave me meaning: I was a black man dedicated to the improvement of myself and my black family, and that small story connected me to a community, living and dead. My ancestors, the great mass of them, had not lived in times of hope. Most of them were not the Harriet Tubmans or Martin Luther Kings, living on the precipice of monumental change, but were strugglers wending their way through the murky before, after, and in-between. They did not alter history. They were Celia, enslaved, hanged in 1855 for murdering her master, but who for a brief moment, stick in hand, lifeless body beneath her, knew freedom, for she had stopped this master from "forcing her." They were Margaret Garner, who would slaughter her own child before submitting her to the slow slaughter of bondage, who with her last breath said to her husband, "Never marry again in slavery." They were Ida B. Wells, who defied the great wave of lynching even when the men whom it victimized would not, even as the country turned away from her. All of these heroes had failed to cajole and coerce the masters of America. Their ambition of a better world had been frustrated. This was the story of my ancestors, the story I expected for myself. These were not stories of hope, but were they without import? If Celia, Margaret, and Ida had failed to help the country at large locate its morality, they had succeeded in living by their own. And that was all they could control. Within the small and narrow frame of their own lives, all they had was their own conscience, their own story. The lessons they passed down were not about an abstract hope, an unknowable dream. They were about the power and necessity of immediate defiance.

That is where I joined them. I understood the problem of black enslavement in America as twofold. First there is the actual enslavement and all that has followed from it, from Reconstruction to Jim

Crow to mass incarceration. But then there was the manufactured story that was told to ennoble and sanctify that enslavement. This was where these heroes took their stand. Celia would go to her death before she would accept the story that gave away her body. Margaret would make herself into a child killer before she would be made an accessory. Ida would scream into the roaring waves before she would believe the story the masters of America told. I was a writer like Ida. And I felt, even in this time, a century later, that I too would gather my words and scream into the roaring waves, because to scream was to defy the story, and that defiance had meaning, no matter that the waves kept coming, would come, maybe, forever. The masters could lie to themselves, lie to the world, but they would never force me to lie to myself. I would never forget that they were liars, that they justified rape, child slavery, and lynching by telling themselves and us and the world that there was something benighted in us, some flaw in our genes, some deficit in our culture, something unfortunate about the shape of our noses, the span of our lips, our style of speech or taste in art, something unsightly in our women or brutal in our men, something wrong with us beyond the misfortune of having been forced, enslaved, and lynched.

If freedom has ever meant anything to me personally, it is this defiance. I remember the first time I heard "Fight the Power," specifically the line where Chuck D assails Elvis and John Wayne as racist. It's true that Elvis was not one, while John Wayne was, but this misses the point. The line evinced a total disrespect and ill regard for America's hallowed heroes and insisted that the pop culture of plunderers be treated as the theft it was. Chuck insisted on treating the claims of our masters with all the contempt they'd earned. When I heard that line, I felt free. I wanted to scream. I drew on that same freedom for my writing. The world might fall off a cliff, but I did not have to be among those pushing it and more, I did not have to nod along while fools insisted that gravity was debatable. This defiance was my firm ground—as real as my wife, my son, my family, my friends, my community. It would not save anyone or anything, least of all me. But it was my way of swinging, stabbing, shooting, doing whatever it took to remain free, to make them know that I was not the one.

There were distinct advantages to black atheism, to a disbelief in dreams and moral appeal. First, it removed the weight of believing that "white people," en masse, were interested listeners. "White people," en masse, are not. They are—like any other people— mostly self-interested, which is why mass appeals to conscience, minus some compelling, existential threat, generally end in disappointment. But I was armed against disappointment because, in defiance, I had no expectations of white people at all.

This lack of expectation dovetailed with my writing, because writers, too, must learn to abandon appeal and expectation. Failure is the norm for writers—firings and layoffs, rejected pitches, manuscripts tossed into the wastebins, bad reviews, uninterested editors, your own woeful rough drafts, they all form a chorus telling you to quit with whatever dignity you still have intact. And if you are going to write, you must learn to work in defiance of this chorus, in defiance of the unanswered pitches, of the books that find no audience, and most of all, in defiance of the terror radiating from the blank white page. And so, in writing, I found that black atheism and defiance morphed into a general theory of the life. No one was coming to save me, and no one was going to read me. My reasons for writing had to be my own, divorced from expectation. There would be no reward.

Except there was.

This was near the end of Barack Obama's first term, and I had become *The Atlantic*'s "Black Writer"—a phrase that described both my identity and my interests. There was always a sense that African American journalists should avoid being tagged as "black" lest they be "boxed in" and unable to pursue more "universal" topics such as the economy and global policy. But the more I wrote, the more I saw I wasn't boxed in as much as those who dismissed my chosen beat were boxed out. The notion that writing about race, which is to say, the force of white supremacy, is marginal and provincial is itself parcel to white supremacy, premised on the notion that the foundational crimes of this country are mostly irrelevant to its existence.

I knew by then that I was not reporting and writing from some corner of American society but from the very heart of it, from the plunder that was essential to it and the culture that animated it. If you really wanted to understand this country, this alleged two-hundred-year attempt to establish a society on Enlightenment values, I could think of no better place to study that effort than from the perspective of those whom that society excluded and pillaged in order to bring those values into practice. I did not feel pigeonholed in my role. I felt advantaged.

And now it was time to take all of that advantage and synthesize it into some assessment of our first black president. I had gathered stories that became the threads of a theory, even if I did not know exactly how these threads should be woven together. One story in particular stood out to me: the termination of Shirley Sherrod early in the president's tenure. Sherrod was a political appointee under Obama. In 2009, the right-wing provocateur Andrew Breitbart released footage of a speech she'd given before a local NAACP meeting. The footage appeared to show Sherrod reveling in taking revenge on a white farmer for all the racist slights and abuses she'd endured. Sherrod was quickly and gracelessly fired. E-mails were later released showing administration officials congratulating each other on quickly handling a potential crisis. Sherrod was well-known in the community of civil rights activists. Sherrod's cousin had been lynched in 1943. Her father had been murdered by a white farmer in a land dispute. She'd been a member of SNCC, been among the leaders of the Albany Movement, and later fought on behalf of black farmers in her native southwest Georgia. The comments, as rendered, were at odds with her life as a nonviolent integrationist—a fact made apparent when the full speech came into view the next day. Sherrod was not reveling in vengeance; she was detailing how she'd overcome the impulse toward it.

The episode embarrassed the Obama administration, but it also pointed to the great power of white innocence—the need to believe that whatever might befall the country, white America is ultimately blameless. The possibility of Shirley Sherrod's anger or desire for revenge—however fallacious—had to be effaced before it was allowed to raise uncomfortable questions about white innocence. Likewise, when Obama claimed that the Cambridge police officer had "acted stupidly," the assertion that the officer bore some amount of responsibility for arresting a senior citizen at his own home was met with howls of protest. Conversely, in his first race speech, Obama's sympathetic portrait of whites who roll up their windows in the inner city, a defense of white innocence, was cheered as a political masterstroke. (His recollection of his grandmother's racist remarks were not—and he was attacked for throwing her under the bus.)

How should Obama have grappled with the force of that innocence? Should he have spoken more directly to the painful truths? What would likely be the result of this truth-telling? It was well and true to say Obama's words and actions were constricted by a fear of offending white innocence. But Obama was the first black president of a majority-white country: *He should've feared white innocence.* Presumably, all those black people who voted for Obama supported him because they thought he would advance policies that advanced them. It was hard to see how truth-telling would have improved that prospect.

Obama's first term was almost over, and the limitations of his ascendancy now came into view: a black president whose power was bracketed by the same forces that bracketed the lives of black people everywhere. He represented our aspirations and hopes but could never forthrightly address the source of our agony. And should he ever attempt to ("The officer acted stupidly"; "If I had a son he'd look like Trayvon"), white innocence would be there waiting for him, threatening to derail his agenda and destroy him. And there was another price to Obama's ascendancy that was becoming clear: The crimes of the American state against its own people, along with its bombings in Yemen, Afghanistan, and Iraq, now had the imprimatur of a black man. We were at once the most segregated and disenfranchised community in the country and somehow now even more complicit in all of its sins. On one hand, paralyzing constriction; on the other, an assumption of the full weight of America's crimes. This was our black president. Was it worth it?

Yes is what I thought at the time I wrote this piece, and even now, if I am unsure it's only because I don't know how else to answer the question. Obama was the realization of generations, a black ambition as old as this country. From the moment George Washington stepped into the office, likely somewhere on his sprawling Virginia plantation, there was a black person who knew that they too could have been Washington, better than Washington, if only given the chance. And now I had found myself in an era where, from the seat of power, a black man, his black wife, and his black daughters waved to the world from across the White House lawn. This may have been a half-victory, but weren't all of our victories in this country half-victories? Had emancipation not given way to second slavery throughout the South? Had integration only ultimately applied to a select few? Was this not what winning always looked like for us?

The price of a black president captivated me and became the central question animating the essay "Fear of a Black President." What I remember most about this essay is that it was the first time, after over fifteen years of practice, that I felt in control of the form. All those years I had attempted to mix my influences—poetry, hiphop, history, memoir, reportage—and produce something original and beautiful. This was the first time I felt I succeeded, and more, felt I understood the how and why. It did not make the task easier, but understanding brought a great joy.

External events followed. I won a National Magazine Award for the essay. At thirty-six, with a now eleven-year-old son, I felt, for the first time in my life, a sense of financial stability. Kenyatta was back in school and had transformed herself into a scientist. She still worked part-time, but it was less necessary. Soon it would not be necessary at all. I took pride in watching her grow. She was always introducing me to things—Paris, pre-Code Hollywood, E. L. Doctorow. And now she was adding the wonder of cells and biological systems to her repertoire. I had not been prepared for the simple charm of watching someone you love grow. I had not known to look forward to it, and I guess that is because so often it does not happen, or perhaps when it does people generally grow apart. I don't really know. All I can say is seeing Kenyatta remake herself from liberal arts savant to med student, and doing so in service of her own mission, has been one of the great pleasures of my life. It was resistance: We do not have to be what they say about us. And it was more, something that I was actually lacking in my own life: service.

That same year, I consented to be profiled in a newspaper and was dubbed "America's best writer on race." The idea made me retch.

The work of Adolph Reed was never far from mind. I often thought of his essay "What Are the Drums Saying, Booker?" which condemned the black intellectuals who came of age in the '90s as interpreters of "the opaquely black heart of darkness for whites." I'd read it as a college student, annoyed with the same class of intellectuals Reed condemned, and when I began writing seriously a year after Reed's essay was published I was determined to never be an interpreter. It did not occur to me that writing is always some form of interpretation, some form of translating the specificity of one's roots or expertise or even one's own mind into language that can be absorbed and assimilated into the consciousness of a broader audience. Almost any black writer publishing in the mainstream press would necessarily be read by whites. Reed was not exempt. He was not holding forth from *The Chicago Defender* but from *The*

Village Voice, interpreting black intellectuals for that audience, most of whom were white.

But all interpreters do not hold the same authority to that mainstream readership, and that authority is not granted on the strict basis of merit. I saw this directly. E-mails now came constantly from show bookers, documentarians, panel producers, and magazine editors requesting interpretation of black life from angles beyond my expertise, such as it was. If the subject was deemed "black," I must have something to say about it. And so it might be proposed that I expound on the history of jazz, the Mau-Mau struggle, or direct a hip-hop video. I almost always declined. I should have declined more. A question—from other black writers and readers and a voice inside me now began to hover over my work—*Why do white people like what I write?* The question would eventually overshadow the work, or maybe it would just feel like it did. Either way, there was a lesson in this: God might not save me, but neither would defiance. How do you defy a power that insists on claiming you? What does the story you tell matter, if the world is set upon hearing a different one?

FEAR OF A
BLACK PRESIDENT

THE IRONY OF PRESIDENT BARACK OBAMA IS BEST CAPTURED
in his comments on the death of Trayvon Martin, and the ensuing
fray. Obama has pitched his presidency as a monument to moderation. He peppers his speeches with nods to ideas originally held
by conservatives. He routinely cites Ronald Reagan. He effusively
praises the enduring wisdom of the American people, and believes
that the height of insight lies in the town square. Despite his slogan-
eering for change and progress, Obama is a conservative revolutionary, and nowhere is his conservative character revealed more
than in the very sphere where he holds singular gravity—race.

Part of that conservatism about race has been reflected in his
reticence: For most of his term in office, Obama has declined to talk
about the ways in which race complicates the American present
and, in particular, his own presidency. But then, last February,
George Zimmerman, a twenty-eight-year-old insurance under-
writer, shot and killed a black teenager, Trayvon Martin, in San-
ford, Florida. Zimmerman, armed with a 9-mm handgun, believed

himself to be tracking the movements of a possible intruder. The possible intruder turned out to be a boy in a hoodie, bearing nothing but candy and iced tea. The local authorities at first declined to make an arrest, citing Zimmerman's claim of self-defense. Protests exploded nationally. Skittles and Arizona Iced Tea assumed totemic power. Celebrities—the actor Jamie Foxx, the former Michigan governor Jennifer Granholm, members of the Miami Heat—were photographed wearing hoodies. When Representative Bobby Rush of Chicago took to the House floor to denounce racial profiling, he was removed from the chamber after donning a hoodie mid-speech.

The reaction to the tragedy was, at first, trans-partisan. Conservatives either said nothing or offered tepid support for a full investigation—and in fact it was the Republican governor of Florida, Rick Scott, who appointed the special prosecutor who ultimately charged Zimmerman with second-degree murder. As civil rights activists descended on Florida, *National Review,* a magazine that once opposed integration, ran a column proclaiming "Al Sharpton Is Right." The belief that a young man should be able to go to the store for Skittles and an iced tea and not be killed by a neighborhood-watch patroller seemed uncontroversial.

By the time reporters began asking the White House for comment, the president likely had already given the matter considerable thought. Obama is not simply America's first black president—he is the first president who could credibly teach a black-studies class. He is fully versed in the works of Richard Wright and James Baldwin, Frederick Douglass and Malcolm X. Obama's two autobiographies are deeply concerned with race, and in front of black audiences he is apt to cite important but obscure political figures such as George Henry White, who served from 1897 to 1901 and was the last African American congressman to be elected from the South until 1970. But with just a few notable exceptions, the president had, for the first three years of his presidency, strenuously avoided talk of race. And yet, when Trayvon Martin died, talk Obama did:

When I think about this boy, I think about my own kids, and I think every parent in America should be able to understand why it is absolutely imperative that we investigate every aspect of this, and that everybody pulls together—federal, state, and local—to figure out exactly how this tragedy happened. . . .

But my main message is to the parents of Trayvon Martin. If I had a son, he'd look like Trayvon. I think they are right to expect that all of us as Americans are going to take this with the seriousness it deserves, and that we're going to get to the bottom of exactly what happened.

The moment Obama spoke, the case of Trayvon Martin passed out of its national-mourning phase and lapsed into something darker and more familiar—racialized political fodder. The illusion of consensus crumbled. Rush Limbaugh denounced Obama's claim of empathy. *The Daily Caller,* a conservative website, broadcast all of Martin's tweets, the most loutish of which revealed him to have committed the unpardonable sin of speaking like a seventeen-year-old boy. A white supremacist site called Stormfront produced a photo of Martin with pants sagging, flipping the bird. *Business Insider* posted the photograph and took it down without apology when it was revealed to be a fake.

Newt Gingrich pounced on Obama's comments: "Is the president suggesting that if it had been a white who had been shot, that would be okay because it wouldn't look like him?" Reverting to form, *National Review* decided the real problem was that we were interested in the deaths of black youths only when nonblacks pulled the trigger. John Derbyshire, writing for *Taki's Magazine,* an iconoclastic libertarian publication, composed a racist advice column for his children inspired by the Martin affair. (Among Derbyshire's tips: Never help black people in any kind of distress; avoid large gatherings of black people; cultivate black friends to shield yourself from charges of racism.)

The notion that Zimmerman might be the real victim began seeping out into the country, aided by PR efforts by his family and legal team, as well as by various acts of stupidity—Spike Lee tweeting Zimmerman's address (an act made all the more repugnant by the fact that he had the wrong Zimmerman), NBC misleadingly editing a tape of Zimmerman's phone conversation with a police dispatcher to make Zimmerman seem to be racially profiling Martin. In April, when Zimmerman set up a website to collect donations for his defense, he raised more than $200,000 in two weeks, before his lawyer asked that he close the site and launched a new, independently managed legal-defense fund. Although the trial date has yet to be set, as of July the fund was still raking in up to $1,000 in donations daily.

But it would be wrong to attribute the burgeoning support for Zimmerman to the blunders of Spike Lee or an NBC producer. Before President Obama spoke, the death of Trayvon Martin was generally regarded as a national tragedy. After Obama spoke, Martin became material for an Internet vendor flogging paper gun-range targets that mimicked his hoodie and his bag of Skittles. (The vendor sold out within a week.) Before the president spoke, George Zimmerman was arguably the most reviled man in America. After the president spoke, Zimmerman became the patron saint of those who believe that an apt history of racism begins with Tawana Brawley and ends with the Duke lacrosse team.

The irony of Barack Obama is this: He has become the most successful black politician in American history by avoiding the radioactive racial issues of yesteryear, by being "clean" (as Joe Biden once labeled him)—and yet his indelible blackness irradiates everything he touches. This irony is rooted in the greater ironies of the country he leads. For most of American history, our political system was premised on two conflicting facts—one, an oft-stated love of democracy; the other, an undemocratic white supremacy inscribed at every level of government. In warring against that paradox, African Americans have historically been restricted to the realm of protest and agitation. But when President Barack Obama pledged to "get to the bottom of exactly what happened," he was not protesting or agitating. He was not appealing to federal power—he was employing it. The power was black—and, in certain quarters, was received as such.

No amount of rhetorical moderation could change this. It did not matter that the president addressed himself to "every parent in America." His insistence that "everybody [pull] together" was irrelevant. It meant nothing that he declined to cast aspersions on the investigating authorities, or to speculate on events. Even the fact that Obama expressed his own connection to Martin in the quietest way imaginable—"If I had a son, he'd look like Trayvon"—would not mollify his opposition. It is, after all, one thing to hear "I am Trayvon Martin" from the usual placard-waving rabble-rousers. Hearing it from the commander of the greatest military machine in human history is another.

By virtue of his background—the son of a black man and a white woman, someone who grew up in multiethnic communities around the world—Obama has enjoyed a distinctive vantage point on race relations in America. Beyond that, he has displayed enviable dexterity at navigating between black and white America, and at finding a language that speaks to a critical mass in both communities. He emerged into national view at the Democratic National Convention in 2004, with a speech heralding a nation uncolored by old prejudices and shameful history. There was no talk of the effects of racism. Instead Obama stressed the power of parenting, and condemned those who would say that a black child carrying a book was "acting white." He cast himself as the child of a father from Kenya and a mother from Kansas and asserted, "In no other country on Earth is my story even possible." When, as a senator, he was asked if the response to Hurricane Katrina evidenced racism, Obama responded by calling the "ineptitude" of the response "color-blind."

Racism is not merely a simplistic hatred. It is, more often, broad sympathy toward some and broader skepticism toward others. Black America ever lives under that skeptical eye. Hence the old admonishments to be "twice as good." Hence the need for a special "talk" administered to black boys about how to be extra careful when relating to the police. And hence Barack Obama's insisting that there was no racial component to Katrina's effects; that name-calling among children somehow has the same import as one of the oldest guiding principles of American policy—white supremacy. The election of an African American to our highest political office was alleged to demonstrate a triumph of integration. But when President Obama addressed the tragedy of Trayvon Martin, he demonstrated integration's great limitation—that acceptance depends not just on being twice as good but on being half as black. And even then, full acceptance is still withheld. The larger effects of this withholding constrict Obama's presidential potential in areas affected tangentially—or seemingly not at all—by race. Meanwhile, across the country, the community in which Obama is rooted sees this fraudulent equality, and quietly seethes.

Obama's first term has coincided with a strategy of massive resistance on the part of his Republican opposition in the House, and a record number of filibuster threats in the Senate. It would be nice if this were merely a reaction to Obama's politics or his policies—if this resistance truly were, as it is generally described, merely one more sign of our growing "polarization" as a nation. But the greatest abiding challenge to Obama's national political standing has always rested on the existential fact that if he had a son, he'd look like Trayvon Martin. As a candidate, Barack Obama understood this.

"The thing is, a *black man* can't be president in America, given the racial aversion and history that's still out there," Cornell Belcher, a pollster for Obama, told the journalist Gwen Ifill after the 2008 election. "However, an extraordinary, gifted, and talented young man who happens to be black can be president."

Belcher's formulation grants the power of anti-black racism, and proposes to defeat it by not acknowledging it. His is the perfect statement of the Obama era, a time marked by a revolution that must never announce itself, by a democracy that must never acknowledge the weight of race, even while being shaped by it. Barack Obama governs a nation enlightened enough to send an African American to the White House, but not enlightened enough to accept a black man as its president.

BEFORE BARACK OBAMA, the "black president" lived in the African American imagination as a kind of cosmic joke, a phantom of all that could never be. White folks, whatever their talk of freedom and liberty, would not allow a black president. They could not tolerate Emmett's boyish gaze. Dr. King turned the other cheek, and they blew it off. White folks shot Lincoln over "nigger equality," ran Ida Wells out of Memphis, beat Freedom Riders over bus seats, slaughtered Medgar in his driveway like a dog. The comedian Dave Chappelle joked that the first black president would need a "Vice President Santiago"—because the only thing that would ensure his life in the White House was a Hispanic president-in-waiting. A black president signing a bill into law might as well sign his own death certificate.

And even if white folks could moderate their own penchant for violence, we could not moderate our own. A long-suffering life on the wrong side of the color line had denuded black people of the delicacy necessary to lead the free world. In a skit on his 1977 TV comedy show, Richard Pryor, as a black president, conceded that he was "courting an awful lot of white women" and held a press conference that erupted into a riot after a reporter requested that the president's momma clean his house. More recently, the comedian Cedric the Entertainer joked that a black president would never have made it through Monicagate without turning a press conference into a battle royal. When Chappelle tried to imagine how a black George W. Bush would have justified the war against Saddam Hussein, his character ("Black Bush") simply yelled, "The nigger tried to kill my father!"

Thus, in hard jest, the paradoxes and problems of a theoretical black presidency were given voice. Racism would not allow a black president. Nor would a blackness, forged by America's democratic double-talk, that was too ghetto and raw for the refinement of the Oval Office. Just beneath the humor lurked a resonant pain, the scars of history, an aching doubt rooted in the belief that "they" would never accept us. And so in our Harlems and Paradise Valleys, we invoked a black presidency the way a legion of five-foot point guards might invoke the dunk—as evidence of some great cosmic injustice, weighty in its import, out of reach.

And yet Spud Webb lives.

When presidential candidate Barack Obama presented himself to the black community, he was not to be believed. It strained credulity to think that a man sporting the same rigorously managed haircut as Jay-Z, a man who was a hard-core pickup basketball player, and who was married to a dark-skinned black woman from the South Side, could coax large numbers of white voters into the booth. Obama's blackness quotient is often a subject of debate. (He himself once joked, while speaking to the National Association of Black Journalists in 2007, "I want to apologize for being a little bit late, but you guys keep on asking whether I'm black enough.") But despite Obama's post-election reluctance to talk about race, he has always displayed both an obvious affinity for black culture and a distinct ability to defy black America's worst self-conceptions.

The crude communal myth about black men is that we are in some manner unavailable to black women—either jailed, dead, gay, or married to white women. A corollary myth posits a direct and negative relationship between success and black culture. Before we actually had one, we could not imagine a black president who loved being black. In *The Audacity of Hope,* Obama describes his first kiss with the woman who would become his wife as tasting "of chocolate." The line sounds ripped from *Essence* magazine. That's the point.

These cultural cues became important during Obama's presidential run and beyond. Obama doesn't merely evince blackness; he uses his blackness to signal and court African Americans, semaphoring in a cultural dialect of our creation—crooning Al Green at the Apollo, name-checking Young Jeezy, regularly appearing on the cover of black magazines, weighing the merits of Jay-Z versus Kanye West, being photographed in the White House with a little black boy touching his hair. There is often something mawkish about this signaling—like a Virginia politico thickening his southern accent when talking to certain audiences. If you've often been the butt of political signaling (Sister Souljah, Willie Horton), and rarely the recipient, these displays of cultural affinity are powerful. And they are all the more powerful because Obama has been successful. Whole sections of America that we had assumed to be negrophobic turned out in support of him in 2008. Whatever Obama's other triumphs, arguably his greatest has been an expansion of the black imagination to encompass this: the idea that a man can be culturally black and many other things also—biracial, Ivy League, intellectual, cosmopolitan, temperamentally conservative, presidential.

It is often said that Obama's presidency has given black parents the right to tell their kids with a straight face that they can do anything. This is a function not only of Obama's election to the White House but of the way his presidency broadcasts an easy, almost mystic, blackness to the world. The Obama family represents our ideal imagining of ourselves—an ideal we so rarely see on any kind of national stage.

What black people are experiencing right now is a kind of privilege previously withheld—seeing our most sacred cultural practices and tropes validated in the world's highest office. Throughout the whole of American history, this kind of cultural power was wielded solely by whites, and with such ubiquity that it was not even commented upon. The expansion of this cultural power beyond the private province of whites has been a tremendous advance for black America. Conversely, for those who've long treasured white exclusivity, the existence of a President Barack Obama is discombobulating, even terrifying. For as surely as the iconic picture of the young black boy reaching out to touch the president's curly hair sends one message to black America, it sends another to those who have enjoyed the power of whiteness.

IN AMERICA, THE RIGHTS to own property, to serve on a jury, to vote, to hold public office, to rise to the presidency have historically been seen as belonging only to those people who showed particular integrity. Citizenship was a social contract in which persons of moral standing were transformed into stakeholders who swore to defend the state against threats external and internal. Until a century and a half ago, slave rebellion ranked high in the fevered American imagination of threats necessitating such an internal defense.

In the early years of our republic, when democracy was still an unproven experiment, the founders were not even clear that all white people should be entrusted with this fragile venture, much less the bestial African. Thus Congress, in 1790, declared the following:

> All free white persons who have, or shall migrate into the United States, and shall give satisfactory proof, before a magistrate, by oath, that they intend to reside therein, and shall take an oath of allegiance, and shall have resided in the United States for one whole year, shall be entitled to all the rights of citizenship.

In such ways was the tie between citizenship and whiteness in America made plain from the very beginning. By the nineteenth century, there was, as Matthew Jacobson, a professor of history and American studies at Yale, has put it, "an unquestioned acceptance of whiteness as a prerequisite for naturalized citizenship." Debating Abraham Lincoln during the race for a U.S. Senate seat in Illinois in 1858, Stephen Douglas asserted that "this government was made on the white basis" and that the Framers had made "no reference either to the Negro, the savage Indians, the Feejee, the Malay, or any other inferior and degraded race, when they spoke of the equality of men."

After the Civil War, Andrew Johnson, Lincoln's successor as president and a unionist, scoffed at awarding the Negro the franchise:

> The peculiar qualities which should characterize any people who are fit to decide upon the management of public affairs for a great state have seldom been combined. It is the glory of white men to know that they have had these qualities in sufficient measure to build upon this continent a great political fabric and to preserve its stability for more than ninety years, while in every other part of the world all similar experiments have failed. But if anything can be proved by known facts, if all reasoning upon evidence is not abandoned, it must be acknowledged that in the progress of nations Negroes have shown less capacity for government than any other race of people. No independent government of any form has ever been successful in their hands. On the contrary, wherever they have been left to their own devices they have shown a constant tendency to relapse into barbarism.

The notion of blacks as particularly unfit for political equality persisted well into the twentieth century. As the nation began considering integrating its military, a young West Virginian wrote to a senator in 1944:

> I am a typical American, a southerner, and 27 years of age. . . .
> I am loyal to my country and know but reverence to her flag,

BUT I shall never submit to fight beneath that banner with a negro by my side. Rather I should die a thousand times, and see Old Glory trampled in the dirt never to rise again, than to see this beloved land of ours become degraded by race mongrels, a throw back to the blackest specimen from the wilds.

The writer—who never joined the military, but did join the Ku Klux Klan—was Robert Byrd, who died in 2010 as the longest-serving U.S. senator in history. Byrd's rejection of political equality was echoed in 1957 by William F. Buckley Jr., who addressed the moral disgrace of segregation by endorsing disenfranchisement strictly based on skin color:

The central question that emerges—and it is not a parliamentary question or a question that is answered by merely consulting a catalog of the rights of American citizens, born Equal—is whether the White community in the South is entitled to take such measures as are necessary to prevail, politically and culturally, in areas in which it does not predominate numerically? The sobering answer is Yes—the White community is so entitled because, for the time being, it is the advanced race.

Buckley, the founder of *National Review,* went on to assert, "The great majority of the Negroes of the South who do not vote do not care to vote and would not know for what to vote if they could."

The idea that blacks should hold no place of consequence in the American political future has affected every sector of American society, transforming whiteness itself into a monopoly on American possibilities. White people like Byrd and Buckley were raised in a time when, by law, they were assured of never having to compete with black people for the best of anything. Blacks used inferior public pools and inferior washrooms, attended inferior schools. The nicest restaurants turned them away. In large swaths of the country, blacks paid taxes but could neither attend the best universities nor exercise the right to vote. The best jobs, the richest neighborhoods, were giant set-asides for whites—universal affirmative action, with no pretense of restitution.

Slavery, Jim Crow, segregation: These bonded white people into a broad aristocracy united by the salient fact of unblackness. What Byrd saw in an integrated military was the crumbling of the ideal of whiteness, and thus the crumbling of an entire society built around it. Whatever the saintly nonviolent rhetoric used to herald it, racial integration was a brutal assault on whiteness. The American presidency, an unbroken streak of nonblack men, was, until 2008, the greatest symbol of that old order.

Watching Obama rack up victories in states like Virginia, New Mexico, Ohio, and North Carolina on Election Night in 2008, anyone could easily conclude that racism, as a national force, had been defeated. The thought should not be easily dismissed: Obama's victory demonstrates the incredible distance this country has traveled. (Indeed, William F. Buckley Jr. later revised his early positions on race; Robert Byrd spent decades in Congress atoning for his.) That a country that once took whiteness as the foundation of citizenship would elect a black president is a victory. But to view this victory as racism's defeat is to forget the precise terms on which it was secured, and to ignore the quaking ground beneath Obama's feet.

During the 2008 primary, *The New Yorker*'s George Packer journeyed to Kentucky and was shocked by the brazen declarations of white identity. "I think he would put too many minorities in positions over the white race," one voter told Packer. "That's my opinion." That voter was hardly alone. In 2010, Michael Tesler, a political scientist at Brown University, and David Sears, a professor of psychology and political science at UCLA, were able to assess the impact of race in the 2008 primary by comparing data from two 2008 campaign and election studies with previous surveys of racial resentment and voter choice. As they wrote in *Obama's Race: The 2008 Election and the Dream of a Post-Racial America*:

No other factor, in fact, came close to dividing the Democratic primary electorate as powerfully as their feelings about African Americans. The impact of racial attitudes on individual vote decisions . . . was so strong that it appears to have even outstripped the substantive impact of racial attitudes on Jesse Jackson's more racially charged campaign for the nomination in 1988.

Seth Stephens-Davidowitz, a doctoral candidate in economics at Harvard, is studying how racial animus may have cost Obama votes in 2008. First, Stephens-Davidowitz ranked areas of the country according to how often people there typed racist search terms into Google. (The areas with the highest rates of racially charged search terms were West Virginia, western Pennsylvania, eastern Ohio, upstate New York, and southern Mississippi.) Then he compared Obama's voting results in those areas with John Kerry's four years earlier. So, for instance, in 2004 Kerry received 50 percent of the vote in the media markets of both Denver and Wheeling (which straddles the Ohio–West Virginia border). Based on the Democratic groundswell in 2008, Obama should have received about 57 percent of the popular vote in both regions. But that's not what happened. In the Denver area, which had one of the nation's lowest rates of racially charged Google searching, Obama received the predicted 57 percent. But in Wheeling, which had a high rate of racially charged Google searching, Obama's share of the popular vote was only 48 percent. Of course, Obama also picked up some votes because he is black. But, aggregating his findings nationally, Stephens-Davidowitz has concluded that Obama lost between 3 and 5 percentage points of the popular vote to racism.

After Obama won, the longed-for post-racial moment did not arrive; on the contrary, racism intensified. At rallies for the nascent Tea Party, people held signs saying things like Obama Plans White Slavery. Steve King, an Iowa congressman and Tea Party favorite, complained that Obama "favors the black person." In 2009, Rush

Limbaugh, bard of white decline, called Obama's presidency a time when "the white kids now get beat up, with the black kids cheering 'Yeah, right on, right on, right on.' And of course everybody says the white kid deserved it—he was born a racist, he's white." On *Fox & Friends,* Glenn Beck asserted that Obama had exposed himself as a guy "who has a deep-seated hatred for white people or the white culture. . . . This guy is, I believe, a racist." Beck later said he was wrong to call Obama a racist. That same week he also called the president's healthcare plan "reparations."

One possible retort to this pattern of racial paranoia is to cite the Clinton years, when an ideological fever drove the right wing to derangement, inspiring militia movements and accusations that the president had conspired to murder his own lawyer, Vince Foster. The upshot, by this logic, is that Obama is experiencing run-of-the-mill political opposition in which race is but a minor factor among much larger ones, such as party affiliation. But the argument assumes that party affiliation itself is unconnected to race. It pretends that only Toni Morrison took note of Clinton's particular appeal to black voters. It forgets that Clinton felt compelled to attack Sister Souljah. It forgets that whatever ignoble labels the right wing pinned on Clinton's healthcare plan, "reparations" did not rank among them.

Michael Tesler, following up on his research with David Sears on the role of race in the 2008 campaign, recently published a study assessing the impact of race on opposition to and support for healthcare reform. The findings are bracing. Obama's election effectively racialized white Americans' views, even of healthcare policy. As Tesler writes in a paper published in July in the *American Journal of Political Science,* "Racial attitudes had a significantly greater impact on health care opinions when framed as part of President Obama's plan than they had when the exact same policies were attributed to President Clinton's 1993 health care initiative."

While Beck and Limbaugh have chosen direct racial assault, others choose simply to deny that a black president actually exists. One in four Americans (and more than half of all Republicans) believe

Obama was not born in this country, and thus is an illegitimate president. More than a dozen state legislatures have introduced "birther bills" demanding proof of Obama's citizenship as a condition for putting him on the 2012 ballot. Eighteen percent of Republicans believe Obama to be a Muslim. The goal of all this is to delegitimize Obama's presidency. If Obama is not truly American, then America has still never had a black president.

White resentment has not cooled as the Obama presidency has proceeded. Indeed, the GOP presidential-primary race featured candidates asserting that the black family was better off under slavery (Michele Bachmann, Rick Santorum); claiming that Obama, as a black man, should oppose abortion (Santorum again); or denouncing Obama as a "food-stamp president" (Newt Gingrich).

The resentment is not confined to Republicans. Earlier this year, West Virginia gave 41 percent of the popular vote during the Democratic primary to Keith Judd, a white incarcerated felon (Judd actually defeated Obama in ten counties). Joe Manchin, one of West Virginia's senators, and Earl Ray Tomblin, its governor, are declining to attend this year's Democratic convention, and will not commit to voting for Obama.

It is often claimed that Obama's unpopularity in coal-dependent West Virginia stems from his environmental policies. But recall that no state ranked higher on Seth Stephens-Davidowitz's racism scale than West Virginia. Moreover, Obama was unpopular in West Virginia before he became president: even at the tail end of the Democratic primaries in 2008, Hillary Clinton walloped Obama by 41 points. A fifth of West Virginia Democrats openly professed that race played a role in their vote.

What we are now witnessing is not some new and complicated expression of white racism—rather, it's the dying embers of the same old racism that once rendered the best pickings of America the exclusive province of unblackness. Confronted by the thoroughly racialized backlash to Obama's presidency, a stranger to American politics might conclude that Obama provoked the response by relentlessly pushing an agenda of radical racial reform. Hardly. Daniel Gillion, a political scientist at the University of Pennsylvania who studies race and politics, examined the Public Papers of the Presidents, a compilation of nearly all public presidential utterances—proclamations, news-conference remarks, executive orders—and found that in his first two years as president, Obama talked less about race than any other Democratic president since 1961. Obama's racial strategy has been, if anything, the opposite of radical: He declines to use his bully pulpit to address racism, using it instead to engage in the time-honored tradition of black self-hectoring, railing against the perceived failings of black culture.

His approach is not new. It is the approach of Booker T. Washington, who, amid a sea of white terrorists during the era of Jim Crow, endorsed segregation and proclaimed the South to be a land of black opportunity. It is the approach of L. Douglas Wilder, who, in 1986, not long before he became Virginia's first black governor, kept his distance from Jesse Jackson and told an NAACP audience: "Yes, dear Brutus, the fault is not in our stars, but in ourselves. . . . Some blacks don't particularly care for me to say these things, to speak to values. . . . Somebody's got to. We've been too excusing." It was even, at times, the approach of Jesse Jackson himself, who railed against "the rising use of drugs, and babies making babies, and violence . . . cutting away our opportunity."

The strategy can work. Booker T.'s Tuskegee University still stands. Wilder became the first black governor in America since Reconstruction. Jackson's campaign moved the Democratic nominating process toward proportional allocation of delegates, a shift that Obama exploited in the 2008 Democratic primaries by staying competitive enough in big states to rack up delegates even where he was losing, and rolling up huge vote margins (and delegate-count victories) in smaller ones.

And yet what are we to make of an integration premised, first, on the entire black community's emulating the Huxtables? An equality that requires blacks to be twice as good is not equality—it's a double standard. That double standard haunts and constrains the Obama presidency, warning him away from candor about America's sordid birthmark.

ANOTHER POLITICAL TRADITION IN black America, running counter to the one publicly embraced by Obama and Booker T. Washington, casts its skepticism not simply upon black culture but upon the entire American project. This tradition stretches back to Frederick Douglass, who, in 1852, said of his native country, "There is not a nation on the earth guilty of practices more shocking and bloody than are the people of the United States at this very hour." It extends through Martin Delany, through Booker T.'s nemesis W.E.B. Du Bois, and through Malcolm X. It includes Martin Luther King Jr., who at the height of the Vietnam War called America "the greatest purveyor of violence in the world today." And it includes Obama's former pastor, he of the famous "God Damn America" sermon, Jeremiah Wright.

The Harvard Law professor Randall Kennedy, in his 2011 book *The Persistence of the Color Line: Racial Politics and the Obama Presidency,* examines this tradition by looking at his own father and Reverend Wright in the context of black America's sense of patriotism. Like Wright, the elder Kennedy was a veteran of the U.S. military, a man seared and radicalized by American racism, forever remade as a vociferous critic of his native country: In virtually any American conflict, Kennedy's father rooted for the foreign country.

The deep skepticism about the American project that Kennedy's father and Reverend Wright evince is an old tradition in black America. Before Frederick Douglass worked, during the Civil War, for the preservation of the Union, he called for his country's destruction. "I have no love for America," he declaimed in a lecture to the American Anti-Slavery Society in 1847. "I have no patriotism. . . . I desire to see [the government] overthrown as speedily as possible and its Constitution shivered in a thousand fragments."

Kennedy notes that Douglass's denunciations were the words of a man who not only had endured slavery but was living in a country where whites often selected the Fourth of July as a special day to prosecute a campaign of racial terror:

On July 4, 1805, whites in Philadelphia drove blacks out of the square facing Independence Hall. For years thereafter, blacks attended Fourth of July festivities in that city at their peril. On July 4, 1834, a white mob in New York City burned down the Broadway Tabernacle because of the antislavery and antiracist views of the church's leaders. Firefighters in sympathy with the arsonists refused to douse the conflagration. On July 4, 1835, a white mob in Canaan, New Hampshire, destroyed a school open to blacks that was run by an abolitionist. The antebellum years were liberally dotted with such episodes.

Jeremiah Wright was born into an America of segregation—overt in the South and covert in the North, but wounding wherever. He joined the Marines, vowing service to his country, at a time when he wouldn't have been allowed to vote in some states. He built his ministry in a community reeling from decades of job and housing discrimination, and heaving under the weight of drugs, gun violence, and broken families. Wright's world is emblematic of the African Americans he ministered to, people reared on the anti-black-citizenship tradition—poll taxes, states pushing stringent voter-ID laws—of Stephen Douglas and Andrew Johnson and William F. Buckley Jr. The message is "You are not American." The countermessage—God Damn America—is an old one, and is surprising only to people unfamiliar with the politics of black life in this country. Unfortunately, that is an apt description of large swaths of America.

Whatever the context for Wright's speech, the surfacing of his remarks in 2008 was utterly inconvenient not just for the Obama campaign but for much of black America. One truism holds that black people are always anxious to talk about race, eager to lecture white people at every juncture about how wrong they are and about the price they must pay for past and ongoing sins. But one reason Obama rose so quickly was that African Americans are war-weary. It was not simply the country at large that was tired of the old baby boomer debates. Blacks, too, were sick of talking about affirmative action and school busing. There was a broad sense that integration had failed us, and a growing disenchantment with our appointed spokespeople. Obama's primary triumphs in predominantly white states gave rise to rumors of a new peace, one many blacks were anxious to achieve.

And even those black Americans who embrace the tradition of God Damn America do so not with glee but with deep pain and anguish. Both Kennedy's father and Wright were military men. My own father went to Vietnam dreaming of John Wayne, but came back quoting Malcolm X. The poet Lucille Clifton once put it succinctly:

> They act like they don't love their country
> No
> what it is
> is they found out
> their country don't love them.

In 2008, as Obama's election became imaginable, it seemed possible that our country had indeed, at long last, come to love us. We did not need our Jeremiah Wrights, our Jesse Jacksons, our products of the polarized '60s getting in the way. Indeed, after distancing himself from Wright, Obama lost almost no black support.

Obama offered black America a convenient narrative that could be meshed with the larger American story. It was a narrative premised on Crispus Attucks, not the black slaves who escaped plantations and fought for the British; on the 54th Massachusetts, not Nat

Turner; on stoic and saintly Rosa Parks, not young and pregnant Claudette Colvin; on a Christ-like Martin Luther King Jr., not an avenging Malcolm X. Jeremiah Wright's presence threatened to rupture that comfortable narrative by symbolizing that which makes integration impossible—black rage.

From the "inadequate black male" diatribe of the Hillary Clinton supporter Harriet Christian in 2008, to Rick Santelli's 2009 rant on CNBC against subsidizing "losers' mortgages," to Representative Joe Wilson's "You lie!" outburst during Obama's September 2009 address to Congress, to John Boehner's screaming "Hell no!" on the House floor about Obamacare in 2010, politicized rage has marked the opposition to Obama. But the rules of our racial politics require that Obama never respond in like fashion. So frightening is the prospect of black rage given voice and power that when Obama was a freshman senator, he was asked, on national television, to denounce the rage of Harry Belafonte. This fear continued with demands that he keep his distance from Louis Farrakhan and culminated with Reverend Wright and a presidency that must never betray any sign of rage toward its white opposition.

Thus the myth of "twice as good" that makes Barack Obama possible also smothers him. It holds that African Americans—enslaved, tortured, raped, discriminated against, and subjected to the most lethal homegrown terrorist movement in American history—feel no anger toward their tormentors. Of course, very little in our history argues that those who seek to tell bold truths about race will be rewarded. But it was Obama himself, as a presidential candidate in 2008, who called for such truths to be spoken. "Race is an issue that I believe this nation cannot afford to ignore right now," he said in his "More Perfect Union" speech, which he delivered after a furor erupted over Reverend Wright's "God Damn America" remarks. And yet, since taking office, Obama has virtually ignored race.

Whatever the political intelligence of this calculus, it has broad and deep consequences. The most obvious result is that it prevents

Obama from directly addressing America's racial history, or saying anything meaningful about present issues tinged by race, such as mass incarceration or the drug war. There have been calls for Obama to take a softer line on state-level legalization of marijuana or even to stand for legalization himself. Indeed, there is no small amount of inconsistency in our black president's either ignoring or upholding harsh drug laws that every day injure the prospects of young black men—laws that could have ended his own, had he been of another social class and arrested for the marijuana use he openly discusses. But the intellectual argument doubles as the counter-argument. If the fact of a black president is enough to racialize the wonkish world of healthcare reform, what havoc would the Obama touch wreak upon the already racialized world of drug policy?

The political consequences of race extend beyond the domestic. I am, like many liberals, horrified by Obama's embrace of a secretive drone policy, and particularly the killing of American citizens without any restraints. A president aware of black America's tenuous hold on citizenship, of how the government has at times secretly conspired against its advancement—a black president with a broad sense of the world—should know better. Except a black president with Obama's past is the perfect target for right-wing attacks depicting him as weak on terrorism. The president's inability to speak candidly on race cannot be bracketed off from his inability to speak candidly on everything. Race is not simply a portion of the Obama story. It is the lens through which many Americans view all his politics.

But whatever the politics, a total submission to them is a disservice to the country. No one knows this better than Obama himself, who once described patriotism as more than pageantry and the scarfing of hot dogs. "When our laws, our leaders, or our government are out of alignment with our ideals, then the dissent of ordinary Americans may prove to be one of the truest expressions of patriotism," Obama said in Independence, Missouri, in June 2008. Love of country, like all other forms of love, requires that you tell those you care about not simply what they want to hear but what they need to hear.

But in the age of the Obama presidency, expressing that kind of patriotism is presumably best done quietly, politely, and with great deference.

THIS SPRING I FLEW down to Albany, Georgia, and spent the day with Shirley Sherrod, a longtime civil rights activist who embodies exactly the kind of patriotism that Obama esteems. Albany is in Dougherty County, where the poverty rate hangs around 30 percent—double that of the rest of the state. On the drive in from the airport, the selection of vendors—payday loans, title loans, and car dealers promising no credit check—evidenced the statistic.

When I met Sherrod at her office, she was working to get a birthday card out to Roger Spooner, whose farm she'd once fought to save. In July 2010, the conservative commentator Andrew Breitbart posted video clips on his website of a speech Sherrod had delivered to the NAACP the previous March. The video was edited so that Sherrod, then an official at the U.S. Department of Agriculture, appeared to be bragging about discriminating against a white farmer and thus enacting a fantasy of racial revenge. The point was to tie Obama to the kind of black rage his fevered enemies often impute to him. Fearing exactly that, Sherrod's supervisors at the USDA called her in the middle of a long drive and had her submit her resignation via BlackBerry, telling her, "You're going to be on *Glenn Beck* tonight."

Glenn Beck did eventually do a segment on Sherrod—one in which he attacked the administration for forcing her out. As it turned out, the full context showed that Sherrod was actually documenting her own turn *away* from racial anger. The farmer who was the subject of the story came forward, along with his wife, and explained that Sherrod had worked tirelessly to help the family. The farmer was Roger Spooner.

Sherrod's career as an activist, first in civil rights and then later in the world of small farmers like Roger Spooner, was not chosen so much as thrust upon her. Her cousin had been lynched in 1943. Her father was shot and killed by a white relative in a dispute over some cows. There were three witnesses, but the grand jury in her native Baker County did not indict the suspect. Sherrod became an activist with the Student Nonviolent Coordinating Committee, registering voters near her hometown. Her husband, Charles Sherrod, was instrumental in leading the Albany Movement, which attracted Martin Luther King Jr. to town. But when Stokely Carmichael rose to lead SNCC and took it in a black-nationalist direction, the Sherrods, committed to nonviolence and integration, faced a weighty choice. Carmichael himself had been committed to nonviolence, until the killings and beatings he encountered as a civil rights activist took their toll. Sherrod, with a past haunted by racist violence, would have seemed ripe for recruitment to the nationalist line. But she, along with her husband, declined, leaving SNCC in order to continue in the tradition of King and nonviolence.

Her achievements from then on are significant. She helped pioneer the farm-collective movement in America, and co-founded New Communities—a sprawling six-thousand-acre collective that did everything from growing crops to canning sugarcane and sorghum. New Communities folded in 1985, largely because Ronald Reagan's USDA refused to sign off on a loan, even as it was signing off on money for smaller-scale white farmers. Sherrod went on to work with Farm Aid. She befriended Willie Nelson, held a fellowship with the Kellogg Foundation, and was short-listed for a job in President Clinton's Agriculture Department. Still, she remained relatively unknown except to students of the civil rights movement and activists who promoted the rights of small farmers. And unknown she would have remained, had she not been very publicly forced out of her position by the administration of the country's first black president.

Through most of her career as an agriculture activist, Sherrod had found the USDA to be a barrier to the success of black farmers. What hurt black farms the most were the discriminatory practices of local officials in granting loans. Sherrod spent years protesting these practices. But then, after the election of Barack Obama, she was hired by the USDA, where she would be supervising the very people she'd once fought. Now she would have a chance to ensure fair and nondiscriminatory lending practices. Her appointment represented the kind of unnoticed but significant changes Obama's election brought.

But then the administration, intimidated by a resurgent right wing specializing in whipping up racial resentment, compelled Sherrod to resign on the basis of the misleading clips. When the full tape emerged, the administration was left looking ridiculous.

And cowardly. An e-mail chain later surfaced in which the White House congratulated Agriculture Secretary Tom Vilsack's staff for getting ahead of the news cycle. None of them had yet seen the full tape. That the Obama administration would fold so easily gives some sense of how frightened it was of a protracted fight with any kind of racial subtext, particularly one that had a subtext of black rage. Its enemies understood this, and when no black rage could be found, they concocted some. And the administration, in a panic, knuckled under.

Violence at the hands of whites robbed Shirley Sherrod of a cousin and a father. White rage outlined the substantive rules of her life: Don't quarrel with white people. Don't look them in the eye. Avoid Route 91 after dark. White racism destroyed New Communities, a fact validated by the nearly $13 million the organization received in the class-action suit it joined alleging racial discrimination by the local USDA officials granting loan applications. (Which means that her being forced out by Vilsack was the second time the USDA had wronged her directly.) And yet through it all, Sherrod has hewed to the rule of "twice as good." She has preached nonviolence and integration. The very video that led to her dismissal was of a speech aimed at black people, warning them against the dangers of succumbing to rage.

Driving down a sparse country road, Sherrod and I pulled over to a grassy footpath and stepped out at the spot where her father had been shot and killed in 1965. We then drove a few miles into Newton, and stopped at a large brick building that used to be the courthouse where Sherrod had tried to register to vote a few months after her father's death but had been violently turned back by the sheriff; where a year later Sherrod's mother pursued a civil case against her husband's killer. (She lost.) For this, Sherrod's mother enjoyed routine visits from white terrorists, which abated only after she, pregnant with her dead husband's son, appeared in the doorway with a gun and began calling out names of men in the mob.

When we got back into the car, I asked Sherrod why she hadn't given in to rage against her father's killers and sided with Stokely Carmichael. "It was simple for me," she said. "I really wanted to work. I wanted to win."

I asked Sherrod if she thought the president had a grasp of the specific history of the region and of the fights waged and the sacrifices made in order to make his political journey possible. "I don't think he does," Sherrod said. "When he called me [shortly after the incident], he kept saying he understood our struggle and all we'd fought for. He said, 'Read my book and you'll see.' But I *had* read his book."

In 2009, Sergeant James Crowley arrested Henry Louis Gates Jr., the eminent professor of African American studies at Harvard, at his front door in Cambridge, for, essentially, sassing him. When President Obama publicly asserted the stupidity of Crowley's action, he was so besieged that the controversy threatened to derail what he hoped would be his signature achievement—healthcare reform. Obama, an African American male who had risen through the ranks of the American elite, was no doubt sensitive to untoward treatment at the hands of the police. But his expounding upon it so provoked right-wing rage that he was forced away from doing the kind of truth-telling he'd once lauded. "I don't know if you've noticed," Obama said at the time, "but nobody's been paying much attention to health care."

Shirley Sherrod has worked all her life to make a world where the rise of a black president born of a biracial marriage is both conceivable and legal. She has endured the killing of relatives, the ruination of enterprises, and the defaming of her reputation. Crowley, for his actions, was feted in the halls of American power, honored by being invited to a "beer summit" with the man he had arrested and the leader of the free world. Shirley Sherrod, unjustly fired and defamed, was treated to a brief phone call from a man whose career, in some profound way, she had made possible. Sherrod herself is not immune to this point. She talked to me about crying with her husband while watching Obama's Election Night speech. In her new memoir, *The Courage to Hope,* she writes about a different kind of tears: When she discussed her firing with her family, her mother, who'd spent her life facing down racism at its most lethal, simply wept. "What will my babies say?" Sherrod cried to her husband, referring to their four small granddaughters. "How can I explain to my children that I got fired by the first black president?"

IN 2000, AN UNDERCOVER police officer followed a young man named Prince Jones from suburban Maryland through Washington, D.C., into Northern Virginia and shot him dead, near the home of his girlfriend and eleven-month-old daughter. Jones was a student at Howard University. His mother was a radiologist. He was also my friend. The officer tracking Prince thought he was on the trail of a drug dealer. But the dealer he was after was short and wore dreadlocks—Prince was tall and wore his hair cropped close. The officer was black. He wore dreadlocks and a T-shirt, in an attempt to look like a drug dealer. The ruse likely worked. He claimed that after Prince got out of his car and confronted him, he drew his gun and said "Police"; Prince returned to his car and repeatedly rammed the officer's unmarked car with his own vehicle. The story sounded wildly at odds with the young man I knew. But even if it was accurate, I could easily see myself frightened by a strange car following me for miles, and then reacting wildly when a man in civilian clothes pulled out a gun and claimed to be a cop. (The officer never showed a badge.)

No criminal charges were ever brought against Carlton Jones, the officer who killed my friend and rendered a little girl fatherless. It was as if society barely blinked. A few months later, I moved to New York. When 9/11 happened, I wanted nothing to do with any kind of patriotism, with the broad national ceremony of mourning. I had no sympathy for the firefighters, and something bordering on hatred for the police officers who had died. I lived in a country where my friend—twice as good—could be shot down mere footsteps from his family by agents of the state. God damn America, indeed.

I grew. I became a New Yorker. I came to understand the limits of anger. Watching Barack Obama crisscross the country to roaring white crowds, and then get elected president, I became convinced that the country really had changed—that time and events had altered the nation, and that progress had come in places I'd never imagined it could. When Osama bin Laden was killed, I cheered like everyone else. God damn al-Qaeda.

When trans-partisan mourning erupted around Trayvon Martin, it reinforced my conviction that the world had changed since the death of Prince Jones. Like Prince, Trayvon was suspected of being a criminal chiefly because of the color of his skin. Like Prince's, Trayvon's killer claimed self-defense. Again, with little effort, I could see myself in the shoes of the dead man. But this time, society's response seemed so very different, so much more heartening.

Then the first black president spoke, and the Internet bloomed. Young people began "Trayvoning"—mocking the death of a black boy by photographing themselves in hoodies, with Skittles and iced tea, in a death pose.

In a democracy, so the saying goes, the people get the government they deserve. Part of Obama's genius is a remarkable ability to soothe race consciousness among whites. Any black person who's worked in the professional world is well acquainted with this trick. But never has it been practiced at such a high level, and never have its limits been so obviously exposed. This need to talk in dulcet tones, to never be angry regardless of the offense, bespeaks a strange and compromised integration indeed, revealing a country so infantile that it can countenance white acceptance of blacks only when they meet an Al Roker standard.

And yet this is the uncertain foundation of Obama's historic victory—a victory that I, and my community, hold in the highest esteem. Who would truly deny the possibility of a black presidency in all its power and symbolism? Who would rob that little black boy of the right to feel himself affirmed by touching the kinky black hair of his president?

I think back to the first time I wrote Shirley Sherrod, requesting an interview. Here was a black woman with every reason in the world to bear considerable animosity toward Barack Obama. But she agreed to meet me only with great trepidation. She said she didn't "want to do anything to hurt" the president.

6.

NOTES FROM
THE
SIXTH YEAR

———

I N ALL OF AMERICAN LIFE, THERE IS A BIAS TOWARD THE HAPPY
ending, toward the notion that human resilience and intellect will
be a match for any problem. This holds especially true for the problem of white supremacy. For white people who have not quite
taken on the full load of ancestral debt but can sense its weight,
there is a longing for some magic that might make the burden of
slavery and all that followed magically vanish. For blacks born
under the burden, there is a need to believe that a better day is on
the horizon, that their lives, their children's lives, and their grandchildren's lives are not forever condemned to carry that weight,
which white people can only but sense. I felt this need whenever I
spoke to audiences about my writing since, invariably, I would be
asked what I could say that would give the audience hope. I never
knew how to answer the question. The writers I loved, whom I
sought to emulate, were mostly unconcerned with "hope." But
moreover—what if there was no hope at all? Sometimes, I said as
much and was often met with a kind of polite and stunned disappointment.

By then the title "public intellectual" had been attached to me, and I saw that what came with it was not just the air of the dilettante but the air of the solutionist. The black public intellectual need not be wise, but he had better have answers. There were dissenters in the tradition. There was Derrick Bell, for instance. But mostly I felt the expectation that if I was writing or talking about problems, I should also be able to identify an immediately actionable way out—preferably one that could garner a sixty-vote majority in the Senate. There was a kind of insanity to this—like telling doctors to only diagnose that which they could immediately and effortlessly cure. But that was the job of the black public intellectual—not to stimulate, not to ask the questions that kept them up at night, not even just to interpret the drums but to interpret them in some way that promised redemption. This was not work for writers and scholars, who thrive in privacy and study, but performance-prophets who live for the roar of the crowd.

Imagining the smallness of my own life span against the span of American history, and thinking how many lifetimes went into the creation of the problem of white supremacy, meant that any solutions I gave would likely require the work of generations. Moreover, my solution might seem crazy in this moment—much as abolition seemed "crazy" for decades, right up until it happened—but must be considered anyway. It's likely that should white supremacy fall, the means by which that happens might be unthinkable to those of us bound by present realities and politics. But part of the joy of writing in exploration was the freedom to think beyond the present and consider ideas roundly dismissed as crazy. Even when I had been part of that dismissal.

At the onset of these eight years, my own views on what was so often and obscenely called "race relations" were not so different from those of any other liberal. Like all other Americans confronted with this "problem," I could see that some fifty years after the civil rights movement black people could still be found at the bottom of virtually every socioeconomic metric of note. I subscribed, like most, to the theories of the sociologist William Julius Wilson: that the decline of the kind of industrial high-paying low-skill jobs that built America's white middle class had left large numbers of young black men unemployed, and the government made no real effort to ameliorate this shift. An array of unfortunate consequences issued from this shift—family poverty, violent streets, poor schools.

This way of thinking appealed to me because it directly matched events I had seen in my own life. When I recalled the Baltimore of my youth, it did not seem to suffer from anything so quaint and simple as "segregation" or "white supremacy," terms that conjured COLORED ONLY signs, night rides, and thuggish sheriffs with ominous nicknames. Instead, the pox represented itself in an abundance of men hanging out on corners, single mothers working night shifts, teen parents in all my high school classes, and kids with ready and easy access to guns. White supremacy was not in direct evidence, because there were no white people around. I had the quasi-nationalist pride that marked hip-hop in the '80s and marked my home. I had a vague sense of "white supremacy" as a kind of historical wrong. And I understood that this wrong was not unconnected to the yawning gap in resources between black people and white people. But the awareness was imprecise and could not match the visceral power of Wilson's theory, which was not historical but observable, as Jay would say, on any Martin Luther.

For those seeking immediately actionable solutions, there was also something useful about this perspective. If white supremacy was not the primary injury, if what injured black people was the same deindustrialization and governmental retreat that threatened working people everywhere, then there was no need for solutions that took racism into account. Instead, programs could be targeted at those in need, and the residual problems of a presumably historical racism could be solved while eliding any discussion of their origins. True, it was widely accepted, racism is "part" of the problem. But it was not the whole problem, and overheated accusations of bigotry had done great harm and clouded the mutual interest of all working and poor people, regardless of color. The idea behind the old Kennedy maxim, "a rising tide lifts all boats," was embraced, and this became the dominant liberal response to any demand for a "black agenda" or directly "anti-racist" program. What passed for anti-racist programs—affirmative action, for instance—came under attack, not just from conservatives, but from liberals who believed that the true vector for attacking all that bedeviled African Americans was class, not race.

Affinity to the "rising tide" theory was genuinely felt. It also offered certain advantages. Though often proffered by the self-styled "New Democrats," the theory connected to the ancient leftist dream of a broad coalition of working people. For those interested in electoral politics, the "rising tide" theory meant never having to confront white voters, still the mass of voters, with the weight of ancestral sins and all the privileges accrued from them. If race was declining in significance, then there really would be no need to talk about it. All one need do is urge the white working class, so often cruelly tricked into acting "against their interest," to see that they had cast their lot with their oppressors.

The promise of a cost-free escape from history should have made me suspicious. But what ultimately made me question the "rising tide" idea was not the theory itself but all the attendant theories that so often went with it. There is a long tradition among liberal intellectuals, and even among black intellectuals, of insisting that some amount of the racial chasm is the fault of black people themselves.

To the credit of leftists, to them this argument was anathema. But it was not the leftists who had power, it was the New Democrats. And likely for reasons of political expediency and some legitimate belief, they married their "rising tide" rhetoric with the idea that something in black culture had gone wrong and was contributing to the panoply of negative outcomes. And so it was said that there was an unwillingness to work among black men, a disdain for marriage in black men, an allegiance to gangsta rap among black youth, and that these cultural forces had more explanatory power than racism ever could.

As much as Wilson's theory matched the facts of my life, black pathology matched none of it. I was from the kind of home that would have been labeled, on paper, pathological. I had six siblings born to four women, two of them born in the same year, two of them born to friends. All of us had, in turn, had children before we were married. We were also all college graduates, save me. We were writers, engineers, computer programmers, prosecutors, and PR specialists.

I could grant that my family was exceptional, but even among those black families I knew, I saw, not so much a culture of pathology, as a culture fitted for a pathological world. To fight, stab, or shoot over respect seemed ridiculous to those who already had the society's respect. But all the boys and young men of my youth were keenly aware of how little they owned, how little of their lives they actually controlled. And so some of them made their stand on the scuff mark on their suede Pumas, on the trespassing of some corner, on the hard looks of strangers. "I ain't no punk," was the motto then, and the motto was adopted by those who knew what they were not but had no power to declare what they were.

Memoir is not data. But even the unbiased statistics did not say what they appeared to say. I recall, for instance, that there was much fretting over the increase in the percentage of out-of-wedlock births as the marker of a culture in decline. But the percentage of out-of-wedlock births did not say what its inveighers thought it did. That is because the rate of out-of-wedlock births is the result of the number of children born to married women and the number born to unmarried women. It could have been true that unmarried black women were having the same number of children today as they had thirty years ago, but a drop in births to married women could still cause the percentage of out-of-wedlock births to increase. I called the Census Bureau and pulled as much data as I could on both categories. The birth rate for unmarried women had spiked in the late '80s but was now declining and was at its lowest level since 1969, the furthest back I could trace census numbers. The early aughts saw a historic drop in teen pregnancy numbers, and much of that drop happened in the black community. It was a small thing to learn this, but it fixed my opposition to lazy cultural arguments.

The final thing that got me was the vaguely insulting way that "rising tide" rhetoric addressed the masses of whites. The presumption that they had, for centuries, acted "against their interests" struck me as saying that these whites had been, for generations, so gullible as to be fooled by a prejudice that paid no dividends. When rich Hollywood actors supported higher taxes, no one criticized them for "acting against their interests," presumably because paying higher taxes aligns with those wealthy actors' vision of the world as they would like it to be. Could it also be true that the masses of poorer whites might support lowering those same taxes for the rich in response to a different vision of the world? What if it was true that the masses of white Americans had not been fooled at all but that a critical mass of them had simply identified with a set of "interests" that were not purely economic and so powerful they overawed the class interests that liberals and leftists presumed should be broadly shared?

In fact, I knew of such a set of interests—one so powerful that it brought on a war that killed more Americans than every other American war combined. And I knew that that war ended in the dissolution of slavery, an institution that had provided the seed money for the country itself. And I knew that the force that reaped all that death did not dissipate into the ether at the end of the war but instead gave birth to a century of outright terrorism against black people. And I knew that slavery and the terrorism that followed were not incidental elements in American history, but at its core.

I was not always a believer in reparations. I'd read TransAfrica founder Randall Robinson's work on the subject in the late '90s, which convinced me that the negative conditions of black people were tied to the fact of slavery and that recompense for that crime made sense in the broadest way. But like most people who agreed with the idea in principle, I thought it was a wildly impractical solution. Some years later I read *Crabgrass Frontier,* Kenneth Jackson's history of the suburbs and the cities they ringed. I remembered the bracing section on how black families had been cut out of the FHA loan program and thus excluded from much of the suburban housing development in the postwar years. Jackson argued that there was a link between the impoverished cities where black people lived and the relatively affluent suburbs where they did not, and the link was neither mystical nor natural but was the knowable actions of our government. I knew that housing was a great source of the wealth for American families. So was the gap in wealth between black and white families tied to this government action?

Still later, I read Ira Katznelson's history of discrimination, *When Affirmative Action Was White,* which argued that similar exclusions applied to other "color-blind" New Deal programs, such as the beloved GI Bill, social security, and unemployment insurance. I was slowly apprehending that a rising tide, too, could be made to discriminate. A raft of well-researched books and articles pointed me this way. From historians, I learned that the New Deal's exclusion of blacks was the price FDR paid to the southern senators for its passage. The price black people paid was being forced out of the greatest government-backed wealth-building opportunity in the twentieth century. The price of discrimination had more dimensions than those that were immediately observable. Since the country's wealth was distributed along the lines of race and because black families were cordoned off, resources accrued and compounded for whites while relative poverty accrued for blacks. And so it was not simply that black people were more likely to be poor but that black people—of all classes—were more likely to live in poor neighborhoods. So thick was the barrier of segregation that upper-class blacks were more likely to live in poor neighborhoods than poor whites.

The "rising tide" theory rested on a notion of separate but equal class ladders. And so there was a class of black poor and an equivalent class of white poor, a black middle class and a white middle class, a black elite and a white elite. From this angle, the race problem was merely the result of too many blacks being found at the bottom of their ladder—too many who were poor and too few who were able to make their way to the next rung. If one could simply alter the distribution, the old problem of "race" could be solved. But any investigation into the actual details revealed that the ladders themselves were not equal—that to be a member of the "black race" in America had specific, quantifiable consequences. Not only did poor blacks tend to be much less likely to advance up their ladder, but those who did stood a much greater likelihood of tumbling back. That was because the middle-class rung of the black ladder lacked the financial stability enjoyed by the white ladder. Whites in the middle class often brought with them generational wealth—the home of a deceased parent, a modest inheritance, a gift from a favorite uncle. Blacks in the middle class often brought with them generational debt—an incarcerated father, an evicted niece, a mother forced to take in her sister's kids. And these conditions, themselves, could not be separated out from the specific injury of racism, one that was not addressed by simply moving up a rung. Racism was not a singular one-dimensional vector but a pandemic, afflicting black communities at every level, regardless of what rung they occupied. From that point forward the case for reparations seemed obvious and the case against it thin. The sins of slavery did not stop with slavery. On the contrary, slavery was but the initial crime in a long tradition of crimes, of plunder even, that could be traced into the present day. And whereas a claim for reparations for slavery rested in the ancestral past, it was now clear that one could make a claim on behalf of those who were very much alive.

All the threads I had been working on in my blog and other work came together in "The Case for Reparations": the critique of respectability politics, the realization that history could be denied but could not be escaped, the understanding of the Civil War's long shadow, the attempt to discover my own voice and language, and, finally, the deeply held belief that white supremacy was so foundational to this country that it would not be defeated in my lifetime, my child's lifetime, or perhaps ever. There would be no happy endings, and if there were, they would spring from chance, not from any preordained logic of human morality. I believed this because the reparations claim was so old, so transparently correct, so clearly the only solution, and yet it remained far outside the borders of American politics. To believe anything else was to believe that a robbery spanning generations could somehow be ameliorated while never acknowledging the scope of the crime and never making recompense. And yet that was the thinking that occupied mainstream American politics. And why wouldn't it? To enact reparations would mean not simply an outlay of money but also a deep reconsideration of America's own autobiography. The implications could not be confined to the presumably narrow realm of "race." What would it mean for American foreign policy, so often rooted in its image as the oldest enlightened republic and pioneer of the free world, to forthrightly note that that freedom and enlightenment were only made possible through a plunder that stretched from the country's prehistory up into living memory? For Americans, the hardest part of paying reparations would not be the outlay of money. It would be acknowledging that their most cherished myth was not real.

The essay has two problems that deserve to be acknowledged here. I pride myself on citing the sources of my thinking, research, and understanding. But Beryl Satter, whose book *Family Properties* provided much of the narrative background for the story, was not properly acknowledged. I wish to say here that this essay could never have happened without her book but also without her willingness to assist me in tracking down people in Chicago who'd long fought against the city's racist housing practices. The lack of proper citation did not originate in any desire to erase or appropriate Beryl's work but out of my own sloppiness while closing out this huge enterprise on deadline. That makes it neither better, nor right, nor acceptable. The second is the reference in the article to the reparations offered to Israel after World War II. I was aware that this inclusion would provoke some strong reactions, given that country's policies toward the Palestinian people. In part I included it because that seeming paradox—that Israel was both worthy of reparations and used those reparations to advance policies that I thought were categorically wrong—did not seem to me to be a paradox at all. There is nothing ennobling about being a victim. The Irish so victimized by Cromwell escaped to America, where they swiftly joined in violence against African Americans. The Cherokee, warred against by white Americans, held blacks as slaves. And those blacks, emancipated after the Civil War, joined the war against the Plains Indians. The point here is that reparations are not reserved for the unimpeachably virtuous and cannot solve the problems of human morality, and this has never been, nor should it have been, the criterion for past reparation efforts. But that point is not made in the essay. Moreover, the entire section about Israel is the least informed part of the essay. I was writing about a region I had never visited and people I did not know from the luxurious position of my armchair. In short, I was behaving like the very "public intellectuals" whom I so despised.

After the publication of "The Case for Reparations," I could feel the world reacting differently to me. This was writer fame, not George Clooney fame. But it was disturbing. People began stopping me on the street, and others, too embarrassed to speak to me directly, would look over and whisper, then tweet out something later. At the café where I regularly wrote, people would stop by the table to say an encouraging word or ask an opinion. One morning I was boarding the 1 train downtown, headphones on, blasting

M.O.P. A middle-aged white man began gesturing toward me. I took off my headphones. He lauded the article. And then another white man, a few feet away, mentioned he'd read it, too. "I'm a pretty educated guy," he said. "But I had no idea. I really had no idea."

The adolescent in me loved the attention and admiration. The senior citizen in me loved the financial security that came from the fame, since it meant the payoff of old debts and the possibility of a respectable retirement. But the part of me that I most identified as "me," the part that felt the truest, was mortified. I had come to love the invisibility of writing—the safe distance between my face and the work. The distance was closing. And to complicate matters more there was something else—a civic part of me, which was heartened to see the reparations argument make its way to people who'd never seriously considered it before.

It was a lesson in what serious writing married to the right platform could actually achieve. The fact was that *The Atlantic* was regarded in a way other publications that had made the reparations argument before were not. *The Atlantic* was seen as serious and respectable. If it was putting an argument for reparations on the cover, reparations had to be considered. I don't think that's something to brag about. Indeed, it's quite sad and partially speaks to the ways legitimate ideas are dismissed, because people of the right "reputation" have yet to vouch for them. How bizarre and confusing it was to look up one day and see that I, who'd begun in failure, who held no degrees or credentials, had become such a person.

THE CASE
FOR REPARATIONS

And if thy brother, a Hebrew man, or a Hebrew
woman, be sold unto thee, and serve thee six years; then
in the seventh year thou shalt let him go free from thee.
And when thou sendest him out free from thee, thou
shalt not let him go away empty: thou shalt furnish him
liberally out of thy flock, and out of thy floor, and out
of thy winepress: of that wherewith the LORD thy
God hath blessed thee thou shalt give unto him. And
thou shalt remember that thou wast a bondman in the
land of Egypt, and the LORD thy God redeemed thee:
therefore I command thee this thing today.

—DEUTERONOMY 15:12–15

Besides the crime which consists in violating the law, and
varying from the right rule of reason, whereby a man so
far becomes degenerate, and declares himself to quit the
principles of human nature, and to be a noxious creature,
there is commonly injury done to some person or other,
and some other man receives damage by his transgression:
in which case he who hath received any damage, has, be-

sides the right of punishment common to him with other men, a particular right to seek reparation.

—JOHN LOCKE, "SECOND TREATISE"

By our unpaid labor and suffering, we have earned the right to the soil, many times over and over, and now we are determined to have it.

—ANONYMOUS, 1861

I.
"SO THAT'S JUST ONE OF MY LOSSES"

Clyde Ross was born in 1923, the seventh of thirteen children, near Clarksdale, Mississippi, the home of the blues. Ross's parents owned and farmed a forty-acre tract of land, flush with cows, hogs, and mules. Ross's mother would drive to Clarksdale to do her shopping in a horse and buggy, in which she invested all the pride one might place in a Cadillac. The family owned another horse, with a red coat, which they gave to Clyde. The Ross family wanted for little, save that which all black families in the Deep South then desperately desired—the protection of the law.

In the 1920s, Jim Crow Mississippi was, in all facets of society, a kleptocracy. The majority of the people in the state were perpetually robbed of the vote—a hijacking engineered through the trickery of the poll tax and the muscle of the lynch mob. Between 1882 and 1968, more black people were lynched in Mississippi than in any other state. "You and I know what's the best way to keep the nigger from voting," blustered Theodore Bilbo, a Mississippi senator and a proud Klansman. "You do it the night before the election."

The state's regime partnered robbery of the franchise with robbery of the purse. Many of Mississippi's black farmers lived in debt peonage, under the sway of cotton kings who were at once their landlords, their employers, and their primary merchants. Tools and necessities were advanced against the return on the crop, which was determined by the employer. When farmers were deemed to be in debt—and they often were—the negative balance was then carried over to the next season. A man or woman who protested this arrangement did so at the risk of grave injury or death. Refusing to work meant arrest under vagrancy laws and forced labor under the state's penal system.

Well into the twentieth century, black people spoke of their flight from Mississippi in much the same manner as their runagate ancestors had. In her 2010 book *The Warmth of Other Suns,* Isabel Wilkerson tells the story of Eddie Earvin, a spinach picker who fled Mississippi in 1963, after being made to work at gunpoint. "You didn't talk about it or tell nobody," Earvin said. "You had to sneak away."

When Clyde Ross was still a child, Mississippi authorities claimed his father owed $3,000 in back taxes. The elder Ross could not read. He did not have a lawyer. He did not know anyone at the local courthouse. He could not expect the police to be impartial. Effectively, the Ross family had no way to contest the claim and no protection under the law. The authorities seized the land. They seized the buggy. They took the cows, hogs, and mules. And so for the upkeep of separate but equal, the entire Ross family was reduced to sharecropping.

This was hardly unusual. In 2001, the Associated Press published a three-part investigation into the theft of black-owned land stretching back to the antebellum period. The series documented some 406 victims and 24,000 acres of land valued at tens of millions of dollars. The land was taken through means ranging from legal chicanery to terrorism. "Some of the land taken from black families has become a country club in Virginia," the AP reported, as well as "oil fields in Mississippi" and "a baseball spring training facility in Florida."

Clyde Ross was a smart child. His teacher thought he should attend a more challenging school. There was very little support for educating black people in Mississippi. But Julius Rosenwald, a part owner of Sears, Roebuck, had begun an ambitious effort to build schools for black children throughout the South. Ross's teacher believed he should attend the local Rosenwald school. It was too far for Ross to walk and get back in time to work in the fields. Local white children had a school bus. Clyde Ross did not, and thus lost the chance to better his education.

Then, when Ross was ten years old, a group of white men demanded his only childhood possession—the horse with the red coat. "You can't have this horse. We want it," one of the white men said. They gave Ross's father $17.

"I did everything for that horse," Ross told me. "Everything. And they took him. Put him on the racetrack. I never did know what happened to him after that, but I know they didn't bring him back. So that's just one of my losses."

The losses mounted. As sharecroppers, the Ross family saw their wages treated as the landlord's slush fund. Landowners were supposed to split the profits from the cotton fields with sharecroppers. But bales would often disappear during the count, or the split might be altered on a whim. If cotton was selling for fifty cents a pound, the Ross family might get fifteen cents, or only five. One year Ross's mother promised to buy him a seven-dollar suit for a summer program at their church. She ordered the suit by mail. But that year Ross's family was paid only five cents a pound for cotton. The mailman arrived with the suit. The Rosses could not pay. The suit was sent back. Clyde Ross did not go to the church program.

It was in these early years that Ross began to understand himself as an American—he did not live under the blind decree of justice, but under the heel of a regime that elevated armed robbery to a governing principle. He thought about fighting. "Just be quiet," his father told him. "Because they'll come and kill us all."

Clyde Ross grew. He was drafted into the Army. The draft officials offered him an exemption if he stayed home and worked. He preferred to take his chances with war. He was stationed in California. He found that he could go into stores without being bothered. He could walk the streets without being harassed. He could go into a restaurant and receive service.

Ross was shipped off to Guam. He fought in World War II to save the world from tyranny. But when he returned to Clarksdale, he found that tyranny had followed him home. This was 1947, eight years before Mississippi lynched Emmett Till and tossed his broken body into the Tallahatchie River. The Great Migration, a mass exodus of 6 million African Americans that spanned most of the twentieth century, was now in its second wave. The black pilgrims did not journey north simply seeking better wages and work, or bright lights and big adventures. They were fleeing the acquisitive warlords of the South. They were seeking the protection of the law.

Clyde Ross was among them. He came to Chicago in 1947 and took a job as a taster at Campbell's Soup. He made a stable wage. He married. He had children. His paycheck was his own. No Klansmen stripped him of the vote. When he walked down the street, he did not have to move because a white man was walking past. He did not have to take off his hat or avert his gaze. His journey from peonage to full citizenship seemed near-complete. Only one item was missing—a home, that final badge of entry into the sacred order of the American middle class of the Eisenhower years.

In 1961, Ross and his wife bought a house in North Lawndale, a bustling community on Chicago's West Side. North Lawndale had long been a predominantly Jewish neighborhood, but a handful of middle-class African Americans had lived there starting in the '40s. The community was anchored by the sprawling Sears, Roebuck headquarters. North Lawndale's Jewish People's Institute actively encouraged blacks to move into the neighborhood, seeking to make it a "pilot community for interracial living." In the battle for integration then being fought around the country, North Lawndale seemed to offer promising terrain. But out in the tall grass, highwaymen, nefarious as any Clarksdale kleptocrat, were lying in wait.

Three months after Clyde Ross moved into his house, the boiler blew out. This would normally be a homeowner's responsibility, but in fact, Ross was not really a homeowner. His payments were made to the seller, not the bank. And Ross had not signed a normal mortgage. He'd bought "on contract": a predatory agreement that combined all the responsibilities of homeownership with all the disadvantages of renting—while offering the benefits of neither. Ross had bought his house for $27,500. The seller, not the previous homeowner but a new kind of middleman, had bought it for only $12,000 six months before selling it to Ross. In a contract sale, the seller kept the deed until the contract was paid in full—and, unlike with a normal mortgage, Ross would acquire no equity in the meantime. If he missed a single payment, he would immediately forfeit his $1,000 down payment, all his monthly payments, and the property itself.

The men who peddled contracts in North Lawndale would sell homes at inflated prices and then evict families who could not pay—taking their down payment and their monthly installments as profit. Then they'd bring in another black family, rinse, and repeat. "He loads them up with payments they can't meet," an office secretary told the *Chicago Daily News* of her boss, the speculator Lou Fushanis, in 1963. "Then he takes the property away from them. He's sold some of the buildings three or four times."

Ross had tried to get a legitimate mortgage in another neighborhood, but was told by a loan officer that there was no financing available. The truth was that there was no financing for people like Clyde Ross. From the 1930s through the 1960s, black people across the country were largely cut out of the legitimate home-mortgage market through means both legal and extralegal. Chicago whites employed every measure, from "restrictive covenants" to bomb-ings, to keep their neighborhoods segregated.

Their efforts were buttressed by the federal government. In 1934, Congress created the Federal Housing Administration. The FHA insured private mortgages, causing a drop in interest rates and a de-cline in the size of the down payment required to buy a house. But an insured mortgage was not a possibility for Clyde Ross. The FHA had adopted a system of maps that rated neighborhoods according to their perceived stability. On the maps, green areas, rated "A," indicated "in demand" neighborhoods that, as one appraiser put it, lacked "a single foreigner or Negro." These neighborhoods were considered excellent prospects for insurance. Neighborhoods where black people lived were rated "D" and were usually considered in-eligible for FHA backing. They were colored in red. Neither the percentage of black people living there nor their social class mat-tered. Black people were viewed as a contagion. Redlining went beyond FHA-backed loans and spread to the entire mortgage indus-try, which was already rife with racism, excluding black people from most legitimate means of obtaining a mortgage.

"A government offering such bounty to builders and lenders could have required compliance with a nondiscrimination policy," Charles Abrams, the urban studies expert who helped create the New York City Housing Authority, wrote in 1955. "Instead, the FHA adopted a racial policy that could well have been culled from the Nuremberg laws."

The devastating effects are cogently outlined by Melvin L. Oli-ver and Thomas M. Shapiro in their 1995 book *Black Wealth/White Wealth:*

Locked out of the greatest mass-based opportunity for wealth accumulation in American history, African Americans who desired and were able to afford home ownership found them-selves consigned to central-city communities where their in-vestments were affected by the "self-fulfilling prophecies" of

the FHA appraisers: cut off from sources of new investment[,] their homes and communities deteriorated and lost
value in comparison to those homes and communities that
FHA appraisers deemed desirable.

In Chicago and across the country, whites looking to achieve the
American dream could rely on a legitimate credit system backed by
the government. Blacks were herded into the sights of unscrupu-
lous lenders who took them for money and for sport. "It was like
people who like to go out and shoot lions in Africa. It was the same
thrill," a housing attorney told the historian Beryl Satter in her
2009 book *Family Properties*. "The thrill of the chase and the kill."

The kill was profitable. At the time of his death, Lou Fushanis
owned more than six hundred properties, many of them in North
Lawndale, and his estate was estimated to be worth $3 million. He'd
made much of this money by exploiting the frustrated hopes of
black migrants like Clyde Ross. During this period, according to
one estimate, 85 percent of all black home buyers who bought in
Chicago bought on contract. "If anybody who is well established in
this business in Chicago doesn't earn $100,000 a year," a contract
seller told *The Saturday Evening Post* in 1962, "he is loafing."

Contract sellers became rich. North Lawndale became a ghetto.
Clyde Ross still lives there. He still owns his home. He is ninety-
one, and the emblems of survival are all around him—awards for
service in his community, pictures of his children in cap and gown.
But when I asked him about his home in North Lawndale, I heard
only anarchy.

"We were ashamed. We did not want anyone to know that we
were that ignorant," Ross told me. He was sitting at his dining-
room table. His glasses were as thick as his Clarksdale drawl. "I'd
come out of Mississippi where there was one mess, and come up
here and got in another mess. So how dumb am I? I didn't want
anyone to know how dumb I was.

"When I found myself caught up in it, I said, 'How? I just left this mess. I just left no laws. And no regard. And then I come here and get cheated wide open.' I would probably want to do some harm to some people, you know, if I had been violent like some of us. I thought, 'Man, I got caught up in this stuff. I can't even take care of my kids.' I didn't have enough for my kids. You could fall through the cracks easy fighting these white people. And no law."

But fight Clyde Ross did. In 1968 he joined the newly formed Contract Buyers League—a collection of black homeowners on Chicago's South and West Sides, all of whom had been locked into the same system of predation. There was Howell Collins, whose contract called for him to pay $25,500 for a house that a speculator had bought for $14,500. There was Ruth Wells, who'd managed to pay out half her contract, expecting a mortgage, only to suddenly see an insurance bill materialize out of thin air—a requirement the seller had added without Wells's knowledge. Contract sellers used every tool at their disposal to pilfer from their clients. They scared white residents into selling low. They lied about properties' compliance with building codes, then left the buyer responsible when city inspectors arrived. They presented themselves as real-estate brokers, when in fact they were the owners. They guided their clients to lawyers who were in on the scheme.

The Contract Buyers League fought back. Members—who would eventually number more than five hundred—went out to the posh suburbs where the speculators lived and embarrassed them by knocking on their neighbors' doors and informing them of the details of the contract-lending trade. They refused to pay their installments, instead holding monthly payments in an escrow account. Then they brought a suit against the contract sellers, accusing them of buying properties and reselling in such a manner "to reap from members of the Negro race large and unjust profits."

In return for the "deprivations of their rights and privileges under the Thirteenth and Fourteenth Amendments," the league demanded "prayers for relief"—payback of all moneys paid on contracts and all moneys paid for structural improvement of properties, at 6 percent interest minus a "fair, non-discriminatory" rental price for time of occupation. Moreover, the league asked the court to adjudge that the defendants had "acted willfully and maliciously and that malice is the gist of this action."

Ross and the Contract Buyers League were no longer appealing to the government simply for equality. They were no longer fleeing in hopes of a better deal elsewhere. They were charging society with a crime against their community. They wanted the crime publicly ruled as such. They wanted the crime's executors declared to be offensive to society. And they wanted restitution for the great injury brought upon them by said offenders. In 1968, Clyde Ross and the Contract Buyers League were no longer simply seeking the protection of the law. They were seeking reparations.

II.
"A DIFFERENCE OF KIND, NOT DEGREE"

According to the most recent statistics, North Lawndale is now on the wrong end of virtually every socioeconomic indicator. In 1930 its population was 112,000. Today it is 36,000. The halcyon talk of "interracial living" is dead. The neighborhood is 92 percent black. Its homicide rate is 45 per 100,000—triple the rate of the city as a whole. The infant mortality rate is 14 per 1,000—more than twice the national average. Forty-three percent of the people in North Lawndale live below the poverty line—double Chicago's overall rate. Forty-five percent of all households are on food stamps— nearly three times the rate of the city at large. Sears, Roebuck left the neighborhood in 1987, taking 1,800 jobs with it. Kids in North Lawndale need not be confused about their prospects: Cook County's Juvenile Temporary Detention Center sits directly adjacent to the neighborhood.

North Lawndale is an extreme portrait of the trends that ail black Chicago. Such is the magnitude of these ailments that it can be said that blacks and whites do not inhabit the same city. The average per capita income of Chicago's white neighborhoods is almost three times that of its black neighborhoods. When the Harvard sociologist Robert J. Sampson examined incarceration rates in Chicago in his 2012 book *Great American City,* he found that a black neighborhood with one of the highest incarceration rates (West Garfield Park) had a rate more than forty times as high as the white neighborhood with the highest rate (Clearing). "This is a staggering differential, even for community-level comparisons," Sampson writes. "A difference of kind, not degree."

In other words, Chicago's impoverished black neighborhoods—characterized by high unemployment and households headed by single parents—are not simply poor; they are "ecologically distinct." This "is not simply the same thing as low economic status," writes Sampson. "In this pattern Chicago is not alone."

The lives of black Americans are better than they were half a century ago. The humiliation of WHITES ONLY signs is gone. Rates of black poverty have decreased. Black teen pregnancy rates are at record lows—and the gap between black and white teen pregnancy rates has shrunk significantly. But such progress rests on a shaky foundation, and fault lines are everywhere. The income gap between black and white households is roughly the same today as it was in 1970. Patrick Sharkey, a sociologist at New York University, studied children born from 1955 through 1970 and found that 4 percent of whites and 62 percent of blacks across America had been raised in poor neighborhoods. A generation later, the same study showed, virtually nothing had changed. And whereas whites born into affluent neighborhoods tended to remain in affluent neighborhoods, blacks tended to fall out of them.

This is not surprising. Black families, regardless of income, are significantly less wealthy than white families. The Pew Research Center estimates that white households are worth roughly twenty times as much as black households, and that whereas only 15 percent of whites have zero or negative wealth, more than a third of blacks do. Effectively, the black family in America is working without a safety net. When financial calamity strikes—a medical emergency, divorce, job loss—the fall is precipitous.

And just as black families of all incomes remain handicapped by a lack of wealth, so too do they remain handicapped by their restricted choice of neighborhood. Black people with upper-middle-class incomes do not generally live in upper-middle-class neighborhoods. Sharkey's research shows that black families making $100,000 typically live in the kinds of neighborhoods inhabited by white families making $30,000. "Blacks and whites inhabit such different neighborhoods," Sharkey writes, "that it is not possible to compare the economic outcomes of black and white children."

The implications are chilling. As a rule, poor black people do not work their way out of the ghetto—and those who do often face the horror of watching their children and grandchildren tumble back.

Even seeming evidence of progress withers under harsh light. In 2012, the Manhattan Institute cheerily noted that segregation had declined since the 1960s. And yet African Americans still remained—by far—the most segregated ethnic group in the country.

With segregation, with the isolation of the injured and the robbed, comes the concentration of disadvantage. An unsegregated America might see poverty, and all its effects, spread across the country with no particular bias toward skin color. Instead, the concentration of poverty has been paired with a concentration of melanin. The resulting conflagration has been devastating.

One thread of thinking in the African American community holds that these depressing numbers partially stem from cultural pathologies that can be altered through individual grit and exceptionally good behavior. (In 2011, Philadelphia Mayor Michael Nutter, responding to violence among young black males, put the blame on the family: "Too many men making too many babies they don't want to take care of, and then we end up dealing with your children." Nutter turned to those presumably fatherless babies:

"Pull your pants up and buy a belt, because no one wants to see your underwear or the crack of your butt.") The thread is as old as black politics itself. It is also wrong. The kind of trenchant racism to which black people have persistently been subjected can never be defeated by making its victims more respectable. The essence of American racism is disrespect. And in the wake of the grim numbers, we see the grim inheritance.

The Contract Buyers League's suit brought by Clyde Ross and his allies took direct aim at this inheritance. The suit was rooted in Chicago's long history of segregation, which had created two housing markets—one legitimate and backed by the government, the other lawless and patrolled by predators. The suit dragged on until 1976, when the league lost a jury trial. Securing the equal protection of the law proved hard; securing reparations proved impossible. If there were any doubts about the mood of the jury, the foreman removed them by saying, when asked about the verdict, that he hoped it would help end "the mess Earl Warren made with *Brown v. Board of Education* and all that nonsense."

The Supreme Court seems to share that sentiment. The past two decades have witnessed a rollback of the progressive legislation of the 1960s. Liberals have found themselves on the defensive. In 2008, when Barack Obama was a candidate for president, he was asked whether his daughters—Malia and Sasha—should benefit from affirmative action. He answered in the negative.

The exchange rested upon an erroneous comparison of the average American white family and the exceptional first family. In the contest of upward mobility, Barack and Michelle Obama have won. But they've won by being twice as good—and enduring twice as much. Malia and Sasha Obama enjoy privileges beyond the average white child's dreams. But that comparison is incomplete. The more telling question is how they compare with Jenna and Barbara Bush—the products of many generations of privilege, not just one. Whatever the Obama children achieve, it will be evidence of their family's singular perseverance, not of broad equality.

III.
"WE INHERIT OUR AMPLE PATRIMONY"

In 1783, the freedwoman Belinda Royall petitioned the common-wealth of Massachusetts for reparations. Belinda had been born in modern-day Ghana. She was kidnapped as a child and sold into slavery. She endured the Middle Passage and fifty years of enslave-ment at the hands of Isaac Royall and his son. But the junior Roy-all, a British loyalist, fled the country during the Revolution. Belinda, now free after half a century of labor, beseeched the na-scent Massachusetts legislature:

> The face of your Petitioner, is now marked with the furrows of time, and her frame bending under the oppression of years, while she, by the Laws of the Land, is denied the employment of one morsel of that immense wealth, apart whereof hath been accumilated by her own industry, and the whole augmented by her servitude.
>
> WHEREFORE, casting herself at your feet if your hon-ours, as to a body of men, formed for the extirpation of vassalage, for the reward of Virtue, and the just return of honest industry—she prays, that such allowance may be made her out of the Estate of Colonel Royall, as will pre-vent her, and her more infirm daughter, from misery in the greatest extreme, and scatter comfort over the short and downward path of their lives.

Belinda Royall was granted a pension of 15 pounds and 12 shil-lings, to be paid out of the estate of Isaac Royall—one of the earli-est successful attempts to petition for reparations. At the time, black people in America had endured more than 150 years of enslavement, and the idea that they might be owed something in return was, if not the national consensus, at least not outrageous.

"A heavy account lies against us as a civil society for oppressions committed against people who did not injure us," wrote the Quaker John Woolman in 1769, "and that if the particular case of many individuals were fairly stated, it would appear that there was considerable due to them."

As the historian Roy E. Finkenbine has documented, at the dawn of this country, black reparations were actively considered and often effected. Quakers in New York, New England, and Baltimore went so far as to make "membership contingent upon compensating one's former slaves." In 1782, the Quaker Robert Pleasants emancipated his 78 slaves, granted them 350 acres, and later built a school on their property and provided for their education. "The doing of this justice to the injured Africans," wrote Pleasants, "would be an acceptable offering to him who 'Rules in the kingdom of men.'"

Edward Coles, a protégé of Thomas Jefferson who became a slaveholder through inheritance, took many of his slaves north and granted them a plot of land in Illinois. John Randolph, a cousin of Jefferson's, willed that all his slaves be emancipated upon his death, and that all those older than forty be given ten acres of land. "I give and bequeath to all my slaves their freedom," Randolph wrote, "heartily regretting that I have been the owner of one."

In his book *Forever Free,* Eric Foner recounts the story of a disgruntled planter reprimanding a freedman loafing on the job:

PLANTER: "You lazy nigger, I am losing a whole day's labor by you."
FREEDMAN: "Massa, how many days' labor have I lost by you?"

In the twentieth century, the cause of reparations was taken up by a diverse cast that included the Confederate veteran Walter R. Vaughan, who believed that reparations would be a stimulus for the South; the black activist Callie House; black nationalist leaders like "Queen Mother" Audley Moore; and the civil rights activist James Forman. The movement coalesced in 1987 under an umbrella organization called the National Coalition of Blacks for Reparations in America (N'COBRA). The NAACP endorsed reparations in 1993. Charles J. Ogletree Jr., a professor at Harvard Law School, has pursued reparations claims in court.

But while the people advocating reparations have changed over time, the response from the country has remained virtually the same. "They have been taught to labor," the *Chicago Tribune* editorialized in 1891. "They have been taught Christian civilization, and to speak the noble English language instead of some African gibberish. The account is square with the ex-slaves."

Not exactly. Having been enslaved for 250 years, black people were not left to their own devices. They were terrorized. In the Deep South, a second slavery ruled. In the North, legislatures, mayors, civic associations, banks, and citizens all colluded to pin black people into ghettos, where they were overcrowded, overcharged, and undereducated. Businesses discriminated against them, awarding them the worst jobs and the worst wages. Police brutalized them in the streets. And the notion that black lives, black bodies, and black wealth were rightful targets remained deeply rooted in the broader society. Now we have half-stepped away from our long centuries of despoilment, promising, "Never again." But still we are haunted. It is as though we have run up a credit card bill and, having pledged to charge no more, remain befuddled that the balance does not disappear. The effects of that balance, interest accruing daily, are all around us.

Broach the topic of reparations today and a barrage of questions inevitably follows: Who will be paid? How much will they be paid? Who will pay? But if the practicalities, not the justice, of reparations are the true sticking point, there has for some time been the beginnings of a solution. For the past twenty-five years, Congressman John Conyers Jr., who represents the Detroit area, has marked every session of Congress by introducing a bill calling for a congressional study of slavery and its lingering effects as well as recommendations for "appropriate remedies."

A country curious about how reparations might actually work has an easy solution in Conyers's bill, now called HR 40, the Commission to Study Reparation Proposals for African Americans Act. We would support this bill, submit the question to study, and then assess the possible solutions. But we are not interested.

"It's because it's black folks making the claim," Nkechi Taifa, who helped found N'COBRA, says. "People who talk about reparations are considered left lunatics. But all we are talking about is studying [reparations]. As John Conyers has said, we study everything. We study the water, the air. We can't even study the issue? This bill does not authorize one red cent to anyone."

That HR 40 has never—under either Democrats or Republicans—made it to the House floor suggests our concerns are rooted not in the impracticality of reparations but in something more existential. If we conclude that the conditions in North Lawndale and black America are not inexplicable but are instead precisely what you'd expect of a community that for centuries has lived in America's crosshairs, then what are we to make of the world's oldest democracy?

One cannot escape the question by hand-waving at the past, disavowing the acts of one's ancestors, nor by citing a recent date of ancestral immigration. The last slaveholder has been dead for a very long time. The last soldier to endure Valley Forge has been dead much longer. To proudly claim the veteran and disown the slaveholder is patriotism à la carte. A nation outlives its generations. We were not there when Washington crossed the Delaware, but Emanuel Gottlieb Leutze's rendering has meaning to us. We were not there when Woodrow Wilson took us into World War I, but we are still paying out the pensions. If Thomas Jefferson's genius matters, then so does his taking of Sally Hemings's body. If George Washington crossing the Delaware matters, so must his ruthless pursuit of the runagate Oney Judge.

In 1909, President William Howard Taft told the country that "intelligent" white southerners were ready to see blacks as "useful members of the community." A week later Joseph Gordon, a black man, was lynched outside Greenwood, Mississippi. The high point of the lynching era has passed. But the memories of those robbed of their lives still live on in the lingering effects. Indeed, in America there is a strange and powerful belief that if you stab a black person ten times, the bleeding stops and the healing begins the moment the assailant drops the knife. We believe white dominance to be a fact of the inert past, a delinquent debt that can be made to disappear if only we don't look.

There has always been another way. "It is in vain to alledge, that *our ancestors* brought them hither, and not we," Yale President Timothy Dwight said in 1810.

We inherit our ample patrimony with all its incumbrances; and are bound to pay the debts of our ancestors. *This* debt, particularly, we are bound to discharge: and, when the righteous Judge of the Universe comes to reckon with his servants, he will rigidly exact the payment at our hands. To give them liberty, and stop here, is to entail upon them a curse.

IV.
"THE ILLS THAT SLAVERY FREES US FROM"

America begins in black plunder and white democracy, two features that are not contradictory but complementary. "The men who came together to found the independent United States, dedicated to freedom and equality, either held slaves or were willing to join hands with those who did," the historian Edmund S. Morgan wrote. "None of them felt entirely comfortable about the fact, but neither did they feel responsible for it. Most of them had inherited both their slaves and their attachment to freedom from an earlier generation, and they knew the two were not unconnected."

When enslaved Africans, plundered of their bodies, plundered of their families, and plundered of their labor, were brought to the colony of Virginia in 1619, they did not initially endure the naked racism that would engulf their progeny. Some of them were freed. Some of them intermarried. Still others escaped with the white indentured servants who had suffered as they had. Some even rebelled together, allying under Nathaniel Bacon to torch Jamestown in 1676.

One hundred years later, the idea of slaves and poor whites joining forces would shock the senses, but in the early days of the English colonies, the two groups had much in common. English visitors to Virginia found that its masters "abuse their servantes with intollerable oppression and hard usage." White servants were flogged, tricked into serving beyond their contracts, and traded in much the same manner as slaves.

This "hard usage" originated in a simple fact of the New World—land was boundless but cheap labor was limited. As life spans increased in the colony, the Virginia planters found in the enslaved Africans an even more efficient source of cheap labor. Whereas indentured servants were still legal subjects of the English crown and thus entitled to certain protections, African slaves entered the colonies as aliens. Exempted from the protections of the crown, they became early America's indispensable working class—fit for maximum exploitation, capable of only minimal resistance.

For the next 250 years, American law worked to reduce black people to a class of untouchables and raise all white men to the level of citizens. In 1650, Virginia mandated that "all persons except Negroes" were to carry arms. In 1664, Maryland mandated that any Englishwoman who married a slave must live as a slave of her husband's master. In 1705, the Virginia assembly passed a law allowing for the dismemberment of unruly slaves—but forbidding masters from whipping "a Christian white servant naked, without an order from a justice of the peace." In that same law, the colony mandated that "all horses, cattle, and hogs, now belonging, or that hereafter shall belong to any slave" be seized and sold off by the local church, the profits used to support "the poor of the said parish." At that time, there would have still been people alive who could remember blacks and whites joining to burn down Jamestown only twenty-nine years before. But at the beginning of the eighteenth century, two primary classes were enshrined in America.

"The two great divisions of society are not the rich and poor, but white and black," John C. Calhoun, South Carolina's senior senator, declared on the Senate floor in 1848. "And all the former, the poor as well as the rich, belong to the upper class, and are respected and treated as equals."

In 1860, the majority of people living in South Carolina and Mississippi, almost half of those living in Georgia, and about one-third of all Southerners were on the wrong side of Calhoun's line. The state with the largest number of enslaved Americans was Virginia, where in certain counties some 70 percent of all people labored in chains. Nearly one-fourth of all white Southerners owned slaves, and upon their backs the economic basis of America—and much of the Atlantic world—was erected. In the seven cotton states, one-third of all white income was derived from slavery. By 1840, cotton produced by slave labor constituted 59 percent of the country's exports. The web of this slave society extended north to the looms of New England, and across the Atlantic to Great Britain, where it powered a great economic transformation and altered the trajectory of world history. "Whoever says Industrial Revolution," wrote the historian Eric J. Hobsbawm, "says cotton."

The wealth accorded America by slavery was not just in what the slaves pulled from the land but in the slaves themselves. "In 1860, slaves as an asset were worth more than all of America's manu-facturing, all of the railroads, all of the productive capacity of the United States put together," the Yale historian David W. Blight has noted. "Slaves were the single largest, by far, financial asset of prop-erty in the entire American economy." The sale of these slaves—"in whose bodies that money congealed," writes Walter Johnson, a

Harvard historian—generated even more ancillary wealth. Loans were taken out for purchase, to be repaid with interest. Insurance policies were drafted against the untimely death of a slave and the loss of potential profits. Slave sales were taxed and notarized. The vending of the black body and the sundering of the black family became an economy unto itself, estimated to have brought in tens of millions of dollars to antebellum America. In 1860 there were more millionaires per capita in the Mississippi Valley than anywhere else in the country.

Beneath the cold numbers lay lives divided. "I had a constant dread that Mrs. Moore, her mistress, would be in want of money and sell my dear wife," a freedman wrote, reflecting on his time in slavery. "We constantly dreaded a final separation. Our affection for each was very strong, and this made us always apprehensive of a cruel parting."

Forced partings were common in the antebellum South. A slave in some parts of the region stood a 30 percent chance of being sold in his or her lifetime. Twenty-five percent of interstate trades destroyed a first marriage and half of them destroyed a nuclear family.

When the wife and children of Henry Brown, a slave in Richmond, Virginia, were to be sold away, Brown searched for a white master who might buy his wife and children to keep the family together. He failed:

The next day, I stationed myself by the side of the road, along which the slaves, amounting to three hundred and fifty, were to pass. The purchaser of my wife was a Methodist minister, who was about starting for North Carolina. Pretty soon five waggon-loads of little children passed, and looking at the foremost one, what should I see but a little child, pointing its tiny hand towards me, exclaiming, "There's my father; I knew he would come and bid me good-bye." It was my eldest child! Soon the gang approached in which my wife was chained. I looked, and beheld her familiar face; but O, reader, that glance of agony! may God spare me ever again enduring the excruciating horror of that moment! She passed, and came near to where I stood. I seized hold of her hand, intending to bid her farewell; but words failed me; the gift of utterance had fled, and I remained speechless. I followed her for some distance, with her hand grasped in mine, as if to save her from her fate, but I could not speak, and I was obliged to turn away in silence.

In a time when communications were primitive and blacks lacked freedom of movement, the parting of black families was a kind of murder. Here we find the roots of American wealth and democracy—in the for-profit destruction of the most important asset available to any people, the family. The destruction was not incidental to America's rise; it facilitated that rise. By erecting a slave society, America created the economic foundation for its great experiment in democracy. The labor strife that seeded Bacon's rebellion was suppressed. America's indispensable working class existed as property beyond the realm of politics, leaving white Americans free to trumpet their love of freedom and democratic values. Assessing antebellum democracy in Virginia, a visitor from England observed that the state's natives "can profess an unbounded love of liberty and of democracy in consequence of the mass of the people, who in other countries might become mobs, being there nearly altogether composed of their own Negro slaves."

V.
THE QUIET PLUNDER

The consequences of 250 years of enslavement, of war upon black families and black people, were profound. Like homeownership today, slave ownership was aspirational, attracting not just those who owned slaves but those who wished to. Much as homeowners today might discuss the addition of a patio or the painting of a living room, slaveholders traded tips on the best methods for breeding workers, exacting labor, and doling out punishment. Just as a homeowner today might subscribe to a magazine like *This Old House,* slaveholders had journals such as *De Bow's Review,* which recommended the best practices for wringing profits from slaves. By the dawn of the Civil War, the enslavement of black America was thought to be so foundational to the country that those who sought to end it were branded heretics worthy of death. Imagine what would happen if a president today came out in favor of taking all American homes from their owners: The reaction might well be violent.

"This country was formed for the *white,* not for the black man," John Wilkes Booth wrote, before killing Abraham Lincoln. "And looking upon *African slavery* from the same standpoint held by those noble framers of our Constitution, I for one have ever considered *it* one of the greatest blessings (both for themselves and us) that God ever bestowed upon a favored nation."

In the aftermath of the Civil War, Radical Republicans attempted to reconstruct the country upon something resembling universal equality—but they were beaten back by a campaign of "Redemption," led by White Liners, Red Shirts, and Klansmen bent on upholding a society "formed for the *white,* not for the black man." A wave of terrorism roiled the South. In his massive history *Reconstruction,* Eric Foner recounts incidents of black people being attacked for not removing their hats; for refusing to hand over a whiskey flask; for disobeying church procedures; for "using insolent language"; for disputing labor contracts; for refusing to be "tied like a slave." Sometimes the attacks were intended simply to "thin out the niggers a little."

Terrorism carried the day. Federal troops withdrew from the South in 1877. The dream of Reconstruction died. For the next century, political violence was visited upon blacks wantonly, with special treatment meted out toward black people of ambition. Black schools and churches were burned to the ground. Black voters and the political candidates who attempted to rally them were intimidated, and some were murdered. At the end of World War I, black veterans returning to their homes were assaulted for daring to wear the American uniform. The demobilization of soldiers after the war, which put white and black veterans into competition for scarce jobs, produced the Red Summer of 1919: a succession of racist pogroms against dozens of cities ranging from Longview, Texas, to Chicago to Washington, D.C. Organized white violence against blacks continued into the 1920s—in 1921 a white mob leveled Tulsa's "Black Wall Street," and in 1923 another one razed the black town of Rosewood, Florida—and virtually no one was punished.

The work of mobs was a rabid and violent rendition of prejudices that extended even into the upper reaches of American government. The New Deal is today remembered as a model for what progressive government should do—cast a broad social safety net that protects the poor and the afflicted while building the middle class. When progressives wish to express their disappointment with Barack Obama, they point to the accomplishments of Franklin Roosevelt. But these progressives rarely note that Roosevelt's New Deal, much like the democracy that produced it, rested on the foundation of Jim Crow.

"The Jim Crow South," writes Ira Katznelson, a history and political science professor at Columbia, "was the one collaborator America's democracy could not do without." The marks of that collaboration are all over the New Deal. The omnibus programs passed under the Social Security Act in 1935 were crafted in such a way as to protect the southern way of life. Old-age insurance (Social Security proper) and unemployment insurance excluded farmworkers and domestics—jobs heavily occupied by blacks. When President Roosevelt signed Social Security into law in 1935, 65 percent of African Americans nationally and between 70 and 80 percent in the South were ineligible. The NAACP protested, calling the new American safety net "a sieve with holes just big enough for the majority of Negroes to fall through."

The oft-celebrated GI Bill similarly failed black Americans, by mirroring the broader country's insistence on a racist housing policy. Though ostensibly color-blind, Title III of the bill, which aimed to give veterans access to low-interest home loans, left black veterans to tangle with white officials at their local Veterans Administration as well as with the same banks that had, for years, refused to grant mortgages to blacks. The historian Kathleen J. Frydl observes in her 2009 book *The GI Bill* that so many blacks were disqualified from receiving Title III benefits "that it is more accurate simply to say that blacks could not use this particular title."

In Cold War America, homeownership was seen as a means of instilling patriotism, and as a civilizing and anti-radical force. "No man who owns his own house and lot can be a Communist," claimed William Levitt, who pioneered the modern suburb with the development of the various Levittowns, his famous planned communities. "He has too much to do."

But the Levittowns were, with Levitt's willing acquiescence, segregated throughout their early years. Daisy and Bill Myers, the first black family to move into Levittown, Pennsylvania, were greeted with protests and a burning cross. A neighbor who opposed the family said that Bill Myers was "probably a nice guy, but every time I look at him I see $2,000 drop off the value of my house."

The neighbor had good reason to be afraid. Bill and Daisy Myers were from the other side of John C. Calhoun's dual society. If they moved next door, housing policy almost guaranteed that their neighbors' property values would decline.

Whereas shortly before the New Deal, a typical mortgage required a large down payment and full repayment within about ten years, the creation of the Home Owners' Loan Corporation in 1933 and then the Federal Housing Administration the following year allowed banks to offer loans requiring no more than 10 percent down, amortized over twenty to thirty years. "Without federal intervention in the housing market, massive suburbanization would have been impossible," writes Thomas J. Sugrue, a historian at the

University of Pennsylvania. "In 1930, only 30 percent of Americans owned their own homes; by 1960, more than 60 percent were home owners. Home ownership became an emblem of American citizenship."

That emblem was not to be awarded to blacks. The American real-estate industry believed segregation to be a moral principle. As late as 1950, the National Association of Real Estate Boards' code of ethics warned that "a Realtor should never be instrumental in introducing into a neighborhood . . . any race or nationality, or any individuals whose presence will clearly be detrimental to property values." A 1943 brochure specified that such potential undesirables might include madams, bootleggers, gangsters—and "a colored man of means who was giving his children a college education and thought they were entitled to live among whites."

The federal government concurred. It was the Home Owners' Loan Corporation, not a private trade association, that pioneered the practice of redlining, selectively granting loans and insisting that any property it insured be covered by a restrictive covenant—a clause in the deed forbidding the sale of the property to anyone other than whites. Millions of dollars flowed from tax coffers into segregated white neighborhoods.

"For perhaps the first time, the federal government embraced the discriminatory attitudes of the marketplace," the historian Kenneth T. Jackson wrote in his 1985 book *Crabgrass Frontier,* a history of suburbanization. "Previously, prejudices were personalized and individualized; FHA exhorted segregation and enshrined it as public policy. Whole areas of cities were declared ineligible for loan guarantees." Redlining was not officially outlawed until 1968, by the Fair Housing Act. By then the damage was done—and reports of redlining by banks have continued.

The federal government is premised on equal fealty from all its citizens, who in return are to receive equal treatment. But as late as the mid-twentieth century, this bargain was not granted to black people, who repeatedly paid a higher price for citizenship and received less in return. Plunder had been the essential feature of slavery, of the society described by Calhoun. But practically a full century after the end of the Civil War and the abolition of slavery, the plunder—quiet, systemic, submerged—continued even amidst the aims and achievements of New Deal liberals.

VI.
MAKING THE SECOND GHETTO

Today Chicago is one of the most segregated cities in the country, a fact that reflects assiduous planning. In the effort to uphold white supremacy at every level down to the neighborhood, Chicago— a city founded by the black fur trader Jean Baptiste Point Du Sable—has long been a pioneer. The efforts began in earnest in 1917, when the Chicago Real Estate Board, horrified by the influx of southern blacks, lobbied to zone the entire city by race. But after the Supreme Court ruled against explicit racial zoning that year, the city was forced to pursue its agenda by more discreet means.

Like the Home Owners' Loan Corporation, the Federal Housing Administration initially insisted on restrictive covenants, which helped bar blacks and other ethnic undesirables from receiving federally backed home loans. By the 1940s, Chicago led the nation in the use of these restrictive covenants, and about half of all residential neighborhoods in the city were effectively off-limits to blacks.

It is common today to become misty-eyed about the old black ghetto, where doctors and lawyers lived next door to meatpackers and steelworkers, who themselves lived next door to prostitutes and the unemployed. This segregationist nostalgia ignores the actual conditions endured by the people living there—vermin and arson, for instance—and ignores the fact that the old ghetto was premised on denying black people privileges enjoyed by white Americans.

In 1948, when the Supreme Court ruled that restrictive covenants, while permissible, were not enforceable by judicial action, Chicago had other weapons at the ready. The Illinois state legislature had already given Chicago's city council the right to approve—and thus to veto—any public housing in the city's wards. This came in handy in 1949, when a new federal housing act sent millions of tax dollars into Chicago and other cities around the country. Beginning in 1950, site selection for public housing proceeded entirely on the grounds of segregation. By the 1960s, the city had created with its vast housing projects what the historian Arnold R. Hirsch calls a "second ghetto," one larger than the old Black Belt but just as impermeable. More than 98 percent of all the family public-housing units built in Chicago between 1950 and the mid-1960s were built in all-black neighborhoods.

Governmental embrace of segregation was driven by the virulent racism of Chicago's white citizens. White neighborhoods vulnerable to black encroachment formed block associations for the sole purpose of enforcing segregation. They lobbied fellow whites not to sell. They lobbied those blacks who did manage to buy to sell back. In 1949, a group of Englewood Catholics formed block associations intended to "keep up the neighborhood." Translation: Keep black people out. And when civic engagement was not enough, when government failed, when private banks could no longer hold the line, Chicago turned to an old tool in the American repertoire—racial violence. "The pattern of terrorism is easily discernible," concluded a Chicago civic group in the 1940s. "It is at the seams of the black ghetto in all directions." On July 1 and 2 of 1946, a mob of thousands assembled in Chicago's Park Manor neighborhood, hoping to eject a black doctor who'd recently moved in. The mob pelted the house with rocks and set the garage on fire. The doctor moved away.

In 1947, after a few black veterans moved into the Fernwood section of Chicago, three nights of rioting broke out; gangs of whites yanked blacks off streetcars and beat them. Two years later, when a union meeting attended by blacks in Englewood triggered rumors that a home was being "sold to niggers," blacks (and whites thought to be sympathetic to them) were beaten in the streets. In 1951, thousands of whites in Cicero, twenty minutes or so west of downtown Chicago, attacked an apartment building that housed a single black family, throwing bricks and firebombs through the windows and setting the apartment on fire. A Cook County grand jury declined to charge the rioters—and instead indicted the family's NAACP attorney, the apartment's white owner, and the owner's attorney and rental agent, charging them with conspiring to lower property values. Two years after that, whites picketed and planted explosives in South Deering, about thirty minutes from downtown Chicago, to force blacks out.

When terrorism ultimately failed, white homeowners simply fled the neighborhood. The traditional terminology, *white flight,* implies a kind of natural expression of preference. In fact, white flight was a triumph of social engineering, orchestrated by the shared racist presumptions of America's public and private sectors. For should any nonracist white families decide that integration might not be so bad as a matter of principle or practicality, they still had to contend with the hard facts of American housing policy: When the mid-twentieth-century white homeowner claimed that the presence of a Bill and Daisy Myers decreased his property value, he was not merely engaging in racist dogma—he was accurately observing the impact of federal policy on market prices. Redlining destroyed the possibility of investment wherever black people lived.

VII.
"A LOT OF PEOPLE FELL BY THE WAY"

Speculators in North Lawndale, and at the edge of the black ghettos, knew there was money to be made off white panic. They resorted to "block-busting"—spooking whites into selling cheap before the neighborhood became black. They would hire a black woman to walk up and down the street with a stroller. Or they'd hire someone to call a number in the neighborhood looking for "Johnny Mae." Then they'd cajole whites into selling at low prices, informing them that the more blacks who moved in, the more the value of their homes would decline, so better to sell now. With these white-fled homes in hand, speculators then turned to the masses of black people who had streamed northward as part of the Great Migration, or who were desperate to escape the ghettos: The speculators would take the houses they'd just bought cheap through block-busting and sell them to blacks on contract.

To keep up with his payments and keep his heat on, Clyde Ross took a second job at the post office and then a third job delivering pizza. His wife took a job working at Marshall Field's. He had to take some of his children out of private school. He was not able to be at home to supervise his children or help them with their homework. Money and time that Ross wanted to give his children went instead to enrich white speculators.

"The problem was the money," Ross told me. "Without the money, you can't move. You can't educate your kids. You can't give them the right kind of food. Can't make the house look good. They think this neighborhood is where they supposed to be. It changes their outlook. My kids were going to the best schools in this neighborhood, and I couldn't keep them in there."

Mattie Lewis came to Chicago from her native Alabama in the mid-'40s, when she was twenty-one, persuaded by a friend who told her she could get a job as a hairdresser. Instead she was hired by Western Electric, where she worked for forty-one years. I met Lewis in the home of her neighbor Ethel Weatherspoon. Both had owned homes in North Lawndale for more than fifty years. Both had bought their houses on contract. Both had been active with Clyde Ross in the Contract Buyers League's effort to garner restitution from contract sellers who'd operated in North Lawndale, banks who'd backed the scheme, and even the Federal Housing Administration. We were joined by Jack Macnamara, who'd been an organizing force in the Contract Buyers League when it was founded, in 1968. Our gathering had the feel of a reunion, because the writer James Alan McPherson had profiled the Contract Buyers League for *The Atlantic* back in 1972.

Weatherspoon bought her home in 1957. "Most of the whites started moving out," she told me. "'The blacks are coming. The blacks are coming.' They actually said that. They had signs up: DON'T SELL TO BLACKS."

Before moving to North Lawndale, Lewis and her husband tried moving to Cicero after seeing a house advertised for sale there. "Sorry, I just sold it today," the Realtor told Lewis's husband. "I told him, 'You know they don't want you in Cicero,'" Lewis recalls. "'They ain't going to let nobody black in Cicero.'"

In 1958, the couple bought a home in North Lawndale on contract. They were not blind to the unfairness. But Lewis, born in the teeth of Jim Crow, considered American piracy—black people keep on making it, white people keep on taking it—a fact of nature. "All I wanted was a house. And that was the only way I could get it. They weren't giving black people loans at that time," she said. "We thought, 'This is the way it is. We going to do it till we die, and they ain't never going to accept us. That's just the way it is.'

"The only way you were going to buy a home was to do it the way they wanted," she continued. "And I was determined to get me a house. If everybody else can have one, I want one too. I had worked for white people in the South. And I saw how these white people were living in the North and I thought, 'One day I'm going to live just like them.' I wanted cabinets and all these things these other people have."

Whenever she visited white co-workers at their homes, she saw the difference. "I could see we were just getting ripped off," she said. "I would see things and I would say, 'I'd like to do this at my house.' And they would say, 'Do it,' but I would think, 'I can't, because it costs us so much more.'"

I asked Lewis and Weatherspoon how they kept up on payments.

"You paid it and kept working," Lewis said of the contract. "When that payment came up, you knew you had to pay it."

"You cut down on the light bill. Cut down on your food bill," Weatherspoon interjected.

"You cut down on things for your child, that was the main thing," said Lewis. "My oldest wanted to be an artist and my other wanted to be a dancer and my other wanted to take music."

Lewis and Weatherspoon, like Ross, were able to keep their homes. The suit did not win them any remuneration. But it forced contract sellers to the table, where they allowed some members of the Contract Buyers League to move into regular mortgages or simply take over their houses outright. By then they'd been bilked for thousands. In talking with Lewis and Weatherspoon, I was seeing only part of the picture—the tiny minority who'd managed to hold on to their homes. But for all our exceptional ones, for every Barack and Michelle Obama, for every Ethel Weatherspoon or Clyde Ross, for every black survivor, there are so many thousands gone.

"A lot of people fell by the way," Lewis told me. "One woman asked me if I would keep all her china. She said, 'They ain't going to set you out.'"

VIII.
"NEGRO POVERTY IS NOT WHITE POVERTY"

On a recent spring afternoon in North Lawndale, I visited Billy Lamar Brooks Sr. Brooks has been an activist since his youth in the Black Panther Party, when he aided the Contract Buyers League. I met him in his office at the Better Boys Foundation, a staple of North Lawndale whose mission is to direct local kids off the streets and into jobs and college. Brooks's work is personal. On June 14, 1991, his nineteen-year-old son, Billy Jr., was shot and killed. "These guys tried to stick him up," Brooks told me. "I suspect he could have been involved in some things. . . . He's always on my mind. Every day."

Brooks was not raised in the streets, though in such a neighborhood it is impossible to avoid the influence. "I was in church three or four times a week. That's where the girls were," he said, laughing. "The stark reality is still there. There's no shield from life. You got to go to school. I lived here. I went to Marshall High School. Over here were the Egyptian Cobras. Over there were the Vice Lords."

Brooks has since moved away from Chicago's West Side. But he is still working in North Lawndale. If "you got a nice house, you live in a nice neighborhood, then you are less prone to violence, because your space is not deprived," Brooks said. "You got a security point. You don't need no protection." But if "you grow up in a place like this, housing sucks. When they tore down the projects here, they left the high-rises and came to the neighborhood with that gang mentality. You don't have nothing, so you going to take something, even if it's not real. You don't have no street, but in your mind it's yours."

We walked over to a window behind his desk. A group of young black men were hanging out in front of a giant mural memorializing two black men: IN LOVIN MEMORY QUENTIN AKA "Q," JULY 18, 1974 ❤ MARCH 2, 2012. The name and face of the other man had been spray painted over by a rival group. The men drank beer. Occasionally a car would cruise past, slow to a crawl, then stop. One of the men would approach the car and make an exchange, then the car would drive off. Brooks had known all of these young men as boys.

"That's their corner," he said.

We watched another car roll through, pause briefly, then drive off. "No respect, no shame," Brooks said. "That's what they do. From that alley to that corner. They don't go no farther than that. See the big brother there? He almost died a couple of years ago. The one drinking the beer back there. . . . I know all of them. And the reason they feel safe here is cause of this building, and because they too chickenshit to go anywhere. But that's their mentality. That's their block."

Brooks showed me a picture of a Little League team he had coached. He went down the row of kids, pointing out which ones were in jail, which ones were dead, and which ones were doing all right. And then he pointed out his son—"That's my boy, Billy," Brooks said. Then he wondered aloud if keeping his son with him while working in North Lawndale had hastened his death. "It's a definite connection, because he was part of what I did here. And I think maybe I shouldn't have exposed him. But then, I had to," he said, "because I wanted him with me."

From the White House on down, the myth holds that fatherhood is the great antidote to all that ails black people. But Billy Brooks Jr. had a father. Trayvon Martin had a father. Jordan Davis had a father. Adhering to middle-class norms has never shielded black people from plunder. Adhering to middle-class norms is what made Ethel Weatherspoon a lucrative target for rapacious speculators. Contract sellers did not target the very poor. They targeted black people who had worked hard enough to save a down payment and dreamed of the emblem of American citizenship—homeownership. It was not a tangle of pathology that put a target on Clyde Ross's back. It was not a culture of poverty that singled out Mattie Lewis for "the thrill of the chase and the kill." Some black people always will be twice as good. But they generally find white predation to be thrice as fast.

Liberals today mostly view racism not as an active, distinct evil but as a relative of white poverty and inequality. They ignore the long tradition of this country actively punishing black success—and the elevation of that punishment, in the mid-twentieth century, to federal policy. President Lyndon Johnson may have noted in his historic civil rights speech at Howard University in 1965 that "Negro poverty is not white poverty." But his advisers and their successors were, and still are, loath to craft any policy that recognizes the difference.

After his speech, Johnson convened a group of civil rights leaders, including the esteemed A. Philip Randolph and Bayard Rustin, to address the "ancient brutality." In a strategy paper, they agreed with the president that "Negro poverty is a special, and particularly destructive, form of American poverty." But when it came to specifically addressing the "particularly destructive," Rustin's group demurred, preferring to advance programs that addressed "all the poor, black and white."

The urge to use the moral force of the black struggle to address broader inequalities originates in both compassion and pragmatism. But it makes for ambiguous policy. Affirmative action's precise aims, for instance, have always proved elusive. Is it meant to make amends for the crimes heaped upon black people? Not according to the Supreme Court. In its 1978 ruling in *Regents of the University of California v. Bakke,* the court rejected "societal discrimination" as "an amorphous concept of injury that may be ageless in its reach into the past." Is affirmative action meant to increase "diversity"? If so, it only tangentially relates to the specific problems of black people—the problem of what America has taken from them over several centuries.

This confusion about affirmative action's aims, along with our inability to face up to the particular history of white-imposed black disadvantage, dates back to the policy's origins. "There is no fixed and firm definition of affirmative action," an appointee in Johnson's Department of Labor declared. "Affirmative action is anything that you have to do to get results. But this does not necessarily include preferential treatment."

Yet America was built on the preferential treatment of white people—395 years of it. Vaguely endorsing a cuddly, feel-good diversity does very little to redress this.

Today, progressives are loath to invoke white supremacy as an explanation for anything. On a practical level, the hesitation comes from the dim view the Supreme Court has taken of the reforms of the 1960s. The Voting Rights Act has been gutted. The Fair Housing Act might well be next. Affirmative action is on its last legs. In substituting a broad class struggle for an anti-racist struggle, progressives hope to assemble a coalition by changing the subject.

The politics of racial evasion are seductive. But the record is mixed. Aid to Families with Dependent Children was originally written largely to exclude blacks—yet by the 1990s it was perceived as a giveaway to blacks. The Affordable Care Act makes no mention of race, but this did not keep Rush Limbaugh from denouncing it as reparations. Moreover, the act's expansion of Medicaid was effectively made optional, meaning that many poor blacks in the former Confederate states do not benefit from it. The Affordable Care Act, like Social Security, will eventually expand its reach to those left out; in the meantime, black people will be injured.

"All that it would take to sink a new WPA program would be some skillfully packaged footage of black men leaning on shovels smoking cigarettes," the sociologist Douglas S. Massey writes. "Papering over the issue of race makes for bad social theory, bad research, and bad public policy." To ignore the fact that one of the oldest republics in the world was erected on a foundation of white supremacy, to pretend that the problems of a dual society are the same as the problems of unregulated capitalism, is to cover the sin of national plunder with the sin of national lying. The lie ignores the fact that reducing American poverty and ending white supremacy are not the same. The lie ignores the fact that closing the "achievement gap" will do nothing to close the "injury gap," in which black college graduates still suffer higher unemployment rates than white college graduates, and black job applicants without criminal records enjoy roughly the same chance of getting hired as white applicants *with* criminal records.

Chicago, like the country at large, embraced policies that placed black America's most energetic, ambitious, and thrifty countrymen beyond the pale of society and marked them as rightful targets for legal theft. The effects reverberate beyond the families who were robbed to the community that beholds the spectacle. Don't just picture Clyde Ross working three jobs so he could hold on to his home. Think of his North Lawndale neighbors—their children, their nephews and nieces—and consider how watching this affects them. Imagine yourself as a young black child watching your elders play by all the rules only to have their possessions tossed out in the street and to have their most sacred possession—their home—taken from them.

The message the young black boy receives from his country, Billy Brooks says, is " 'You ain't shit. You not no good. The only thing you are worth is working for us. You will never own anything. You not going to get an education. We are sending your ass to the penitentiary.' They're telling you no matter how hard you struggle, no matter what you put down, you ain't shit. 'We're going to take what you got. You will never own anything, nigger.' "

IX.
TOWARD A NEW COUNTRY

When Clyde Ross was a child, his older brother Winter had a seizure. He was picked up by the authorities and delivered to Parchman Farm, a twenty-thousand-acre state prison in the Mississippi Delta region.

"He was a gentle person," Clyde Ross says of his brother. "You know, he was good to everybody. And he started having spells, and he couldn't control himself. And they had him picked up, because they thought he was dangerous."

Built at the turn of the century, Parchman was supposed to be a progressive and reformist response to the problem of "Negro crime." In fact it was the gulag of Mississippi, an object of terror to African Americans in the Delta. In the early years of the twentieth century, Mississippi Governor James K. Vardaman used to amuse himself by releasing black convicts into the surrounding wilderness and hunting them down with bloodhounds. "Throughout the American South," writes David M. Oshinsky in his book *Worse Than Slavery*, "Parchman Farm is synonymous with punishment and brutality, as well it should be. . . . Parchman is the quintessential penal farm, the closest thing to slavery that survived the Civil War."

When the Ross family went to retrieve Winter, the authorities told them that Winter had died. When the Ross family asked for his body, the authorities at Parchman said they had buried him. The family never saw Winter's body.

And this was just one of their losses.

Scholars have long discussed methods by which America might make reparations to those on whose labor and exclusion the country was built. In the 1970s, the Yale Law professor Boris Bittker argued in *The Case for Black Reparations* that a rough price tag for reparations could be determined by multiplying the number of African Americans in the population by the difference in white and black per capita income. That number—$34 billion in 1973, when Bittker wrote his book—could be added to a reparations program each year for a decade or two. Today Charles Ogletree, the Harvard Law School professor, argues for something broader: a program of job training and public works that takes racial justice as its mission but includes the poor of all races.

To celebrate freedom and democracy while forgetting America's origins in a slavery economy is patriotism à la carte.

Perhaps no statistic better illustrates the enduring legacy of our country's shameful history of treating black people as sub-citizens, sub-Americans, and sub-humans than the wealth gap. Reparations would seek to close this chasm. But as surely as the creation of the wealth gap required the cooperation of every aspect of the society, bridging it will require the same.

Perhaps after a serious discussion and debate—the kind that HR

40 proposes—we may find that the country can never fully repay African Americans. But we stand to discover much about ourselves in such a discussion—and that is perhaps what scares us. The idea of reparations is frightening not simply because we might lack the ability to pay. The idea of reparations threatens something much deeper—America's heritage, history, and standing in the world.

THE EARLY AMERICAN ECONOMY was built on slave labor. The Capitol and the White House were built by slaves. President James K. Polk traded slaves from the Oval Office. The laments about "black pathology," the criticism of black family structures by pundits and intellectuals, ring hollow in a country whose existence was predicated on the torture of black fathers, on the rape of black mothers, on the sale of black children. An honest assessment of America's relationship to the black family reveals the country to be not its nurturer but its destroyer.

And this destruction did not end with slavery. Discriminatory laws joined the equal burden of citizenship to unequal distribution of its bounty. These laws reached their apex in the mid-twentieth century, when the federal government—through housing policies—engineered the wealth gap, which remains with us to this day. When we think of white supremacy, we picture COLORED ONLY signs, but we should picture pirate flags.

On some level, we have always grasped this.

"Negro poverty is not white poverty," President Johnson said in his historic civil rights speech.

Many of its causes and many of its cures are the same. But there are differences—deep, corrosive, obstinate differences— radiating painful roots into the community and into the family, and the nature of the individual. These differences are not racial differences. They are solely and simply the consequence of ancient brutality, past injustice, and present prejudice.

We invoke the words of Jefferson and Lincoln because they say something about our legacy and our traditions. We do this because we recognize our links to the past—at least when they flatter us. But black history does not flatter American democracy; it chastens it. The popular mocking of reparations as a harebrained scheme authored by wild-eyed lefties and intellectually unserious black nationalists is fear masquerading as laughter. Black nationalists have always perceived something unmentionable about America that integrationists dare not acknowledge—that white supremacy is not merely the work of hotheaded demagogues, or a matter of false consciousness, but a force so fundamental to America that it is difficult to imagine the country without it.

And so we must imagine a new country. Reparations—by which I mean the full acceptance of our collective biography and its consequences—is the price we must pay to see ourselves squarely. The recovering alcoholic may well have to live with his illness for the rest of his life. But at least he is not living a drunken lie. Reparations beckon us to reject the intoxication of hubris and see America as it is—the work of fallible humans.

Won't reparations divide us? Not any more than we are already divided. The wealth gap merely puts a number on something we feel but cannot say—that American prosperity was ill gotten and selective in its distribution. What is needed is an airing of family secrets, a settling with old ghosts. What is needed is a healing of the American psyche and the banishment of white guilt.

What I'm talking about is more than recompense for past injustices—more than a handout, a payoff, hush money, or a reluctant bribe. What I'm talking about is a national reckoning that would lead to spiritual renewal. Reparations would mean the end of scarfing hot dogs on the Fourth of July while denying the facts of our heritage. Reparations would mean the end of yelling "patriotism" while waving a Confederate flag. Reparations would mean a revolution of the American consciousness, a reconciling of our self-image as the great democratizer with the facts of our history.

X.
"THERE WILL BE NO 'REPARATIONS' FROM GERMANY"

We are not the first to be summoned to such a challenge.

In 1952, when West Germany began the process of making amends for the Holocaust, it did so under conditions that should be instructive to us. Resistance was violent. Very few Germans believed that Jews were entitled to anything. Only 5 percent of West Germans surveyed reported feeling guilty about the Holocaust, and only 29 percent believed that Jews were owed restitution from the German people.

"The rest," the historian Tony Judt wrote in his 2005 book *Postwar,* "were divided between those (some two-fifths of respondents) who thought that only people 'who really committed something' were responsible and should pay, and those (21 percent) who thought 'that the Jews themselves were partly responsible for what happened to them during the Third Reich.' "

Germany's unwillingness to squarely face its history went beyond polls. Movies that suggested a societal responsibility for the Holocaust beyond Hitler were banned. "The German soldier fought bravely and honorably for his homeland," claimed President Eisenhower, endorsing the Teutonic national myth. Judt wrote, "Throughout the fifties West German officialdom encouraged a comfortable view of the German past in which the Wehrmacht was heroic, while Nazis were in a minority and properly punished."

Konrad Adenauer, the postwar German chancellor, was in favor of reparations, but his own party was divided, and he was able to get an agreement passed only with the votes of the Social Democratic opposition.

Among the Jews of Israel, reparations provoked violent and venomous reactions ranging from denunciation to assassination plots. On January 7, 1952, as the Knesset—the Israeli parliament— convened to discuss the prospect of a reparations agreement with West Germany, Menachem Begin, the future prime minister of Israel, stood in front of a large crowd, inveighing against the country that had plundered the lives, labor, and property of his people. Begin claimed that all Germans were Nazis and guilty of murder. His condemnations then spread to his own young state. He urged the crowd to stop paying taxes and claimed that the nascent Israeli nation characterized the fight over whether or not to accept reparations as a "war to the death." When alerted that the police watching the gathering were carrying tear gas, allegedly of German manufacture, Begin yelled, "The same gases that asphyxiated our parents!"

Begin then led the crowd in an oath to never forget the victims of the Shoah, lest "my right hand lose its cunning" and "my tongue cleave to the roof of my mouth." He took the crowd through the streets toward the Knesset. From the rooftops, police repelled the crowd with tear gas and smoke bombs. But the wind shifted, and the gas blew back toward the Knesset, billowing through windows shattered by rocks. In the chaos, Begin and Prime Minister David Ben-Gurion exchanged insults. Two hundred civilians and 140 police officers were wounded. Nearly four hundred people were arrested. Knesset business was halted.

Begin then addressed the chamber with a fiery speech condemning the actions the legislature was about to take. "Today you arrested hundreds," he said. "Tomorrow you may arrest thousands. No matter, they will go, they will sit in prison. We will sit there with them. If necessary, we will be killed with them. But there will be no 'reparations' from Germany."

Survivors of the Holocaust feared laundering the reputation of Germany with money, and mortgaging the memory of their dead. Beyond that, there was a taste for revenge. "My soul would be at rest if I knew there would be 6 million German dead to match the 6 million Jews," said Meir Dworzecki, who'd survived the concentration camps of Estonia.

Ben-Gurion countered this sentiment, not by repudiating vengeance but with cold calculation: "If I could take German property without sitting down with them for even a minute but go in with jeeps and machine guns to the warehouses and take it, I would do that—if, for instance, we had the ability to send a hundred divisions and tell them, 'Take it.' But we can't do that."

The reparations conversation set off a wave of bomb attempts by Israeli militants. One was aimed at the foreign ministry in Tel Aviv. Another was aimed at Chancellor Adenauer himself. And one was aimed at the port of Haifa, where the goods bought with reparations money were arriving. West Germany ultimately agreed to pay Israel 3.45 billion deutsche marks, or more than $7 billion in today's dollars. Individual reparations claims followed—for psychological trauma, for offense to Jewish honor, for halting law careers, for life insurance, for time spent in concentration camps. Seventeen percent of funds went toward purchasing ships. "By the end of 1961, these reparations vessels constituted two-thirds of the Israeli merchant fleet," writes the Israeli historian Tom Segev in his book *The Seventh Million*. "From 1953 to 1963, the reparations money funded about a third of the total investment in Israel's electrical system, which tripled its capacity, and nearly half the total investment in the railways."

Israel's GNP tripled during the twelve years of the agreement. The Bank of Israel attributed 15 percent of this growth, along with forty-five thousand jobs, to investments made with reparations money. But Segev argues that the impact went far beyond that. Reparations "had indisputable psychological and political importance," he writes.

Reparations could not make up for the murder perpetrated by the Nazis. But they did launch Germany's reckoning with itself, and perhaps provided a road map for how a great civilization might make itself worthy of the name.

Assessing the reparations agreement, David Ben-Gurion said:

For the first time in the history of relations between people, a precedent has been created by which a great State, as a result of moral pressure alone, takes it upon itself to pay compensation to the victims of the government that preceded it. For the first time in the history of a people that has been persecuted, oppressed, plundered and despoiled for hundreds of years in the countries of Europe, a persecutor and despoiler has been obliged to return part of his spoils and has even undertaken to make collective reparation as partial compensation for material losses.

Something more than moral pressure calls America to reparations. We cannot escape our history. All of our solutions to the great problems of health care, education, housing, and economic inequality are troubled by what must go unspoken. "The reason black people are so far behind now is not because of now," Clyde Ross told me. "It's because of then." In the early 2000s, Charles Ogletree went to Tulsa, Oklahoma, to meet with the survivors of the 1921 race riot that had devastated "Black Wall Street." The past was not the past to them. "It was amazing seeing these black women and men who were crippled, blind, in wheelchairs," Ogletree told me. "I had no idea who they were and why they wanted to see me. They said, 'We want you to represent us in this lawsuit.'"

A commission authorized by the Oklahoma legislature produced a report affirming that the riot, the knowledge of which had been suppressed for years, had happened. But the lawsuit ultimately failed, in 2004. Similar suits pushed against corporations such as Aetna (which insured slaves) and Lehman Brothers (whose cofounding partner owned them) also have thus far failed. These results are dispiriting, but the crime with which reparations activists charge the country implicates more than just a few towns or corporations. The crime indicts the American people themselves, at every level, and in nearly every configuration. A crime that implicates the entire American people deserves its hearing in the legislative body that represents them.

John Conyers's HR 40 is the vehicle for that hearing. No one can know what would come out of such a debate. Perhaps no number can fully capture the multi-century plunder of black people in America. Perhaps the number is so large that it can't be imagined, let alone calculated and dispensed. But I believe that wrestling publicly with these questions matters as much as—if not more than—the specific answers that might be produced. An America that asks what it owes its most vulnerable citizens is improved and humane. An America that looks away is ignoring not just the sins of the past but the sins of the present and the certain sins of the future. More important than any single check cut to any African American, the payment of reparations would represent America's maturation out of the childhood myth of its innocence into a wisdom worthy of its founders.

IN 2010, JACOB S. RUGH, then a doctoral candidate at Princeton, and the sociologist Douglas S. Massey published a study of the recent foreclosure crisis. Among its drivers, they found an old foe: segregation. Black home buyers—even after controlling for factors like creditworthiness—were still more likely than white home buyers to be steered toward subprime loans. Decades of racist housing policies by the American government, along with decades of racist housing practices by American businesses, had conspired to concentrate African Americans in the same neighborhoods. As in North Lawndale half a century earlier, these neighborhoods were filled with people who had been cut off from mainstream financial institutions. When subprime lenders went looking for prey, they found black people waiting like ducks in a pen.

"High levels of segregation create a natural market for subprime lending," Rugh and Massey write, "and cause riskier mortgages, and thus foreclosures, to accumulate disproportionately in racially segregated cities' minority neighborhoods."

Plunder in the past made plunder in the present efficient. The banks of America understood this. In 2005, Wells Fargo promoted a series of Wealth Building Strategies seminars. Dubbing itself "the nation's leading originator of home loans to ethnic minority customers," the bank enrolled black public figures in an ostensible effort to educate blacks on building "generational wealth." But the "wealth building" seminars were a front for wealth theft. In 2010, the Justice Department filed a discrimination suit against Wells Fargo alleging that the bank had shunted blacks into predatory loans regardless of their creditworthiness. This was not magic or coincidence or misfortune. It was racism reifying itself. According to *The New York Times,* affidavits found loan officers referring to their black customers as "mud people" and to their subprime products as "ghetto loans."

"We just went right after them," Beth Jacobson, a former Wells Fargo loan officer, told the *Times.* "Wells Fargo mortgage had an emerging-markets unit that specifically targeted black churches because it figured church leaders had a lot of influence and could convince congregants to take out subprime loans."

In 2011, Bank of America agreed to pay $355 million to settle charges of discrimination against its Countrywide unit. The following year, Wells Fargo settled its discrimination suit for more than $175 million. But the damage had been done. In 2009, half the properties in Baltimore whose owners had been granted loans by Wells Fargo between 2005 and 2008 were vacant; 71 percent of these properties were in predominantly black neighborhoods.

7.

NOTES FROM
THE
SEVENTH YEAR

BY THE SEVENTH YEAR, I FELT LIKE I'D FIGURED SOMETHING out. "The Case for Reparations" was, for me, the settling of an internal argument, the final unraveling of an existential mystery. The American story, which was my story, was not the tale of triumph but a majestic tragedy. Pilgrims and revolutionaries fled oppression and dreamed of a world where they might be free. And to pull the dream out of their imaginings, to bring the theory into reality, they broke our backs, taking up the very cudgel of oppression that had first sent them to flight. And I now knew that the line dividing black and white America was neither phenotypical, nor cultural, nor even genetic. In fact, there was no line at all, no necessary division of any kind. We were not two sides of a coin. We were not the photonegative of each other. To be black in America was to be plundered. To be white was to benefit from, and at times directly execute, this plunder. No national conversation, no invocations to love, no moral appeals, no pleas for "sensitivity" and "diversity," no lamenting of "race relations" could make this right. Racism was banditry, pure and simple. And the banditry was not incidental to America, it was essential to it.

It is somewhat ridiculous to say it this way—as though it were some sort of grand revelation and not a feeling that haunted every black person I knew. And I too had felt it. But black people in America do not generally have the luxury of recording their "feelings" as though they were fact, at least those feelings that do not credit the broader American myth of "race relations," of two neighbors engaged in an unfortunate dispute about fences. The theory of banditry not only failed to credit that myth, it directly assaulted it. And so it was not enough to "feel" the myth to be false, to feel somewhat off-put by it. I had to evidence the error in all the exacting detail I could summon.

I did not do this in the hope of convincing any of the disciples of raw myth that they were wrong, at least not in any critical numbers. I did it to know that *I* was not crazy, that what I felt in my bones, what I saw in my people, was real. And I did it for others who know they have been robbed even if they cannot quite draw out the full story behind that feeling in all its horror. I could not shield them from banditry. But all around us there was a machinery meant to verify the myth and validate the illusion. Some black people believed but most of us would look out at the illusion, on a particular day, at a particular angle, in a particular light, and the strings and mirrors would be, if only for an instant, revealed. What I wanted most was to shine an unblinking light on the entire stage, to tell my people with all the authority I could muster that they were right, that they were not crazy, that it really was all a trick.

Much of black literature—or the black literature that interests me—aims to do the same. I didn't feel like my aims were original or pathbreaking but part of something; I aspired to join a long line of dream-breakers. If atheism is important to me, my sense of ancestry is its equal. This goes back to my days as a young nationalist, to libations poured into aloe vera plants, to kneeling on the floor muttering "Ashé," while men in mud cloth and women in head wraps hailed Malcolm X, Toussaint L'Ouverture, Harriet Tubman, and Yaa Asantewaa. Later I came to feel that nationalism was, ultimately, its own kind of dream. But it was nationalism that gave me a sense of politics separate from the whims of white people. The weakness in the case for integration was that it ultimately rested on a critical mass of white people playing along, either out of their own particular interests or some sense of morality. History has produced few instances for the former and virtually none of the latter. This made sense. If there is a power that has ever surrendered itself purely out of some altruistic sense of justice, I have yet to come across it. Nationalism had its flights of fancy—the vision of a separate state outside America or a separate society within it. Neither could work. A separate society without would almost certainly replicate the very same problems of power we found here. Niggers would make more niggers, either of themselves or of the unfortunate group they settled upon. And as for a distinct society within the borders of the United States, well, the ruins of Tulsa and Black Wall Street showed that flaw. And those pogroms against independent black enclaves were just the extreme case. A separate society within America would depend on the mechanisms of American wealth creation, and wealth in America has never been created in absence of government policy, of banks willing to lend and a justice system willing to protect. And so this separatist nationalism revealed itself to be as flawed as integration, in that it, too, ultimately depended on the good graces of white people.

But if nationalism offered no way out, its sense of ancestry and tradition was a balm. It taught me that Nat Turner did not fight alone, did not die alone, but was part of a resistance that was as old as the banditry that made the West and would be here until the West crumbles to dust. That sense of ancestry did not give me hope for America or even for the ultimate fate of black people, but it filled me with purpose and meaning. Howard University also preached ancestry and tradition, told me that it meant something to walk in the path of Alain Locke, Zora Neale Hurston, Toni Morrison, and Amiri Baraka. To be a black writer was to be drafted into the greatest questions of freedom and democracy. Some black writers, searching for their most individual selves, resisted this draft and fled from this tradition. And others like me, in search of meaning and mission, ran toward it.

THE NEED FOR PURPOSE and community, for mission, is human. It's embedded in our politics, which are not simply fights over health coverage, tax credits, and farm subsidies but parcel to the search for meaning. It is that search that bedeviled the eight years of power. Much has been made of the meaning Barack Obama instilled in his supporters during the '08 campaign, the sense that a new America was rising up out of its misbegotten wars and blighted history to finally fulfill the promise of its charter. The old debates of baby boomers and Reagan Democrats were burned out, and from their ashes would emerge a millennial America ushering in a clean, frictionless future. But as sure as this vision granted meaning to one group, it assaulted the meaning of another, one whose own vision was built on centuries of straight white male dominance. Whatever one might say about that dominance, about its propensity to plunder, it offered a coherent story around which purpose and community could be built. The WHITES ONLY signs were not for decoration but to tell a certain tribe that, no matter their station in life, some part of the world, indeed the best part of the world, was carved out for them. The most important sentence in George Wallace's "Segregation Now" speech is not the famous battle cry but the statement detailing on whose behalf the battle cry is made. It was not delivered simply on behalf of white Southerners but "the greatest people that have ever trod this earth." Wallace is not an outlier in this. The popular notion that America is so exceptional in its virtue that even its invasions are alchemized into liberations lends meaning to the political lives of citizens. Through war, hatred, violence, communities draw fences and define themselves.

When the homophobe says that same-sex marriage will alter the definition of marriage, he is still a homophobe but he is not a liar. The right of exclusion is part of his definition of an institution that is vital for him and gives his life meaning. The governors who seek to tie the state's willingness to pay for medical care to drug tests and work requirements are not pursuing a healthcare policy—they are awarding virtue and meaning to one group by warring upon another. White supremacy is a crime and a lie, but it's also a machine that generates meaning. This existential gift, as much as anything, is the source of its enormous, centuries-spanning power.

I hope that my own sense of meaning, rooted in ancestry, is better than this. I like to think that the stories we tell do not have to involve the degradation of others. My ancestry is not in my blood, which, in itself, holds little meaning for me. The specific ancestry of black literature appealed to me not because of racial affinity but because it thrust me directly into the muck of the deepest questions of our age and my age particularly.

The most direct example in my life of the price we black people paid for living under the weight of someone else's purpose—of being a disposable prop in someone else's national saga—was my friend Prince Jones, murdered by a police officer shortly after I'd left Howard. There were no smartphones to record the encounter. No charges were pressed by anyone. The officer was not relieved of his job. Prince was dead, and it was my feeling that the world could have cared less. I had quietly raged over this killing for a decade. But now I saw his death directly connected to the machinery of plunder. More, I saw it as ancestral, an episode in a series stretching back to the dawn of this country up through Prince and then on through Shem Walker, Rekia Boyd, and Tamir Rice. And it then occurred to me that to make sense of that strain of ancestry, I might turn back to my own more specific ancestry—black writing. That is when I turned again to James Baldwin.

I first read *The Fire Next Time* as a nineteen-year-old student at Howard University. I hadn't really understood it. But if comprehension defied me on one level, its beauty connected with me on another. I read more Baldwin and, as a young writer and a young journalist, came not just to admire his clarity, his scorning of sentiment, but to feel in it the legacy of black life in America, the reflex to strip away illusion, to break away from dreams. I felt that to write in that fashion and with that same purpose was to take up an heirloom and a tradition. And the beauty of Baldwin's prose that I connected to was not ancillary to the dream-breaking but central to it. The beauty in his writing wasn't just style or ornament but an unparalleled ability to see what was before him clearly and then lay that vision, with that same clarity, before the world.

I think of him, in his fourteenth year, beginning to perceive the dangers that swirled around his native Harlem:

> For the wages of sin were visible everywhere, in every wine-stained and urine-splashed hallway, in every clanging ambulance bell, in every scar on the faces of the pimps and their whores, in every helpless, newborn baby being brought into this danger, in every knife and pistol fight on the Avenue, and in every disastrous bulletin: a cousin, mother of six, suddenly gone mad, the children parcelled out here and there; an indestructible aunt rewarded for years of hard labor by a slow, agonizing death in a terrible small room; someone's bright son blown into eternity by his own hand; another turned robber and carried off to jail. It was a summer of dreadful speculations and discoveries, of which these were not the worst.

This is beauty, but it is not mystical. It arises from the fine detailing of Baldwin's Harlem—from the dank hallways to the diminished and dying aunt—and through his inerrant word choice—the children "parcelled out," the "bright son blown into eternity." It is crafted from a deliberate attempt to organize those words, at the level of syllables, into a choir. Without those details, a vision could not be sketched onto the mind of the reader, and without the word choice, the sketch would not be crisp, and without the choir, the vision would not haunt the reader, as it haunted me for twenty years from the first time I read those words. Baldwin's beauty—like all real beauty—is not style apart from substance but indivisible from it. It is not the icing on the cake but the eggs within it, giving it texture, color, and shape.

And Baldwin baked goods of all kinds. He conjured from memoir:

My friends were now "downtown," busy, as they put it, "fighting the man." They began to care less about the way they looked, the way they dressed, the things they did; presently, one found them in twos and threes and fours, in a hallway, sharing a jug of wine or a bottle of whisky, talking, cursing, fighting, sometimes weeping. . . .

Invoked from analysis:

White people in this country will have quite enough to do in learning how to accept and love themselves and each other, and when they have achieved this—which will not be tomorrow and may very well be never—the Negro problem will no longer exist, for it will no longer be needed.

Summoned from reportage:

The central quality in Elijah's face is pain, and his smile is a witness to it—pain so old and deep and black that it becomes personal and particular only when he smiles. One wonders what he would sound like if he could sing. He turned to me, with that smile, and said something like "I've got a lot to say to you, but we'll wait until we sit down." And I laughed. He made me think of my father and me as we might have been if we had been friends.

When I reread *The Fire Next Time* in this seventh year, it seemed clear to me that no one was writing like him. More, I felt that no one was trying. Beauty, I felt, had been handed over to poets and novelists, to essays that never escape the living room. I wanted it back. I called my agent, Gloria Loomis, to tell her about this feeling. "Well Jimmy, he was one of a kind," she said. "No one could ever write like Jimmy."

I cut her off. "Gloria, I think I want to try."

SOMETHING ELSE WAS HAPPENING in the background—I had met Barack Obama. I was still holding on to my general admiration of the man, but I had also written several blog posts criticizing him, for his insistence on "color-blind policy" and for his tendency to hector black people on their alleged shortcomings. Obama would regularly invite journalists who disagreed with him to the White House to spar. From time to time, I found myself among the summoned—usually after I'd written something critical. In the first of these, I was intimidated and left thinking I'd failed to do my job. The second time I was responding to the embarrassment of the first. I thought of my days back in Baltimore, back on the block, insisting that "I ain't no punk." Before I left for D.C. for that second trip to the White House, Kenyatta looked at me and said, "What would Baldwin do?" Hmmm. I suspect something more elegant than what I did. I arrived to the meeting late. I was wearing jeans. I'd gotten rained on along the way. I argued, at length, with the president about health care and vulnerable people in Mississippi. I wasn't lying, but the debate was also performative. I was trying to prove to myself that I would not be cowed or seduced by power. It was ridiculous. But it was also an exchange with the first black president in the history of the most powerful nation in the world.

I walked from the White House to Union Station to take the train home. I called my editor, Chris Jackson. I talked about the meeting—"Yo you shoulda seen it, Chris. I was the only other nigga in the room and fools was looking at us like, 'These niggers are fighting!!!!'" But I found myself again talking about Baldwin and the beauty of what he'd done in *The Fire Next Time*. I talked about how I'd read the book in one sitting and the challenge I imagined of crafting a singular essay, in the same fashion, meant to be read in a few hours but to haunt for years. I told him we were in an extraordinary moment—the era of a black president and Black Lives Matter—much like Baldwin had written amid the fight for desegregation. Here he offered this admonition—"The road is littered with knockoffs of *The Fire Next Time*." But he still encouraged me to try.

To invoke the name James Baldwin, these days, is to invoke the name of both a prophet and a God. More than his actual work, Baldwin, himself, has been beatified. That is why young writers descend on his long-abandoned house, like pilgrims into the Holy Land. That is why they have founded an entire genre of essay to document the hajj. The beatification is understandable. Baldwin owes his prominence as much to his image as to his words. And we don't simply have the beauty of his words, we have the force of his presence. I am not immune—Baldwin the Legend was the ancestor Kenyatta sought to summon up when she asked, "What would Baldwin do?"

But all the magic I wanted was on the page. And when I looked closely, when I began to study, I did not even see magic, so much as a machinery so elegant, so wondrous, so imaginative as to seem supernatural. I am talking to young writers now. Your heroes are not mystics nor sorcerers but humans practiced at the work of typing and revising, and often agonized by it. I know this because I have chased before. I chased the work of Nas. I chased the work of E. L.

Doctorow. I chased the work of Black Thought. From *Dust Tracks on a Road* to *Jonah's Gourd Vine,* I chased the work of Zora Neale Hurston. From "The Colonel" to "The Museum of Stones," I chased the work of Carolyn Forché. I chased them all, in the hope that somewhere in the underlined sentences, in the dog-eared pages, in the conversations with other writers, who too were chasing, I would find my own work, and that work would fill someone out there with the same magic, which is not magic, that had filled me that day, sitting in Founders Library, in awe of James Baldwin.

So when I began *Between the World and Me,* I did not begin in humility but with the desire to make something that would leave its mark. I would like to be self-deprecating about this, to soften this recollection with a joke. I would like to tell you that I am a man of small and internal motives, that I do not write for the world but in flagrant disregard of it. This view of things underrates the world that shaped me, in both its rejections and its acceptances. Perhaps I was born to write. But more likely, I simply wasn't born to much else. The path never felt chosen so much as an arranged marriage that somehow grew into a loving home. And having found that home, I saw how it could connect me to that broader tradition of black writers, of dream-breakers. I wrote *Between the World and Me,* in some part at least, to honor them, to honor my ancestry. I know of that other literary tradition where one writes, as they say Baldwin did, to break traditions, to kill your elders and displace your ancestors. But I had been raised to honor tradition, to believe that I stood on the shoulders of elders, not against them. And more than I wanted to write something original and new, I wanted to write something that black people would recognize as original and old, something both classic and radical.

Black books were all over my childhood home. When I was a toddler my dad would play the Last Poets to calm me. When I was a teenager, I played Rakim to calm myself. And when I was in college, I read Sonia Sanchez to keep myself sane. In every way, black writing saved me. The epigraphs from Wright, Baraka, and Sanchez in the book's interior testified to that. The one endorsement affixed to *Between the World and Me,* from Toni Morrison, was the only one I wanted. This was born not just out of appreciation for her actual work but for the consistency with which she represented the tradition.

Perhaps there is also something generational to this understanding of heritage. I think of hip-hop forged from an alloy of the funk and soul of one era and the lyrics of another. I think of the drum, so central to this music, and how that drum is a line stretching across an ocean to our ancient black selves. I think of how much I listened to Kendrick Lamar while writing *Between the World and Me* and marveled at his fusion of new and old. My chain of ancestry was different than these musicians', though it stretched across the same plane. To join that chain, to join that lineage, to link up with Baldwin, I had to try to create something worthy of that tradition, something that would not "just shine," as Jay said, but "illuminate the whole show."

Between the World and Me came out, shot up the bestseller list, won some awards, and launched an indecent number of hot takes, warmed-over think pieces, and prefab ruminations. A dream, which was not my dream, came true. I did not wish to be recognized on the subway. But I did wish to be recognized by the tradition. And so there was a certain joy, perhaps narcissistic joy, in public appearances with Toni Morrison and Sonia Sanchez, in returning to Howard University to discuss *Between the World and Me.* I felt honored to present the book to people to whom Prince Jones was not theory or literary device, who were family in a way the rest of the world could never be.

BETWEEN THE WORLD AND ME OBSCURED another piece that, if not born from chasing Baldwin, was still important to me. *The Atlantic* prided itself on tackling the "big" issues of the day, and mass incarceration was, and is, perhaps the preeminent moral domestic issue of our time. By then I had earned enough trust from my editors that I could declare my interest and go. For much of the time I was finishing *Between the World and Me,* I was reporting another story that sought to understand the specific ways in which mass incarceration had hurt black families. I was excited about this story because I believed that "family" had been ceded to moral scolds who cared more about shaming people than actually helping families.

The man the scolders loved to cite was Daniel Patrick Moynihan. Before coming to mass incarceration, I'd read his Johnson-era report "The Negro Family: The Case for National Action" and a lot about the subsequent reaction. In reading more about Moynihan, both as a liberal wonk and his turn under Nixon, I thought I sensed many of the biases and preconceptions that made mass incarceration seem a plausible answer to the social problems that beset black communities. It was not, to my mind, so simple as racist conservatives; it was self-professed liberals too who embraced solutions for black people that I was convinced they would not embrace for white ones.

The resulting piece, "The Black Family in the Age of Mass Incarceration," had the misfortune of arriving a few months after *Between the World and Me.* It was, in many ways, an end point for my inquiries. A problem—the problem of the color line—that I had not understood had clarified for me. The answer was plunder. The answer was exactly what black people in their hearts believe it to be. The exploration was almost finished for me. And if the voyage had not given me hope, it had, at least, granted clarity.

THE BLACK FAMILY IN THE AGE OF MASS INCARCERATION

Never marry again in slavery.

—MARGARET GARNER, 1858

Wherever the law is, crime can be found.

—ALEKSANDR SOLZHENITSYN, 1973

I.
"LOWER-CLASS BEHAVIOR IN OUR CITIES IS SHAKING THEM APART"

BY HIS OWN LIGHTS, DANIEL PATRICK MOYNIHAN, AMBASSADOR, senator, sociologist, and itinerant American intellectual, was the product of a broken home and a pathological family.* He was born in 1927 in Tulsa, Oklahoma, but raised mostly in New York City. When Moynihan was ten years old, his father, John, left the family, plunging it into poverty. Moynihan's mother, Margaret, remarried, had another child, divorced, moved to Indiana to stay with rela-

---

* James Patterson's *Freedom Is Not Enough* furnished much of the biographical information in this section. Patterson's book is deeply sympathetic to Moynihan in ways that I don't quite agree with, but I found it invaluable for understanding Moynihan as a human.

tives, then returned to New York, where she worked as a nurse. Moynihan's childhood—a tangle of poverty, remarriage, relocation, and single motherhood—contrasted starkly with the idyllic American family life he would later extol. "My relations are obviously those of divided allegiance," Moynihan wrote in a diary he kept during the 1950s. "Apparently I loved the old man very much yet had to take sides . . . choosing mom in spite of loving pop." In the same journal, Moynihan, subjecting himself to the sort of analysis to which he would soon subject others, wrote, "Both my mother and father—They let me down badly. . . . I find through the years this enormous emotional attachment to Father substitutes—of whom the least rejection was cause for untold agonies—the only answer is that I have repressed my feelings towards dad."

As a teenager, Moynihan divided his time between his studies and working at the docks in Manhattan to help out his family. In 1943, he tested into the City College of New York, walking into the examination room with a longshoreman's loading hook in his back pocket so that he would not "be mistaken for any sissy kid." After a year at CCNY, he enlisted in the Navy, which paid for him to go to Tufts University for a bachelor's degree. He stayed for a master's degree and then started a doctorate program, which took him to the London School of Economics, where he did research. In 1959, Moynihan began writing for Irving Kristol's magazine *The Reporter,* covering everything from organized crime to auto safety. The election of John F. Kennedy as president, in 1960, gave Moynihan a chance to put his broad curiosity to practical use; he was hired as an aide in the Department of Labor. Moynihan was, by then, an anticommunist liberal with a strong belief in the power of government to both study and solve social problems. He was also something of a scenester. His fear of being taken for a "sissy kid" had diminished. In London, he'd cultivated a love of wine, fine cheeses, tailored suits, and the mannerisms of an English aristocrat. He stood six feet five inches tall. A cultured civil servant not to the manor born, Moynihan—witty, colorful, loquacious—

charmed the Washington elite, moving easily among congressional aides, politicians, and journalists. As the historian James Patterson writes in *Freedom Is Not Enough,* his book about Moynihan, he was possessed by "the optimism of youth." He believed in the marriage of government and social science to formulate policy. "All manner of later experiences in politics were to test this youthful faith."

Moynihan stayed on at the Labor Department during Lyndon B. Johnson's administration, but became increasingly disillusioned with Johnson's War on Poverty. He believed that the initiative should be run through an established societal institution: the patriarchal family. Fathers should be supported by public policy, in the form of jobs funded by the government. Moynihan believed that unemployment, specifically male unemployment, was the biggest impediment to the social mobility of the poor. He was, it might be said, a conservative radical who disdained service programs such as Head Start and traditional welfare programs such as Aid to Families with Dependent Children, and instead imagined a broad national program that subsidized families through jobs programs for men and a guaranteed minimum income for every family.

Influenced by the civil rights movement, Moynihan focused on the black family. He believed that an undue optimism about the pending passage of civil rights legislation was obscuring a pressing problem: a deficit of employed black men of strong character. He believed that this deficit went a long way toward explaining the African American community's relative poverty. Moynihan began searching for a way to press the point within the Johnson administration. "I felt I had to write a paper about the Negro family," Moynihan later recalled, "to explain to the fellows how there was a problem more difficult than they knew." In March 1965, Moynihan printed up one hundred copies of a report he and a small staff had labored over for only a few months.

The report was called "The Negro Family: The Case for National Action." Unsigned, it was meant to be an internal government document, with only one copy distributed at first and the other ninety-nine kept locked in a vault. Running against the tide of optimism around civil rights, "The Negro Family" argued that the federal government was underestimating the damage done to black families by "three centuries of sometimes unimaginable mistreatment" as well as a "racist virus in the American blood stream," which would continue to plague blacks in the future:

That the Negro American has survived at all is extraordinary—a lesser people might simply have died out, as indeed others have. . . . But it may not be supposed that the Negro American community has not paid a fearful price for the incredible mistreatment to which it has been subjected over the past three centuries.

That price was clear to Moynihan. "The Negro family, battered and harassed by discrimination, injustice, and uprooting, is in the deepest trouble," he wrote. "While many young Negroes are moving ahead to unprecedented levels of achievement, many more are falling further and further behind." Out-of-wedlock births were on the rise, and with them welfare dependency, while the unemployment rate among black men remained high. Moynihan believed that at the core of all these problems lay a black family structure mutated by white oppression:

In essence, the Negro community has been forced into a matriarchal structure which, because it is so out of line with the rest of the American society, seriously retards the progress of the group as a whole, and imposes a crushing burden on the Negro male and, in consequence, on a great many Negro women as well.

Moynihan believed this matriarchal structure robbed black men of their birthright—"The very essence of the male animal, from the bantam rooster to the four star general, is to strut," he wrote—

and deformed the black family and, consequently, the black community. In what would become the most famous passage in the report, Moynihan equated the black community with a diseased patient:

> In a word, most Negro youth are in *danger* of being caught up in the tangle of pathology that affects their world, and probably a majority are so entrapped. Many of those who escape do so for one generation only: as things now are, their children may have to run the gauntlet all over again. That is not the least vicious aspect of the world that white America has made for the Negro.

Despite its alarming predictions, "The Negro Family" was a curious government report in that it advocated no specific policies to address the crisis it described. This was intentional. Moynihan had lots of ideas about what government could do—provide a guaranteed minimum income, establish a government jobs program, bring more black men into the military, enable better access to birth control, integrate the suburbs—but none of these ideas made it into the report. "A series of recommendations was at first included, then left out," Moynihan later recalled. "It would have got in the way of the attention-arousing argument that a crisis was coming and that family stability was the best measure of success or failure in dealing with it."

President Johnson offered the first public preview of the Moynihan Report in a speech written by Moynihan and the former Kennedy aide Richard Goodwin at Howard University in June 1965, in which he highlighted "the breakdown of the Negro family structure." Johnson left no doubt about how this breakdown had come about.* "For this, most of all, white America must accept responsi-

---

* In the quest to understand the politics around the Moynihan Report, and how it was written, Lee Rainwater and William L. Yancey's investigation, *The Moynihan*

bility," Johnson said. Family breakdown "flows from centuries of oppression and persecution of the Negro man. It flows from the long years of degradation and discrimination, which have attacked his dignity and assaulted his ability to produce for his family."

The press did not generally greet Johnson's speech as a claim of white responsibility, but rather as a condemnation of "the failure of Negro family life," as the journalist Mary McGrory put it. This interpretation was reinforced as second- and third-hand accounts of the Moynihan Report, which had not been made public, began making the rounds. On August 18, the widely syndicated newspaper columnists Rowland Evans and Robert Novak wrote that Moynihan's document had exposed "the breakdown of the Negro family," with its high rates of "broken homes, illegitimacy, and female-oriented homes." These dispatches fell on all-too-receptive ears. A week earlier, the drunk-driving arrest of Marquette Frye, an African American man in Los Angeles, had sparked six days of rioting in the city, which killed thirty-four people, injured a thousand more, and caused tens of millions of dollars in property damage. Meanwhile, crime rates had begun to rise. People who read the newspapers but were not able to read the report could—and did—conclude that Johnson was conceding that no government effort could match the "tangle of pathology" that Moynihan had said beset the black family. Moynihan's aim in writing "The Negro Family" had been to muster support for an all-out government assault on the structural social problems that held black families down. ("Family as an issue raised the possibility of enlisting the support of conservative groups for quite radical social programs," he would later write.) Instead his report was portrayed as an argument for leaving the black family to fend for itself.

Report and the Politics of Controversy, proved key. It has the advantage of being both well researched and contemporaneous—the book was published two years after the Moynihan Report. It was a rich source of primary documents, collecting the responses to the report, for and against, around the time of publication.

Moynihan himself was partly to blame for this. In its bombastic language, its omission of policy recommendations, its implication that black women were obstacles to black men's assuming their proper station, and its unnecessarily covert handling, the Moynihan Report militated against its author's aims. James Farmer, the civil rights activist and a co-founder of the Congress of Racial Equality, attacked the report from the left as "a massive academic cop-out for the white conscience." William Ryan, the psychologist who first articulated the concept of "blaming the victim," accused Moynihan's report of doing just that. Moynihan had left the Johnson administration in the summer to run for president of the New York City Council. The bid failed, and liberal repudiations of the report kept raining down. "I am now known as a racist across the land," he wrote in a letter to the civil rights leader Roy Wilkins.

In fact, the controversy transformed Moynihan into one of the most celebrated public intellectuals of his era. In the summer of 1966, Moynihan was featured in *The New York Times*. In the fall of 1967, after Detroit had exploded into riots, *Life* magazine dubbed him the "Idea Broker in the Race Crisis," declaring, "A troubled nation turns to Pat Moynihan." Between 1965 and 1979, *The New York Times Magazine* ran five features on Moynihan. His own writing was featured in *The Atlantic, The New Yorker, Commentary, The American Scholar, The Saturday Evening Post, The Public Interest,* and elsewhere. Yet despite the positive coverage, Moynihan remained "distressed not to have any influence on anybody" in Washington, as he put it in a 1968 letter to Harry McPherson, a Johnson aide.

Meanwhile, the civil rights movement was fading and the radical New Left was rising.

In September 1967, worried about political instability in the country, Moynihan gave a speech calling for liberals and conservatives to unite "to preserve democratic institutions from the looming forces of the authoritarian left and right." Impressed by the speech, Richard Nixon offered Moynihan a post in the White House the following year. Moynihan was, by then, embittered by the attacks launched against him* and, like Nixon, horrified by the late-'60s radical spirit.

But Moynihan still professed concern for the family, and for the black family in particular. He began pushing for a minimum income for all American families. Nixon promoted Moynihan's proposal—called the Family Assistance Plan—before the American public in a television address in August 1969, and officially presented it to Congress in October. This was a personal victory for Moynihan—a triumph in an argument he had been waging since the War on Poverty began, over the need to help families, not individuals. "I felt I was finally *rid of a subject*. A subject that just . . . *spoiled* my life," Moynihan told *The New York Times* that November. "*Four—long—years* of being called awful things. The people you would most want to admire you detesting you. Being anathematized and stigmatized. And I said, 'Well, the President's *done* this, and now I'm rid of it.'"

But he was not rid of it. The Family Assistance Plan died in the Senate. In a 1972 essay in *The Public Interest,* Moynihan, who had by then left the White House and was a professor at Harvard, railed against "the poverty professionals" who had failed to support his efforts and the "upper-class" liars who had failed to see his perspective. He pointed out that his pessimistic predictions were now becoming reality. Crime was increasing. So were the number of children in poor, female-headed families. Moynihan issued a dire warning: "Lower-class behavior in our cities is shaking them apart." But America had an app for that.

From the mid-1970s to the mid-1980s, America's incarceration rate doubled, from about 150 people per 100,000 to about 300 per 100,000.

---

* Two books proved helpful in understanding Moynihan in his post-Johnson years: *Daniel Patrick Moynihan: A Portrait in Letters of an American Visionary,* edited by Steven R. Weisman, and *The Professor and the President: Daniel Patrick Moynihan in the Nixon White House,* by Stephen Hess. The first is a compilation of primary sources on Moynihan that allows one to get past the rhetoric and get to the man himself. Hess's book is a sympathetic memoir of Nixon and Moynihan's time together in the White House.

From the mid-1980s to the mid-1990s, it doubled again. By 2007, it had reached a historic high of 767 people per 100,000, before registering a modest decline to 707 people per 100,000 in 2012. In absolute terms, America's prison and jail population from 1970 until today has increased sevenfold, from some 300,000 people to 2.2 million. The United States now accounts for less than 5 percent of the world's inhabitants—and about 25 percent of its incarcerated inhabitants. In 2000, one in 10 black males between the ages of 20 and 40 was incarcerated—10 times the rate of their white peers. In 2010, a third of all black male high-school dropouts between the ages of 20 and 39 were imprisoned, compared with only 13 percent of their white peers.

Our carceral state banishes American citizens to a gray wasteland far beyond the promises and protections the government grants its other citizens. Banishment continues long after one's actual time behind bars has ended, making housing and employment hard to secure. And banishment was not simply a well-intended response to rising crime. It was the method by which we chose to address the problems that preoccupied Moynihan, problems resulting from "three centuries of sometimes unimaginable mistreatment." At a cost of $80 billion a year, American correctional facilities are a social-service program—providing health care, meals, and shelter for a whole class of people.

As the civil rights movement wound down, Moynihan looked out and saw a black population reeling under the effects of 350 years of bondage and plunder. He believed that these effects could be addressed through state action. They were—through the mass incarceration of millions of black people.

II.
"WE ARE INCARCERATING TOO FEW CRIMINALS"

The Gray Wastes—our carceral state, a sprawling netherworld of prisons and jails—are a relatively recent invention. Through the middle of the twentieth century, America's imprisonment rate hovered at about 110 people per 100,000. Presently, America's incarceration rate (which accounts for people in prisons *and* jails) is roughly twelve times the rate in Sweden, eight times the rate in Italy, seven times the rate in Canada, five times the rate in Australia, and four times the rate in Poland. America's closest to-scale competitor is Russia—and with an autocratic Vladimir Putin locking up about 450 people per 100,000, compared with our 700 or so, it isn't much of a competition.

China has about four times America's population, but American jails and prisons hold half a million more people. "In short," an authoritative report issued last year by the National Research Council concluded, "the current U.S. rate of incarceration is unprecedented by both historical and comparative standards."

What caused this? Crime would seem the obvious culprit: Between 1963 and 1993, the murder rate doubled, the robbery rate quadrupled, and the aggravated-assault rate nearly quintupled. But the relationship between crime and incarceration is more discordant than it appears. Imprisonment rates actually fell from the 1960s through the early 1970s, even as violent crime increased. From the mid-1970s to the late 1980s, both imprisonment rates and violent-crime rates rose. Then, from the early 1990s to the present, violent-crime rates fell while imprisonment rates increased.

The incarceration rate rose independent of crime—but not of criminal-justice policy.*

Derek Neal, an economist at the University of Chicago, has found that by the early 2000s, a suite of tough-on-crime laws had made prison sentences much more likely than in the past. Examining a sample of states, Neal found that from 1985 to 2000, the likelihood of a long prison sentence nearly doubled for drug possession,

---

* For more, see Derek Neal and Armin Rick's working paper "The Prison Boom and the Lack of Black Progress after Smith and Welch." It's a very technical paper, but indispensable for understanding how we got here.

tripled for drug trafficking, and quintupled for nonaggravated assault.

That explosion in rates and duration of imprisonment might be justified on grounds of cold pragmatism if a policy of mass incarceration actually caused crime to decline. Which is precisely what some politicians and policy makers of the tough-on-crime '90s were claiming. "Ask many politicians, newspaper editors, or criminal justice 'experts' about our prisons, and you will hear that our problem is that we put too many people in prison," a 1992 Justice Department report read. "The truth, however, is to the contrary; we are incarcerating too *few* criminals, and the public is suffering as a result."

History has not been kind to this conclusion.* The rise and fall in crime in the late twentieth century was an international phenomenon. Crime rates rose and fell in the United States and Canada at roughly the same clip—but in Canada, imprisonment rates held steady. "If greatly increased severity of punishment and higher imprisonment rates caused American crime rates to fall after 1990," the researchers Michael Tonry and David P. Farrington have written, then "what caused the Canadian rates to fall?" The riddle is not particular to North America. In the latter half of the twentieth century, crime rose and then fell in Nordic countries as well. During the period of rising crime, incarceration rates held steady in Denmark, Norway, and Sweden—but declined in Finland. "If punishment affects crime, Finland's crime rate should have shot up," Tonry and Farrington write, but it did not. After studying California's tough "Three Strikes and You're Out" law—which mandated at least a twenty-five-year sentence for a third "strikeable offense,"

---

* For more, see Michael Tonry and David P. Farrington's "Punishment and Crime Across Space and Time." For calculations on the effects of mass incarceration on crime, see Bruce Western, *Punishment and Inequality in America,* chapter 7—"Did the Prison Boom Cause the Crime Drop?" Beyond the numbers on this, Western's text was indispensable in helping me understand the mechanics of mass incarceration and how it affected the lives of young black men.

such as murder or robbery—researchers at UC Berkeley and the University of Sydney, in Australia, determined in 2001 that the law had reduced the rate of felony crime by no more than 2 percent. Bruce Western, a sociologist at Harvard and one of the leading academic experts on American incarceration, looked at the growth in state prisons in recent years and concluded that a 66 percent increase in the state prison population between 1993 and 2001 had reduced the rate of serious crime by a modest 2 to 5 percent—at a cost to taxpayers of $53 billion.

This bloating of the prison population may not have reduced crime much, but it increased misery among the group that so concerned Moynihan. Among all black males born since the late 1970s, one in four went to prison by their midthirties; among those who dropped out of high school, seven in ten did. "Prison is no longer a rare or extreme event among our nation's most marginalized groups," Devah Pager, a sociologist at Harvard, has written. "Rather it has now become a normal and anticipated marker in the transition to adulthood."

The emergence of the carceral state has had far-reaching consequences for the economic viability of black families. Employment and poverty statistics traditionally omit the incarcerated from the official numbers. When Western recalculated the jobless rates for the year 2000 to include incarcerated young black men, he found that joblessness among all young black men went from 24 to 32 percent; among those who never went to college, it went from 30 to 42 percent. The upshot is stark. Even in the booming '90s, when nearly every American demographic group improved its economic position, black men were left out. The illusion of wage and employment progress among African American males was made possible only through the erasure of the most vulnerable among them from the official statistics.

These consequences for black men have radiated out to their families. By 2000, more than 1 million black children had a father in jail or prison—and roughly half of those fathers were living in the same household as their kids when they were locked up. Paternal incarceration is associated with behavior problems and delinquency, especially among boys.

"More than half of fathers in state prison report being the primary breadwinner in their family," the National Research Council report noted. Should the family attempt to stay together through incarceration, the loss of income only increases, as the mother must pay for phone time, travel costs for visits, and legal fees. The burden continues after the father returns home, because a criminal record tends to injure employment prospects.* Through it all, the children suffer.

Many fathers simply fall through the cracks after they're released. It is estimated that between 30 and 50 percent of all parolees in Los Angeles and San Francisco are homeless. In that context— employment prospects diminished, cut off from one's children, nowhere to live—one can readily see the difficulty of eluding the ever-present grasp of incarceration, even once an individual is physically out of prison. Many do not elude its grasp. In 1984, 70 percent of all parolees successfully completed their term without arrest and were granted full freedom. In 1996, only 44 percent did. As of 2013, 33 percent do.

The Gray Wastes differ in both size and mission from the penal systems of earlier eras. As African Americans began filling cells in the 1970s, rehabilitation was largely abandoned in favor of retribution—the idea that prison should not reform convicts but punish them. For instance, in the 1990s, South Carolina cut back on in-prison education, banned air conditioners, jettisoned televisions, and discontinued intramural sports. Over the next ten years, Congress repeatedly attempted to pass a No Frills Prison Act, which

---

* For more, the National Research Council's *The Growth of Incarceration in the United States* is really an atlas of the Gray Wastes. Written by a committee of some of the most distinguished scholars on the subject, the report addresses any question you could possibly have about mass incarceration. You can read it straight through. But it works just as well as an encyclopedia.

would have granted extra funds to state correctional systems working to "prevent luxurious conditions in prisons." A goal of this "penal harm" movement, one criminal-justice researcher wrote at the time, was to find "creative strategies to make offenders suffer."

III.
"YOU DON'T TAKE A SHOWER AFTER NINE O'CLOCK"

Last winter, I visited Detroit to take the measure of the Gray Wastes. Michigan, with an incarceration rate of 628 people per 100,000, is about average for an American state. I drove to the East Side to talk with a woman I'll call Tonya, who had done eighteen years for murder and a gun charge and had been released five months earlier. She had an energetic smile and an edge to her voice that evidenced the time she'd spent locked up. Violence, for her, commenced not in the streets, but at home. "There was abuse in my grandmother's home, and I went to school and I told my teacher," she explained. "I had a spot on my nose because I had a lit cigarette stuck on my nose, and when I told her, they sent me to a temporary foster-care home. . . . The foster parent was also abusive, so I just ran away from her and just stayed on the streets."

Tonya began using crack. One night she gathered with some friends for a party. They smoked crack. They smoked marijuana. They drank. At some point, the woman hosting the party claimed that someone had stolen money from her home. Another woman accused Tonya of stealing it. A fight ensued. Tonya shot the woman who had accused her. She got twenty years for the murder and two for the gun. After the trial, the truth came out. The host had hidden the money, but was so high that she'd forgotten.

When the doors finally close and one finds oneself facing banishment to the carceral state—the years, the walls, the rules, the guards, the inmates—reactions vary. Some experience an intense sickening feeling. Others, a strong desire to sleep. Visions of suicide. A deep shame. A rage directed toward guards and other inmates. Utter disbelief. The incarcerated attempt to hold on to family and old social ties through phone calls and visitations. At first, friends and family do their best to keep up. But phone calls to prison are expensive, and many prisons are located far from one's hometown.

"First I would get one [visit] like every four months," Tonya explained to me. "And then I wouldn't get none for like maybe a year. You know, because it was too far away. And I started to have losses. I lost my mom, my brothers. . . . So it was hard, you know, for me to get visits."

As the visits and phone calls diminish, the incarcerated begins to adjust to the fact that he or she is, indeed, a prisoner. New social ties are cultivated. New rules must be understood. A blizzard of acronyms, sayings, and jargon—PBF, CSC, ERD, "letters but no numbers"—must be comprehended. If the prisoner is lucky, someone—a cell mate, an older prisoner hailing from the same neighborhood—takes him under his wing. This can be the difference between survival and catastrophe. On Richard Braceful's first night in Carson City Correctional Facility, in central Michigan, where he had been sent away at age twenty-nine for armed robbery, he decided to take a shower. It was 10 P.M. His cell mate stopped him. "Where are you going?" the cell mate asked. "I'm going to take a shower," Braceful responded. His cell mate, a fourteen-year veteran of the prison system, blocked his way and said, "You're not going to take a shower." Braceful, reading the signs, felt a fight was imminent. "Calm down," his cell mate told him. "You don't take a shower after nine o'clock. People that are sexual predators, people that are rapists, they go in the showers right behind you." Braceful and the veteran sat down. The veteran looked at him. "It's your first time being locked up, ain't it?" he said. "Yeah, it is," Braceful responded. The veteran said to him, "Listen, this is what you have to do. For the next couple of weeks, just stay with me. I've been here for fourteen years. I'll look out for you until you learn how to move around in here without getting yourself hurt."

Michigan prisons assign each inmate to a level corresponding to the security risk the inmate is believed to pose. As the levels decrease, privileges—yard time, for instance—increase. Level V is maximum security. Level I is for prisoners who will soon be released. At Level IV, you will find many prisoners with life sentences and not many prisoners with fewer than five years left to serve. A prisoner with a life sentence who has reached Level II has generally proved that he or she is not a danger to others. But there are very few such prisoners, because it is very hard to remain at the more draconian levels without acquiring "tickets"—demerits for violating prison protocol, often involving fighting. "It's hard to stay ticket-free for ten years without somebody getting stabbed, somebody getting into a fight," Braceful, who is now out of prison, explained to me when I visited him in Detroit last December. "Because there are people that are there who might look at you and go, 'He's a small guy. I'm gonna take advantage of him.' "

When this happens, a prisoner can decide either to defend himself or to "lock up"—that is, to report to the guards that he fears for his safety. The guards will then place the prisoner in solitary confinement for his own protection. "Those are my only two choices," Braceful explained. "And if you lock up, everybody know you lock up. When you come back out, you gonna have a bigger problem."

"Because you're prey," I said.

"Exactly," he responded. "So you fight, you know. And when the fight gets serious enough, you gotta find something to stab with, you gotta find something, you know, you gotta make your weapon, you gotta do something."

Michigan leads the country in the average length of a prison stay—4.3 years—yet most prisoners do eventually say goodbye. The bliss of freedom, the joy of family reunion, can quickly be tempered by the challenge of staying free. The transition can be jarring. "I panicked," Tonya told me, speaking of how it felt to be out of prison after eighteen years. "I was only used to a cell as opposed to having multiple rooms, and there was always somebody there with me in the cell—whether it was a bunkie or officer, somebody's always in this building. To go from that to this? I stayed on the phone. I made people call me, you know. It was scary. And I still experience that to this day. Everybody looks suspect to me. I'm like, 'He's up to something.' A friend of mine told me, 'You've been gone a long time, over a decade, so it's gonna take you about two years for you to readjust.' "

The challenges of housing and employment bedevil many ex-offenders. "It's very common for them to go homeless," Linda VanderWaal, the associate director of prisoner reentry at a community-action agency in Michigan, told me. In the winter, VanderWaal says, she has a particularly hard time finding places to accommodate all the homeless ex-prisoners. Those who do find a place to live often find it difficult to pay their rent.

The carceral state has, in effect, become a credentialing institution as significant as the military, public schools, or universities—but the credentialing that prison or jail offers is negative. In her book *Marked: Race, Crime, and Finding Work in an Era of Mass Incarceration,* Devah Pager, the Harvard sociologist, notes that most employers say that they would not hire a job applicant with a criminal record. "These employers appear less concerned about specific information conveyed by a criminal conviction and its bearing on a particular job," Pager writes, "but rather view this credential as an indicator of general employability or trustworthiness."

Ex-offenders are excluded from a wide variety of jobs, running the gamut from septic tank cleaner to barber to real estate agent, depending on the state. And in the limited job pool that ex-offenders can swim in, blacks and whites are not equal. For her research, Pager pulled together four testers to pose as men looking for low-wage work. One white man and one black man would pose as job seekers without a criminal record, and another black man and white man would pose as job seekers with a criminal record. The negative credential of prison impaired the employment efforts of both the black man and the white man, but it impaired those of the black man more. Startlingly, the effect was not limited to the black man with a criminal record. The black man *without* a criminal record fared worse than the white man *with* one. "High levels of incarceration cast a shadow of criminality over all black men, implicating even those (in the majority) who have remained crime free," Pager writes. Effectively, the job market in America regards black men who have never been criminals as though they were.*

Just as ex-offenders had to learn to acculturate themselves to prison, they have to learn to re-acculturate themselves to the outside. But the attitude that helps one survive in prison is almost the opposite of the kind needed to make it outside. Craig Haney, a professor at UC Santa Cruz who studies the cognitive and psychological effects of incarceration, has observed:

A tough veneer that precludes seeking help for personal problems, the generalized mistrust that comes from the fear of exploitation, and a tendency to strike out in response to minimal provocations are highly functional in many prison contexts but problematic virtually everywhere else.†

Linda VanderWaal told me that re-acculturation is essential to thriving in an already compromised job market. "I hate to say this, but it's a reality," she said. "Making eye contact, the way they walk—people judge you the moment you walk in the doors for an

---

* Devah Pager's book *Marked* gives some sense of how the effects of mass incarceration have spread beyond the prisons, and even beyond the previously imprisoned, and now affect those who are thought to have been imprisoned. One of the great challenges reformers will have to face is not merely reforming the prison system, but reckoning with the broad secondary damage wrought by our policies.

† From Craig Haney's book *Reforming Punishment: Psychological Limits to the Pains of Imprisonment.*

interview. . . . We literally practice eye contact, smiling, handshaking, how you're sitting."

In America, the men and women who find themselves lost in the Gray Wastes are not picked at random. A series of risk factors—mental illness, illiteracy, drug addiction, poverty—increases one's chances of ending up in the ranks of the incarcerated. "Roughly half of today's prison inmates are functionally illiterate," Robert Perkinson, an associate professor of American studies at the University of Hawaii at Mānoa, has noted. "Four out of five criminal defendants qualify as indigent before the courts."* Sixty-eight percent of jail inmates were struggling with substance dependence or abuse in 2002. One can imagine a separate world where the state would see these maladies through the lens of government education or public health programs. Instead it has decided to see them through the lens of criminal justice. As the number of prison beds has risen in this country, the number of public psychiatric hospital beds has fallen. The Gray Wastes draw from the most socioeconomically unfortunate among us, and thus take particular interest in those who are black.

IV.
"THE CRIME-STAINED BLACKNESS OF THE NEGRO"

It is impossible to conceive of the Gray Wastes without first conceiving of a large swath of its inhabitants as both more than crimi-

---

* The quote is from Robert Perkinson's *Texas Tough: The Rise of America's Prison Empire,* a deeply disturbing history of the modern era of mass incarceration. There is a good deal of sociological and economic study on mass incarceration, but considerably less in the way of history. What I would love to see is a book that took the long view of incarceration, crime, and racism. Too many accounts begin in the 1960s. At any rate, Perkinson's book is a crucial contribution to the literature in that it tells us precisely how we got here.

nal and less than human. These inhabitants, black people, are the preeminent outlaws of the American imagination. Black criminality is literally written into the American Constitution—the Fugitive Slave Clause, in Article IV of that document, declared that any "Person held to Service or Labour" who escaped from one state to another could be "delivered up on Claim of the Party to whom such Service or Labour may be due." From America's very founding, the pursuit of the right to labor, and the right to live free of whipping and of the sale of one's children, were verboten for blacks.

The crime of absconding was thought to be linked to other criminal inclinations among blacks. Pro-slavery intellectuals sought to defend the system as "commanded by God" and "approved by Christ." In 1860, *The New York Herald* offered up a dispatch on the doings of runaway slaves residing in Canada. "The criminal calendars would be bare of a prosecution but for the negro prisoners," the report claimed. Deprived of slavery's blessings, blacks quickly devolved into criminal deviants who plied their trade with "a savage ferocity peculiar to the vicious negro." Blacks, the report stated, were preternaturally inclined to rape: "When the lust comes over them they are worse than the wild beast of the forest." Nearly a century and a half before the infamy of Willie Horton, a portrait emerged of blacks as highly prone to criminality, and generally beyond the scope of rehabilitation. In this fashion, black villainy justified white oppression—which was seen not as oppression but as "the corner-stone of our republican edifice."*

---

* Taken from *Cotton Is King, and Pro-Slavery Arguments,* by E. N. Elliot, a crucial text in understanding the perspective of pro-slavery intellectuals. Michelle Alexander has taken some criticism for asserting, in her book *The New Jim Crow,* the connections between slavery, Jim Crow, and mass incarceration. Honestly, I was one of the skeptics. But having finished this research, I really have to applaud Alexander's attempt to connect mass incarceration with American history. I don't totally agree with the book (I think linking crime and black struggle is even older than she does, for instance), but I think *The New Jim Crow* pursues the right line of questioning. I don't think mass incarceration happens without the rise in crime. But there are all kinds of ways one can respond to a crime surge. Mass incarceration is appropriate

To fortify the "republican edifice," acts considered legal when committed by whites were judged criminal when committed by blacks. In 1850, a Missouri man named Robert Newsom purchased a girl named Celia, who was about fourteen years old. For the next five years, he repeatedly raped her. Celia birthed at least one child by Newsom. When she became pregnant again, she begged Newsom to "quit forcing her while she was sick." He refused, and one day in June 1855 informed Celia that he "was coming to her cabin that night." When Newsom arrived and attempted to rape Celia again, she grabbed a stick "about as large as the upper part of a Windsor chair" and beat Newsom to death. A judge rejected Celia's self-defense claim, and she was found guilty of murder and sentenced to death. While she was in jail, she gave birth to the child, who arrived stillborn. Not long after, Celia was hanged.

Celia's status—black, enslaved, female—transformed an act of self-defense into an act of villainy. Randall Kennedy, a law professor at Harvard, writes that "many jurisdictions made slaves into 'criminals' by prohibiting them from pursuing a wide range of activities that whites were typically free to pursue." Among these activities were:

> learning to read, leaving their masters' property without a proper pass, engaging in "unbecoming" conduct in the presence of a white female, assembling to worship outside the supervisory presence of a white person, neglecting to step out of the way when a white person approached on a walkway, smoking in public, walking with a cane, making loud noises, or defending themselves from assaults.

Antebellum Virginia had seventy-three crimes that could garner the death penalty for slaves—and only one for whites.

---

only if you already believe that certain people weren't really fit for freedom in the first place.

The end of enslavement posed an existential crisis for white supremacy, because an open labor market meant blacks competing with whites for jobs and resources, and—most frightening—black men competing for the attention of white women. Postbellum Alabama solved this problem by manufacturing criminals. Blacks who could not find work were labeled vagrants and sent to jail, where they were leased as labor to the very people who had once enslaved them. Vagrancy laws were nominally color-blind but, Kennedy writes, "applied principally, if not exclusively, against Negroes." Some vagrancy laws were repealed during Reconstruction, but as late as the Great Depression, cash-strapped authorities in Miami were found rounding up black "vagrants" and impressing them into sanitation work.

"From the 1890s through the first four decades of the twentieth century," writes Khalil Gibran Muhammad, the director of the Schomburg Center for Research in Black Culture at the New York Public Library, "black criminality would become one of the most commonly cited and longest-lasting justifications for black inequality and mortality in the modern urban world." Blacks were criminal brutes by nature, and something more than the law of civilized men was needed to protect the white public.* Society must defend itself from contamination by "the crime-stained blackness of the negro," asserted Hinton Rowan Helper, a Southern white supremacist writer, in 1868. Blacks were "naturally intemperate," one phy-.

---

* Without the work of Khalil Gibran Muhammad, this section would not be possible. Muhammad's book *The Condemnation of Blackness* is a history of late nineteenth- and twentieth-century social scientists, intellectuals, and reformers elevating the problem of "black criminality." This debate did not take place on dispassionate, objective grounds. Instead the charge was a weapon wielded to claim that blacks were not entitled to the same rights as others. When Frederick Ludwig Hoffman asserts in 1896 that "the criminality of the negro exceeds that of any other race of any numerical importance in this country," he is arguing against the franchise for blacks. Hoffman believed that blacks should be disqualified from the "higher level of citizenship, the first duty of which is to obey the laws and respect the lives and property of others." Muhammad's works lets us see how the psychological and rhetorical groundwork was laid for mass incarceration. Another essential text.

sician claimed in the *New York Medical Journal* in 1886, prone to indulging "every appetite too freely, whether for food, drink, tobacco, or sensual pleasures, and sometimes to such an extent as to appear more of a brute than human."

Rape, according to the mythology of the day, remained the crime of choice for blacks. "There is something strangely alluring and seductive to [black men] in the appearance of a white woman," asserted Philip Alexander Bruce, a nineteenth-century secretary of the Virginia Historical Society. "It moves them to gratify their lust at any cost and in spite of every obstacle." These outrages were marked "by a diabolical persistence" that compelled black men to assault white women with a "malignant atrocity of detail that [has] no reflection in the whole extent of the natural history of the most bestial and ferocious animals."

Before Emancipation, enslaved blacks were rarely lynched, because whites were loath to destroy their own property. But after the Civil War, the number of lynchings rose, peaked at the turn of the century, then persisted at a high level until just before the Second World War, not petering out entirely until the height of the civil rights movement, in the 1960s. The lethal wave was justified by a familiar archetype—"the shadow of the Negro criminal," which, according to John Rankin, a congressman from Mississippi speaking in 1922, hung "like the sword of Damocles over the head of every white woman." Lynching, though extralegal, found support in the local, state, and national governments of America. "I led the mob which lynched Nelse Patton, and I'm proud of it," declared William Van Amberg Sullivan, a former United States senator from Mississippi, on September 9, 1908, the day after Patton's lynching. "I directed every movement of the mob, and I did everything I could to see that he was lynched." Standing before the Senate on March 23, 1900, "Pitchfork Ben" Tillman, of South Carolina, declared to his colleagues that terrorized blacks were the victims not of lynching, but of "their own hot-headedness." Lynching was a prudent act of self-defense. "We will not submit to [the black man's] gratifying his lust on our wives and daughters without lynching him," Tillman said. In 1904, defending southern states' lack of interest in education funding for blacks, James K. Vardaman, the governor of Mississippi, offered a simple rationale, as one report noted: "The strength of [crime] statistics."

Even as African American leaders petitioned the government to stop the lynching, they conceded that the Vardamans of the world had a point.* In an 1897 lecture, W.E.B. Du Bois declared, "The first and greatest step toward the settlement of the present friction between the races—commonly called the Negro problem—lies in the correction of the immorality, crime, and laziness among the Negroes themselves, which still remains as a heritage from slavery." Du Bois's language anticipated the respectability politics of our own era. "There still remain enough well authenticated cases of brutal assault on women by black men in America to make every Negro bow his head in shame," Du Bois claimed in 1904. "This crime must at all hazards stop. Lynching is awful, and injustice and caste are hard to bear; but if they are to be successfully attacked they must cease to have even this terrible justification." Kelly Miller, who was then a leading black intellectual and a professor at Howard University, presaged the call for blacks to be "twice as good," asserting in 1899 that it was not enough for "ninety-five out of every hundred Negroes" to be lawful. "The ninety-five must band themselves together to restrain or suppress the vicious five."

---

* Some of the most painful moments in this research came in looking at the black response to lynching. Mary Church Terrell claimed that black criminals guilty of assault were "ignorant, repulsive in appearance and as near the brute creation as it is possible for a human being to be." William J. Edwards, a black rural Alabama school director, condemned poor blacks as "often ferocious or dangerous" and prone to becoming "a criminal of the lowest type." Edwards believed that there were "criminals in the Negro race for whom no legal form of punishment is too severe." But white supremacists were not in the habit of sorting good blacks from bad. "Little in these appraisals of black criminality by African Americans would have comforted southern whites," writes historian Robert W. Thurston in his book *Lynching,* "who of course paid scant attention to black leaders' ideas in the first place." Thurston's book led me to all of the primary sources cited in this regard.

In this climate of white repression and paralyzed black leadership, the federal government launched, in 1914, its first war on drugs,* passing the Harrison Narcotics Tax Act, which restricted the sale of opiates and cocaine. The reasoning was unoriginal. "The use of cocaine by unfortunate women generally and by negroes in certain parts of the country is simply appalling," the American Pharmaceutical Association's Committee on the Acquirement of the Drug Habit had concluded in 1902. *The New York Times* published an article by a physician saying that the South was threatened by "cocaine-crazed negroes," to whom the drug had awarded expert marksmanship and an immunity to bullets "large enough to 'kill any game in America.'" Another physician, Hamilton Wright, the "father of American narcotic law," reported to Congress that cocaine lent "encouragement" to "the humbler ranks of the negro population in the South." Should anyone doubt the implication of *encouragement*, Wright spelled it out: "It has been authoritatively stated that cocaine is often the direct incentive to the crime of rape by the negroes of the South and other sections of the country."

The persistent and systematic notion that blacks were especially prone to crime extended even to the state's view of black leadership. J. Edgar Hoover, the head of the FBI for nearly half a century, harassed three generations of leaders. In 1919, he attacked the black nationalist Marcus Garvey as "the foremost radical among his race," then ruthlessly pursued Garvey into jail and deportation. In 1964,

---

* When people discuss the drug war, they are usually referring to the one that began in the 1970s, without realizing that this was, at least, our third drug war in the twentieth century. I found David F. Musto's *The American Disease: Origins of Narcotic Control* to be extremely helpful on the subject. It was depressing to see that drug wars, in this country, are almost never launched purely out of concern for public health. In almost every instance that Musto looks at there is some fear of an outsider—blacks and cocaine, Mexican Americans and marijuana, Chinese Americans and opium. I feel compelled to also mention Kathleen J. Frydl's book *The Drug Wars in America, 1940–1973*. It was on my list, but unfortunately I didn't get to it. At any rate, I have great respect for Frydl's work and look forward to reading it in the future.

he attacked Martin Luther King Jr. as "the most notorious liar in the country," and hounded him, bugging his hotel rooms, his office, and his home, until his death. Hoover declared the Black Panther Party to be "the greatest threat to the internal security of the country" and authorized a repressive, lethal campaign against its leaders that culminated in the assassination of Fred Hampton in December 1969.

Today Hoover is viewed unsympathetically as having stood outside mainstream ideas of law and order. But Hoover's pursuit of King was known to both President Kennedy and President Johnson, King's ostensible allies. Moreover, Hoover was operating within an American tradition of criminalizing black leadership. In its time, the Underground Railroad was regarded by supporters of slavery as an interstate criminal enterprise devoted to the theft of property. Harriet Tubman, purloiner of many thousands of dollars in human bodies, was considered a bandit of the highest order. "I appear before you this evening as a thief and a robber," Frederick Douglass told his audiences. "I stole this head, these limbs, this body from my master, and ran off with them."

In Douglass's time, to stand up for black rights was to condone black criminality. The same was true in King's time. The same is true today. Appearing on *Meet the Press* to discuss the death of Michael Brown in Ferguson, Missouri, the former New York City mayor Rudy Giuliani—in the fashion of many others—responded to black critics of law enforcement exactly as his forebears would have: "How about you reduce crime? . . . The white police officers wouldn't be there if you weren't killing each other 70 to 75 percent of the time."

But even in Giuliani's hometown, the relationship between crime and policing is not as clear as the mayor would present it. After Giuliani became mayor, in 1994, his police commissioner William Bratton prioritized a strategy of "order maintenance" in city policing. As executed by Bratton, this strategy relied on a policy of stop-and-frisk, whereby police officers could stop pedestrians on vague premises such as "furtive movements" and then question them and search them for guns and drugs. Jeffrey Fagan, a Columbia University law professor, found that blacks and Hispanics were stopped significantly more often than whites even "after adjusting stop rates for the precinct crime rates" and "other social and economic factors predictive of police activity." Despite Giuliani's claim that aggressive policing is justified because blacks are "killing each other," Fagan found that between 2004 and 2009, officers recovered weapons in less than 1 percent of all stops—and recovered them more frequently from whites than from blacks. Yet blacks were 14 percent more likely to be subjected to force. In 2013 the policy, as carried out under Giuliani's successor, Michael Bloomberg, was ruled unconstitutional.

If policing in New York under Giuliani and Bloomberg was crime prevention tainted by racist presumptions, in other areas of the country ostensible crime prevention has mutated into little more than open pillage. When the Justice Department investigated the Ferguson Police Department in the wake of Michael Brown's death, it found a police force that disproportionately ticketed and arrested blacks and viewed them "less as constituents to be protected than as potential offenders and sources of revenue." This was not because the police department was uniquely evil—it was because Ferguson was looking to make money. "Ferguson's law enforcement practices are shaped by the City's focus on revenue rather than by public safety needs," the report concluded. These findings had been augured by the reporting of *The Washington Post,** which had found a few months earlier that some small, cash-strapped municipalities in the St. Louis suburbs were deriving 40 percent or more of their annual revenue from various fines for traffic violations, loud music, uncut grass, and wearing "saggy pants," among

---

* The reporter for *The Washington Post* deserves to be cited by name—Radley Balko, whose writing and reporting on the problems of modern policing have greatly improved my own understanding of the issue.

other infractions. This was not public safety driving policy—it was law enforcement tasked with the job of municipal plunder.

It is patently true that black communities, home to a class of people regularly discriminated against and impoverished, have long suffered higher crime rates. The historian David M. Oshinsky notes in his book *"Worse Than Slavery": Parchman Farm and the Ordeal of Jim Crow Justice* that from 1900 to 1930, African Americans in Mississippi "comprised about 67 percent of the killers in Mississippi and 80 percent of the victims." As much as African Americans complained of violence perpetrated by white terrorists, the lack of legal protection from everyday neighbor-on-neighbor violence was never then, and has never been, far from their minds. "Law-abiding Negroes point out that there are criminal and treacherous Negroes who secure immunity from punishment because they are fawning and submissive toward whites," observed the Nobel Prize–winning economist Gunnar Myrdal in his famous 1944 book about race in America, *An American Dilemma: The Negro Problem and Modern Democracy.* "Such persons are a danger to the Negro community. Leniency toward Negro defendants in cases involving crimes against other Negroes is thus actually a form of discrimination."

Crime within the black community was primarily seen as a black problem, and became a societal problem mainly when it seemed to threaten the white population. Take the case of New Orleans between the world wars, when, as Jeffrey S. Adler, a historian and criminologist at the University of Florida, has observed, an increase in the proportion of crimes committed by blacks "on the streets and in local shops and bars," as opposed to in black homes and neighborhoods, produced an enduring mix of fear and fury among whites. In response, Louisiana district attorneys promised that "Negro slayers of Negroes will be thoroughly prosecuted." A common tool in homicide cases was to threaten black suspects with capital punishment to extract a guilty plea, which mandated a life sentence. So even as violent crime declined between 1925 and 1940, Louisiana's incarceration rate increased by more than 50 percent.

"Twice as many inmates entered state correctional facilities in low-crime 1940 as in high-crime 1925," Adler writes. At Angola State Penal Farm, the "white population rose by 39 percent while the African American inmate population increased by 143 percent."

The principal source of the intensifying war on crime was white anxiety about social control. In 1927, the Supreme Court had ruled that a racial-zoning scheme in the city was unconstitutional. The black population of New Orleans was growing. And there was increasing pressure from some government officials to spread New Deal programs to black people. "At no time in the history of our State," the city's district attorney claimed in 1935, "has White Supremacy been in greater danger."*

The staggering rise in incarceration rates in interwar Louisiana coincided with a sense among whites that the old order was under siege. In the coming decades, this phenomenon would be replicated on a massive, national scale.

V.
THE "BADDEST GENERATION ANY SOCIETY HAS EVER KNOWN"

The American response to crime cannot be divorced from a history of equating black struggle—individual and collective—with black villainy. And so it is unsurprising that in the midst of the civil rights movement, rising crime was repeatedly linked with black advancement. Elijah Forrester, a Democratic congressman from Georgia, opposed the Eisenhower administration's 1956 civil rights bill on

---

* This account of mass incarceration in Louisiana is drawn from Jeffrey S. Adler's article "Less Crime, More Punishment: Violence, Race, and Criminal Justice in Early Twentieth-Century America." Again, this is a case where things we take to be completely new, are not. One cannot help but note the precedent to cries against "Black on Black crime" in the district attorney vowing to crack down on "Negro slayers of Negroes."

the grounds that "where segregation has been abolished," black villainy soon prospered.* "In the District of Columbia, the public parks have become of no utility whatever to the white race," Forrester claimed, "for they enter at the risk of assaults upon their person or the robbery of their personal effects." Unless segregation was immediately restored, "in ten years, the nation's capital will be unsafe for them in the daytime." Around that time, Basil Whitener, a North Carolina congressman, dismissed the NAACP as an organization pledged to "the assistance of Negro criminals."

In 1966, Richard Nixon picked up the charge, linking rising crime rates to Martin Luther King's campaign of civil disobedience. The decline of law and order "can be traced directly to the spread of the corrosive doctrine that every citizen possesses an inherent right to decide for himself which laws to obey and when to obey them." The cure, as Nixon saw it, was not addressing criminogenic conditions, but locking up more people. "Doubling the conviction rate in this country would do far more to cure crime in America than quadrupling the funds for [the] War on Poverty," he said in 1968.

As president, Nixon did just that: During his second term, incarceration rates began their historic rise. Drugs in particular attracted Nixon's ire. Heroin dealers were "literally the slave traders of our time," he said, "traffickers in living death. They must be hunted to the end of the earth."

Nixon's war on crime was more rhetoric than substance. "I was cranking out that bullshit on Nixon's crime policy before he was elected," wrote White House counsel John Dean, in his memoir

---

* Much of Section V is indebted to Naomi Murakawa's *The First Civil Right: How Liberals Built Prison America.* I was not totally convinced by the subtitle, but some of the evidence that Murakawa musters against Democrats, some of whom are still serving, is damning. Should Joe Biden run for president, he has to be asked about his time spent cheerleading for more prisons. Some of the quotes Murakawa unearths—particularly the ones where Democrats know the bill is bad and vote anyway—are little more than cowardice and put the lie to the notion that mass incarceration is a well-intentioned mistake.

of his time in the administration.* "And it was bullshit, too. We knew it." Indeed, if sinking crime rates are the measure of success, Nixon's war on crime was a dismal failure. The rate of every type of violent crime—murder, rape, robbery, aggravated assault—was up by the end of Nixon's tenure. The true target of Nixon's war on crime lay elsewhere. Describing the Nixon campaign's strategy for assembling enough votes to win the 1972 election, Nixon's aide John Ehrlichman later wrote, "We'll go after the racists. . . . That subliminal appeal to the antiblack voter was always in Nixon's statements and speeches on schools and housing." According to H. R. Haldeman, another Nixon aide, the president believed that when it came to welfare, the "*whole* problem [was] really the blacks." Of course, the civil rights movement had made it unacceptable to say this directly. "The key is to devise a system that recognizes this while not appearing to," Haldeman wrote in his diary. But there was no need to devise new systems from scratch: When Nixon proclaimed drugs "public enemy No. 1," or declared "war against the criminal elements which increasingly threaten our cities, our homes, and our lives," he didn't need to name the threat. A centuries-long legacy of equating blacks with criminals and moral degenerates did the work for him.

In 1968, while campaigning for president, Nixon was taped rehearsing a campaign ad. "The heart of the problem is law and order in our schools," he said. "Discipline in the classroom is essential if our children are to learn." Then, perhaps talking to himself, he added, "Yep, this hits it right on the nose, the thing about this whole teacher—it's all about law and order and the damn Negro–Puerto Rican groups out there."

As incarceration rates rose and prison terms became longer, the idea of rehabilitation was mostly abandoned in favor of incapacita-

---

* Citations from John Dean's memoir *Blind Ambition,* John Ehrlichman's memoir, *Witness to Power,* and H. R. Haldeman's *Diaries.* I wish I could claim to have dug these up. I cannot. I first saw the John Dean quote in Perkinson's *Texas Tough* and the Ehrlichman and Haldeman quotes in Alexander's *The New Jim Crow.*

tion. Mandatory minimums—sentences that set a minimum length of punishment for the convicted—were a bipartisan achievement of the 1980s backed not just by conservatives such as Strom Thurmond but by liberals such as Ted Kennedy. Conservatives believed mandatory sentencing would prevent judges from exercising too much leniency; liberals believed it would prevent racism from infecting the bench. But reform didn't just provide sentencing guidelines—it also cut back on alternatives (parole, for instance) and generally lengthened time served. Before reform, prisoners typically served 40 to 70 percent of their sentences. After reform, they served 87 to 100 percent of their sentences. Moreover, despite what liberals had hoped for, bias was not eliminated, because discretion now lay with prosecutors, who could determine the length of a sentence by deciding what crimes to charge someone with. District attorneys with reelection to consider could demonstrate their zeal to protect the public with the number of criminals jailed and the length of their stay.

Prosecutors were not alone in their quest to appear tough on crime. In the 1980s and '90s, legislators, focusing on the scourge of crack cocaine, vied with one another to appear toughest. There was no real doubt as to who would be the target of this newfound toughness. By then, Daniel Patrick Moynihan had gone from the White House to a U.S. Senate seat in New York. He was respected as a scholar and renowned for his intellect. But his preoccupations had not changed. "We cannot ignore the fact that when we talk about drug abuse in our country, in the main, we are talking about the consequence it has for young males in inner cities," he told the Senate in 1986. This might well have been true as a description of drug *enforcement policies,* but it was not true of actual drug abuse: Surveys have repeatedly shown that blacks and whites use drugs at remarkably comparable rates. Moynihan had by the late Reagan era evidently come to believe the worst distortions of his own 1965 report. Gone was any talk of root causes; in its place was something darker. The young inner-city males who had so concerned Moynihan led "wasted and ruined" lives and constituted a threat that could "bring about the destruction of whole communities and cities across this Nation."

In seeming to abandon scholarship for rhetoric, Moynihan had plenty of company among social scientists and political pundits. James Q. Wilson, the noted social scientist and a co-creator of the "broken windows" theory of policing, retreated to abstract moralizing and tautology. "Drug use is wrong because it is immoral," he claimed, "and it is immoral because it enslaves the mind and destroys the soul." Others went further. "The inner-city crack epidemic is now giving birth to the newest horror," the *Washington Post* columnist Charles Krauthammer declaimed: "A bio-underclass, a generation of physically damaged cocaine babies whose biological inferiority is stamped at birth." In this way, "the crime-stained blackness of the Negro" lived on to haunt white America.

In 1995, Adam Walinsky, a politically liberal lawyer who had been an aide to Senator Robert F. Kennedy, wrote a cover story for *The Atlantic* that, drawing on Moynihan's 1965 report, predicted doom. American policy toward the black family had, Walinsky wrote, "assured the creation of more very violent young men than any reasonable society can tolerate, and their numbers will grow inexorably for every one of the next twenty years." The solutions Walinsky proposed included ending racism, building better schools, and hiring more police. But the thrust of his rhetoric was martial. "We shrink in fear of teenage thugs on every street," he wrote. "More important, we shrink even from contemplating the forceful collective action we know is required."

Even as *The Atlantic* published those words, violent crime had begun to plunge. But thought leaders were slow to catch up. In 1996, William J. Bennett, John P. Walters, and John J. DiIulio Jr. partnered to publish perhaps the most infamous tract of the tough-on-crime era, *Body Count: Moral Poverty . . . and How to Win America's War Against Crime and Drugs*. The authors (wrongly) predicted a new crime wave driven by "inner-city children" who were growing up "almost completely unmoralized and develop[ing] character traits" that would "lead them into a life of illiteracy, illicit drugs, and violent crimes." The threat to America from what the authors called "super-predators" was existential. "As high as America's body count is today, a rising tide of youth crime and violence is about to lift it even higher," the authors warned. "A new generation of street criminals is upon us—the youngest, biggest, and baddest generation any society has ever known." Incarceration was "a solution," DiIulio wrote in *The New York Times,* "and a highly cost-effective one." The country agreed. For the next decade, incarceration rates shot up even further. The justification for resorting to incarceration was the same in 1996 as it was in 1896.

Many African Americans concurred that crime was a problem. When Jesse Jackson confessed, in 1993, "There is nothing more painful to me at this stage in my life than to walk down the street and hear footsteps and start thinking about robbery, then look around and see somebody white and feel relieved," he was speaking to the very real fear of violent crime that dogs black communities. The argument that high crime is the predictable result of a series of oppressive racist policies does not render the victims of those policies bulletproof. Likewise, noting that fear of crime is well grounded does not make that fear a solid foundation for public policy.

The suite of drug laws adopted in the 1980s and '90s did little to reduce crime, but a lot to normalize prison in black communities. "No single offense type has more directly contributed to contemporary racial disparities in imprisonment than drug crimes," Devah Pager, the Harvard sociologist, has written.

Between 1983 and 1997, the number of African Americans admitted to prison for drug offenses increased more than twenty-six-fold, relative to a sevenfold increase for whites. . . . By 2001, there were more than twice as many African Americans as whites in state prison for drug offenses.

In 2013, the ACLU published a report noting a ten-year uptick in marijuana arrests. The uptick was largely explained as "a result of the increase in the arrest rates of Blacks." To reiterate an important point: Surveys have concluded that blacks and whites use drugs at roughly the same rates. And yet by the close of the twentieth century, prison was a more common experience for young black men than college graduation or military service.

By the mid-1990s, both political parties had come to endorse arrest and incarceration as a primary tool of crime-fighting. This conclusion was reached not warily, but lustily. As a presidential candidate, Bill Clinton flew home to Arkansas to preside over the execution of Ricky Ray Rector, a mentally disabled, partially lobotomized black man who had murdered two people in 1981. "No one can say I'm soft on crime," Clinton would say later. Joe Biden, then the junior senator from Delaware, quickly became the point man for showing that Democrats would not go soft on criminals. "One of my objectives, quite frankly," he said, "is to lock Willie Horton up in jail." Biden cast Democrats as the true party without mercy. "Let me define the liberal wing of the Democratic Party," he said in 1994. "The liberal wing of the Democratic Party is now for 60 new death penalties. . . . The liberal wing of the Democratic Party has 70 enhanced penalties. . . . The liberal wing of the Democratic Party is for 100,000 cops. The liberal wing of the Democratic Party is for 125,000 new state prison cells."

In Texas, the Democratic governor, Ann Richards, had come to power in 1991 advocating rehabilitation, but she ended up following the national trend, curtailing the latitude of judges and the parole board in favor of fixed sentencing, which gave power to prosecutors. In 1993, Texas rejected a bid to infuse its schools with $750 million—but approved $1 billion to build more prisons. By the end of her term, Richards had presided over "one of the biggest public works projects in Texas history," according to Robert Perkinson's *Texas Tough: The Rise of America's Prison Empire*. In New

York, another liberal governor, Mario Cuomo, found himself facing an exploding prison population. After voters rejected funding for more prisons, Cuomo pulled the money from the Urban Development Corporation, an agency that was supposed to build public housing for the poor. It did—in prison. Under the avowedly liberal Cuomo, New York added more prison beds than under all his predecessors combined.

This was penal welfarism at its finest. Deindustrialization had presented an employment problem for America's poor and working class of all races. Prison presented a solution: jobs for whites, and warehousing for blacks. Mass incarceration "widened the income gap between white and black Americans," writes Heather Ann Thompson, a historian at the University of Michigan, "because the infrastructure of the carceral state was located disproportionately in all-white rural communities." Some six hundred thousand inmates are released from America's prisons each year, more than the entire population of America's prisons in 1970—enough people, according to Pager, to "fill every one of the fast-food job openings created annually nearly five times over."

Dark predictions of rising crime did not bear out. Like the bestial blacks of the nineteenth century, super-predators proved to be the stuff of myth. This realization cannot be regarded strictly as a matter of hindsight. As the historian Naomi Murakawa has shown in her book *The First Civil Right: How Liberals Built Prison America,* many Democrats knew exactly what they were doing—playing on fear for political gain—and did it anyway. Voting on the Anti–Drug Abuse Act of 1986, Nick Rahall II, a congressman from West Virginia, admitted that he had reservations about mandatory minimums but asked, "How can you get caught voting against them?" Congresswoman Patricia Schroeder of Colorado accused her colleagues of using the 1986 bill to score points before an election. In the end, she voted for it. "Right now, you could put an amendment through to hang, draw, and quarter," said Claude Pepper, a historically liberal congressman from Florida, referring to the same law. Pepper also voted for it.

In 1994, President Clinton signed a new crime bill, which offered grants to states that built prisons and cut back on parole. Clinton recently said that he regrets his pivotal role in driving up the country's incarceration numbers. "I signed a bill that made the problem worse," he told the NAACP in July. "And I want to admit it." In justifying his actions of twenty years earlier, he pointed to the problems of "gang warfare" and of "innocent bystanders" shot down in the streets. Those were, and are, real problems. But even in trying to explain his policies, Clinton neglected to retract the assumption underlying them—that incarcerating large swaths of one population was a purely well-intended, logical, and nonracist response to crime. Even at the time of its passage, Democrats—much like the Republican Nixon a quarter century earlier—knew that the 1994 crime bill was actually about something more than that. Writing about the bill in 1993, Clinton's aides Bruce Reed and Jose Cerda III urged the president to seize the issue "at a time when public concern about crime is the highest it has been since Richard Nixon stole the issue from the Democrats in 1968."

VI.
"IT'S LIKE I'M IN PRISON WITH HIM"

On the evening of December 19, 1973, Odell Newton, who was then sixteen years old, stepped into a cab in Baltimore with a friend, rode half a block, then shot and killed the driver, Edward Mintz. The State of Maryland charged Odell with crimes including murder in the first degree and sentenced him to life in prison. He has now spent forty-one years behind bars, but by all accounts he is a man reformed. He has repeatedly expressed remorse for his crimes. He has not committed an infraction in thirty-six years.

The Maryland Parole Commission has recommended Odell for release three times since 1992. But in Maryland, all release recommendations for lifers are subject to the governor's approval. In the 1970s, when Odell committed his crime, this was largely a formality. But in our era of penal cruelty, Maryland has effectively abolished parole for lifers—even juvenile offenders such as Odell. In 2010, the U.S. Supreme Court ruled that life sentences without the possibility of parole for juveniles found guilty of crimes other than homicide were unconstitutional. Two years later, it held the same for mandatory life sentences without parole for juvenile homicide offenders. But the Court has yet to rule on whether that more recent decision was retroactive. Fifteen percent of Maryland's lifers committed their crimes as juveniles—the largest percentage in the nation, according to a 2015 report by the Maryland Restorative Justice Initiative and the state's ACLU affiliate. The vast majority of them—84 percent—are black.

This summer, I visited Odell's mother, Clara; his sister Jackie; and his brother Tim at Clara's home in a suburb of Baltimore. Clara had just driven seven hours round-trip to visit Odell at Eastern Correctional Institution, on the Eastern Shore of Maryland, and she was full of worry. He was being treated for hepatitis. He'd lost fifty pounds. He had sores around his eyes.

I asked Clara how they managed to visit Odell regularly. She explained that family members trade visits. "It takes a lot out of the family," she explained. "Then you come back home, [after] you've seen him up there like that, [and] you're crying. I got so bad one time, I was losing weight. . . . Just thinking, *Was it gonna be all right? Was it gonna kill him? Was he gonna die?*"

Clara was born and raised in Westmoreland, Virginia. She had her first child, Jackie, when she was only fifteen. The next year she married Jackie's father, John Irvin Newton Sr. They moved to Baltimore so that John could pursue a job at a bakery. "We stuck it out and made things work," Clara told me. They were married for fifty-three years, until John passed away, in 2008.

Odell Newton was born in 1957. When he was four years old, he fell ill and almost died. The family took him to the hospital. Doctors put a hole in his throat to help him breathe. They transferred Odell to another hospital, where he was diagnosed with lead poisoning. It turned out that he had been putting his mouth on the windowsill.

"We didn't sue nobody. We didn't know nothing about that," Clara told me. "And when we finally found out that you could sue, Odell was fifteen. And they said they couldn't do anything, because we waited too long."

In prison, Odell has repeatedly attempted to gain his G.E.D., failing the test several times. "My previous grade school teacher noted that I should be placed in special education," Odell wrote in a 2014 letter to his lawyer. "It is unclear what roll childhood lead poisoning played in my analytical capabilities."

In June 1964, the family moved into a nicer house, in Edmondson Village. Sometime around ninth grade, Clara began to suspect that Odell was lagging behind the other kids in his class. "We didn't find out that he was really delayed until he was almost ready to enter into high school," Jackie told me. "They just passed him on and passed him on." Around this time, Clara says, Odell got "mixed up with the wrong crowd." Not until he wrote his first letter home from prison did Clara understand the depth of his intellectual disability. The letter read as though it had been written by "a child just starting pre-K or kindergarten," Clara told me. "He couldn't really spell. And, I don't know, it just didn't look like a person of his age should be writing like that."

Odell Newton is now fifty-seven. He has spent the lion's share of his life doing time under state supervision. The time he's served has not affected him alone. If men and women like Odell are cast deep within the barrens of the Gray Wastes, their families are held in a kind of orbit, on the outskirts, by the relentless gravity of the carceral state. For starters, the family must contend with the financial expense of having a loved one incarcerated. Odell's parents took out a second mortgage to pay for their son's lawyers, and then a third. Beyond that, there's the expense of having to make long drives to prisons that are commonly built in rural white regions, far from the incarcerated's family. There's the expense of phone calls, and of constantly restocking an inmate's commissary. Taken together, these economic factors fray many a family's bonds.

And then there is the emotional weight, a mix of anger and sadness. While I was in Detroit last winter, I interviewed Patricia Lowe, whose son Edward Span had been incarcerated at age sixteen, sentenced to nine and a half to fifteen years for carjacking, among other offenses. When I met with Patricia, Edward was about three years into his sentence, and she was as worried for him as she was angry at him. He'd recently begun calling home and requesting large sums of money. She was afraid he was being extorted by other prisoners. At the same time, she was unhappy about carrying the burden Edward had placed on her after all the hard work she'd put in as a mother. "He never ate school lunch. I would get up in the morning and make subs, sandwiches, salads, spaghetti, fried chicken," she said. "We had dysfunction, but what family don't? There's no excuse for his misbehavior. So whatever you did out there, you can't do in here. You know what it's about. I told you out here what's going to happen in there. So you gave me heartache out here. You can't give it to me in there."

But the heartache was unavoidable. "It's like I'm in prison with him. I feel like I'm doing every day of that nine-and-a-half to fifteen." When he was seventeen, Edward was taken from juvenile detention and put in an adult prison. Even in juvenile, Edward couldn't sleep at night. "He feared going to prison," Patricia told me. "He calls home and tells me he's okay. But I know different because he has a female friend he calls. He can't sleep. He's worried about his safety."

Odell's brother Tim graduated from Salisbury State College with a degree in sociology in 1982. Two years later, he took a job with the State of Maryland as a corrections officer. For twenty years, while one son, Odell, served time under the state, another son, Tim, worked for it. This gave Tim a front-row seat for observing how Maryland's carceral system grew more punitive. Whereas inmates had once done their time and gone to prerelease facilities, now they were staying longer. Requirements for release became more onerous. Meanwhile, the prisons were filling to capacity and beyond. "They just kept overcrowding and overcrowding and not letting people go home," Tim told me. The prisons began holding two people in cells meant for one. "If you're in an eight-by-ten space that's only big enough for one person and now you got two people in there, it's just more aggravation," Tim said. "And then they cut out a lot of the college programs that they did have. They cut out the weights being in the yard."

The overcrowding, the stripping of programs and resources, were part of the national movement toward punishing inmates more harshly and for longer periods. Officially, Maryland has two kinds of life sentences—life with the possibility of parole, and life without. In the 1970s, Maryland's governor paroled ninety-two lifers. Parole for lifers declined after Marvin Mandel's last term ended, in 1979, and then ground to a halt in 1993, when Rodney Stokes— a lifer out on work release—killed his girlfriend and then himself. Parris Glendening, the Democratic governor elected in 1994, declared, "A life sentence means life." Glendening's Republican successor, Robert L. Ehrlich Jr., commuted five lifers' sentences and granted only a single instance of medical parole.

In 2006, Martin O'Malley (who's currently vying to be the Democrats' nominee for president in 2016) defeated Ehrlich to become governor, but he took an even stricter stance on lifers than his predecessor, failing to act on even a single recommendation of the Parole Commission. Recognizing that the system had broken down, the Maryland legislature changed the law in 2011 so that the commission's recommendations would automatically be carried out if the governor did not reject them within 180 days. This changed almost nothing. After the law's passage, O'Malley vetoed nearly every recommendation that reached his desk.

This is not sound policy for fighting crime or protecting citizens. In Maryland, the average lifer who has been recommended for but not granted release is sixty years old. These men and women are past the age of "criminal menopause," as some put it, and most pose no threat to their community. Even so, the Maryland Parole Commission's recommendation is not easily attained: Between 2006 and 2014, it recommended only about eighty out of more than 2,100 eligible lifers for release. Almost none of those eighty or so men and women, despite meeting a stringent set of requirements, was granted release by the governor. Though Maryland's Parole Commission still offers recommendations for lifers, they are disregarded. The choice given to judges to levy sentences for life either with or without parole no longer has any meaning.

For more than five years, from February 1988 to June 1993, Odell Newton worked in the community through work release; for part of that period, he was able to visit his relatives through the state's family-leave policy. Reports from Odell's former work-release employers are glowing. "His character is above reproach," one wrote in 1991. Another said: "I consider it a privilege to have Mr. Newton as an employee, and would rehire Odell at any time." With his family, he would often go out to eat, or have a cookout or a party. Family leave was supposed to be a bridge to Odell's eventual release. But the program was suspended for lifers in May 1993, after a convicted murderer fled while visiting his son. The Stokes killing followed just weeks later. After that, parole was effectively taken off the table for all lifers, and Maryland ended work release for them as well. Believing for years that Odell was on his way to coming home, and then seeing the road to freedom snatched away, frustrated the family. "I could see you doing it to people that's starting out new, and this is a new law you're putting down," his sister Jackie told me. But this is "like me buying a house and I have it one price, then when you come in and sign the papers, they're going, 'Oh no, I changed my mind, I want $10,000 more for it.'"

I asked Odell's family how they coped with the experience. "You just have to pray and keep praying," his mother told me.

For most of Odell's time in prison, the power to sign the papers has rested in the hands of Democrats, who in recent decades have taken a line on lifers at least as harsh as any Republican has. "The Glendening administration's policies, and Gov. Martin O'Malley policies made a paroleable life sentence a 'non paroleable sentence,'" Odell wrote to his lawyer, "and that's not right."

VII.
"OUR VALUE SYSTEM BECAME
SURVIVING VERSUS LIVING"

Born in the late 1950s, Odell Newton was part of the generation that so troubled Moynihan when he wrote his report on "The Negro Family." But Odell had the very bulwark that Moynihan treasured—a stable family—and it did not save him from incarceration. It would be wrong to conclude from this that family is irrelevant. But families don't exist independent of their environment. Odell was born in the midst of an era of government-backed housing discrimination. Indeed, Baltimore was a pioneer in this practice—in 1910, the city council had zoned the city by race. "Blacks should be quarantined in isolated slums," J. Barry Mahool, Baltimore's mayor, said. After the U.S. Supreme Court ruled such explicit racial-zoning schemes unconstitutional, in 1917, the city turned to other means—restrictive covenants, civic associations, and redlining—to keep blacks isolated.[*]

---

[*]   I first saw this in Richard Rothstein's excellent report "From Ferguson to Baltimore: The Fruits of Government-Sponsored Segregation." Rothstein is brilliant and has the kind of fine understanding of the machinery of government policy as it relates to housing that I deeply envy.

These efforts curtailed the ability of black people to buy better housing, to move to better neighborhoods, and to build wealth. Also, by confining black people to the same neighborhoods, these efforts ensured that people who were discriminated against, and hence had little, tended to be neighbors only with others who also had little. Thus while an individual in that community might be high-achieving, even high-earning, his or her ability to increase that achievement and wealth and social capital, through friendship, marriage, or neighborhood organizations, would always be limited.* Finally, racial zoning condemned black people to the oldest and worst housing in the city—the kind where one was more likely to be exposed, as Odell Newton was, to lead. A lawyer who handled more than four thousand lead-poisoning cases across three decades recently described his client list to *The Washington Post*: "Nearly 99.9 percent of my clients were black."

That families are better off the stronger and more stable they are is self-evidently important. But so is the notion that no family can ever be made impregnable, that families are social structures existing within larger social structures.

Robert Sampson, a sociologist at Harvard who focuses on crime and urban life, notes that in America's ghettos, "like things tend to go together." High rates of incarceration, single-parent households, dropping out of school, and poverty are not unrelated vectors. Instead, taken together, they constitute what

---

* A lot of this section depends on the ever-insightful Robert Sampson, and more broadly the focus on neighborhood dynamics in contemporary sociology. The notion of compounded deprivation, which Rob discusses here, really elucidates the difficulty in making easy comparisons between blacks and whites. And so talking about a white middle class and a black middle class as though they are socioeconomic equals, or as though the only difference is having to give their children "The Talk," really misses that these two groups live in different worlds. Specifically, the world of the black middle class is—because of policy—significantly poorer. Thus to wonder about the difference in outcomes between the black and white middle class, is really to wonder about the difference in weight between humans living on the Earth and humans living on the moon.

Sampson calls "compounded deprivation"—entire families, entire neighborhoods, deprived in myriad ways, must navigate, all at once, a tangle of interrelated and reinforcing perils.

Black people face this tangle of perils at its densest. In a recent study, Sampson and a co-author looked at two types of deprivation—being individually poor, and living in a poor neighborhood. Unsurprisingly, they found that blacks tend to be individually poor and to live in poor neighborhoods. But even blacks who are not themselves individually poor are more likely to live in poor neighborhoods than whites and Latinos who are individually poor. For black people, escaping poverty does not mean escaping a poor neighborhood. And blacks are much more likely than all other groups to fall into compounded deprivation later in life,* even if they managed to avoid it when they were young.

"It's not just being poor; it's discrimination in the housing market, it's subprime loans, it's drug addiction—and then all of that following you over time," Sampson told me recently. "We try to split things out and say, 'Well, you can be poor but still have these other characteristics and qualities.' It's the myth of the American Dream that with initiative and industriousness, an individual can always escape impoverished circumstances. But what the data show is that you have these multiple assaults on life chances that make transcending those circumstances difficult and at times nearly impossible."

On a brisk Thursday morning last December, I climbed into an SUV with Carl S. Taylor and Yusef Bunchy Shakur and drove to the West Side of Detroit, where both men had grown up. Shakur is a community activist and the author of two books chronicling his road to prison, his experience inside, and his return to society. Taylor is a sociologist at Michigan State University, where he researches

* Taken from a forthcoming paper by Sampson and Kristin L. Perkins, "Compounded Deprivation in the Transition to Adulthood: The Intersection of Racial and Economic Inequality among Chicagoans, 1995-2013," in *The Russell Sage Foundation Journal of the Social Sciences*.

urban communities and violence and serves as an adviser to Michigan's prisons and juvenile detention centers. A twenty-four-year age gap separates Taylor and Shakur, a gap that's reflected in their visions of Detroit. Shakur, who is forty-two, recalls a town ravaged by deindustrialization, where unemployment was rampant, social institutions had failed, and gangs had taken their place. "The community collapsed," Shakur said. "Our value system became surviving versus living. Drugs, gangs, lack of education all came to the forefront. And prison and incarceration."

Taylor, who is sixty-six, recalls a more hopeful community where black professionals lived next door to black factory workers and black maids and black gangsters, and the streets were packed with bars, factories, and restaurants. "All of this was filled," Taylor said, pointing out the car window at a row of abandoned housing. "Everybody was working. It was smaller factories all up and down. But the strip was here also. The legendary Chit Chat Lounge was down here, where the Motown and jazz musicians played."

We stopped on the desolate corner of Hazelwood and 12th Street. "I lived in that first house right there that's boarded up," Taylor said. He pointed out at the street, gesturing toward businesses and neighbors long gone. "Right here was a drugstore and produce. There was a black woman right here that owned a drapery-cleaning business. Negroes used to have draperies! Here was the wig shop and the beauty salon for the street girls. Church ladies weren't going in there. I lived right here, and this is a very powerful place for me." In black cities around the country, Jim Crow—with its housing segregation and job discrimination—imposed boundaries. And within those boundaries an order took root. This world was the product of oppression—but it was a world beloved by the people who lived there. It is a matter of some irony that the time period and the communities Taylor was describing with fond nostalgia are the same ones that so alarmed Daniel Patrick Moynihan in 1965. Taylor was not blind to the problems—many of them outlined in Moynihan's report—but he described them as embedded within a larger social fabric, giving them a kind of humanity that Moynihan's alarmism stripped away.

"This was the good time, the good life," Taylor said. "And when the riot hit, this is where it jumped off."

Like so many urban riots during the long, hot summers of the 1960s, Detroit's began with law enforcement. On July 23, 1967, the Detroit police raided an after-hours watering hole on the West Side. For several days, the city's black communities burned. As in other cities, the riot demarcated the end of "the good life." In fact the good life, to the extent it ever existed, had begun decaying long before. As Thomas J. Sugrue, a historian at New York University, observes in his book *The Origins of the Urban Crisis: Race and Inequality in Postwar Detroit,* "Between 1947 and 1963, Detroit lost 134,000 manufacturing jobs, while its population of working-aged men and women actually increased." From the end of the 1940s to the beginning of the 1960s, Detroit suffered four major recessions. Automakers began moving to other parts of the country, and eventually to other parts of the world. The loss of jobs meant a loss of buying power, affecting drugstores, grocery stores, restaurants, and department stores.* "By the late 1950s," Sugrue writes, Detroit's "industrial landscape had become almost unrecognizable."

Black residents of Detroit had to cope not just with the same structural problems as white residents but also with pervasive racism. Within a precarious economy, black people generally worked the lowest-paying jobs. They came home from those jobs to the city's poorest neighborhoods, where most of them used their substandard wages to pay inflated prices for inferior housing. Attempts to escape into white neighborhoods were frustrated by restrictive

---

* One of my great irritants is how so much of our discussions on race and racism proceed from the notion that American history begins in the 1960s. The discussions around Detroit are the obvious example. There is a popular narrative that holds that Detroit was a glorious city and the riots ruined it. Thomas J. Sugrue's *The Origins Of the Urban Crisis* does a great job at dialing back this idea and pointing to the long arc of the city's decline.

covenants, racist real-estate agents, block associations, and residents whose tactics included, as Sugrue writes, "harassment, mass demonstrations, picketing, effigy burning, window breaking, arson, vandalism, and physical attacks." Some blacks were richer than others. Some were better educated than others. But all were constricted, not by a tangle of pathologies, but by a tangle of structural perils.

The fires of 1967 conveniently obscured those perils. But the structural problems, along with the wave of deindustrialization, were what gifted America with the modern "Negro problem." By the 1970s, the government institution charged with mediating these problems was, in the main, the criminal-justice system. As we drove around Detroit, Shakur described the world in which the black men he knew came of age in the 1970s and '80s. Out of every ten men, "probably seven of their fathers have been in prison. Possibly two of their mothers have been killed. The majority of their fathers and mothers haven't graduated from high school." Shakur sounded a lot like Moynihan—except he understood that the family was interacting with something larger. "When you grow up and you seen nothing but drugs, you seen nothing but prostitution, that becomes normal," he said. "So when you talk about Carl"—Taylor, who went to college and graduate school and became a professor—"Carl becomes abnormal, because he's so far from my world. I've never talked with a doctor until he be sewing me up after I got shot. I never talked with a lawyer until he was sending me to prison. I never talked with a judge until he convicted me."

The blacks incarcerated in this country are not like the majority of Americans. They do not merely hail from poor communities—they hail from communities that have been imperiled across both the deep and immediate past, and continue to be imperiled today. Peril is generational for black people in America—and incarceration is our current mechanism for ensuring that the peril continues. Incarceration pushes you out of the job market. Incarceration disqualifies you from feeding your family with food stamps. Incarceration allows for housing discrimination based on a criminal background check. Incarceration increases your risk of homelessness. Incarceration increases your chances of being incarcerated again. "The prison boom helps us understand how racial inequality in America was sustained, despite great optimism for the social progress of African Americans," Bruce Western, the Harvard sociologist, writes. "The prison boom is not the main cause of inequality between blacks and whites in America, but it did foreclose upward mobility and deflate hopes for racial equality."

If generational peril is the pit in which all black people are born, incarceration is the trapdoor closing overhead. "African Americans in our data are distinct from both Latinos and whites," Robert Sampson told me. "Even when we control for marital status and family history of criminality, we still see these strong differences. The compounded deprivation that African Americans experience is a challenge even independent of all the characteristics we think are protective."

Characteristics such as the one Daniel Patrick Moynihan focused on—family.

VIII.
"THE NEGRO POOR HAVING BECOME
MORE OPENLY VIOLENT"

Moynihan is in the midst of a renaissance. Fifty years after the publication of "The Negro Family: The Case for National Action," a coterie of sociologists, historians, and writers is declaring it prophecy. In their version of history, a courageous and blameless Moynihan made one mistake: He told the truth. For his sins—loving the black family enough to be honest—Moynihan was crucified by an intolerant cabal of obstinate leftists and Black Power demagogues.

"Liberals brutally denounced Moynihan as a racist," the columnist Nicholas Kristof wrote in *The New York Times* this past spring. In the eyes of his new acolytes, Moynihan has been vindicated by the rising percentage of female-headed households and the intractable problems of America's inner cities. Intimidated by "the vitriolic attacks and acrimonious debate" over the black family, as the sociologist William Julius Wilson has put it, liberal scholars steered clear of the controversy. Conservatives stepped into the breach, eagerly taking up Moynihan's charge to examine the family, but stripping it of any structural context, and dooming the dream of a benevolent welfare state.

A raft of sociological research has indeed borne out Moynihan's skepticism about black progress, as well as his warnings about the kind of concentrated poverty that flowed from segregation. Moynihan's observation about the insufficiency of civil rights legislation has been proved largely correct.* Moreover, Moynihan's concern about the declining rates of two-parent households would have struck the average black resident of Harlem in 1965 as well placed. Nationalist leaders like Malcolm X drew much of their appeal through their calls for shoring up the black family.

But if Moynihan's past critics exhibited an ignorance of his oeuvre and his intent, his current defenders exhibit a naïveté in defense of their hero. "The Negro Family" is a flawed work in part because it is a fundamentally sexist document that promotes the importance not just of family but of patriarchy, arguing that black men should be empowered at the expense of black women. "Men must have jobs," Moynihan wrote to President Johnson in 1965. "We must not rest until every able-bodied Negro male is working. Even if we have to displace some females." Moynihan was evidently unconcerned that he might be arguing for propping up an order in which

---

* This seems like the right place to thank Peter-Christian Aigner, who is working on a biography of Moynihan. While Peter doesn't yet have a book for me to cite, his insights on Moynihan were crucial in guiding me to sources and thinking about the context for "The Negro Family: The Case for National Action."

women were bound to men by a paycheck,* in which "family" still meant the right of a husband to rape his wife and intramarital violence was still treated as a purely domestic and nonlegal matter.

Moynihan's defenders also overlook his record after he entered the Nixon White House in 1969. Perhaps still smarting from his treatment in the Johnson administration, Moynihan fed Nixon's antipathies—against elites, college students, and blacks—and stoked the president's fears about crime. In a memo to Nixon, he asserted that "a great deal of the crime" in the black community was really a manifestation of anti-white racism: "Hatred—revenge—against whites is now an acceptable excuse for doing what might have been done anyway." Like his forebears who'd criminalized blacks, Moynihan claimed that education had done little to mollify the hatred. "It would be difficult to overestimate the degree to which young well educated blacks detest white America."

Whereas Johnson, guided by Moynihan, had declared that "white America must accept responsibility" for the problems of the black community, Moynihan wrote Nixon that "the Negro lower class would appear to be unusually self-damaging." He continued:

> The Negro poor having become more openly violent—especially in the form of the rioting of the mid 1960's—they have given the black middle class an incomparable weapon with which to *threaten* white America. This has been for many an altogether intoxicating experience. "Do this or the cities will burn." . . . What building contracts and police graft were to the 19th-century urban Irish, the welfare de-

---

* More on this count: In 1967, *Time* magazine put Moynihan on the cover, dubbing him an "urbanologist." Discussing what he'd do about the problem among blacks in cities, Moynihan said, "When these Negro G.I.s come back from Viet Nam, I would meet them with a real estate agent, a girl who looks like Diahann Carroll, and a list of jobs. I'd try to get half of them into the grade schools, teaching kids who've never had anyone but women telling them what to do." Everything about this quote is wrong.

partment, Head Start, and Black Studies programs will be to the coming generation of Negroes. They are of course very wise in this respect.

In this same memo,* Moynihan ominously cited a "rather pronounced revival—in impeccably respectable circles—of the proposition that there is a difference in genetic potential" between the two races. Moynihan claimed that he did not believe in a genetic difference in intelligence, but said he considered the matter "an open question."

Crime really did begin to rise during the early 1970s. But by this point, Moynihan had changed. According to the Moynihan of the Nixon era, middle-class blacks were not hardworking Americans attempting to get ahead—they were mobsters demanding protection money in exchange for the safety of America's cities. And the "unusually self-damaging" black poor were hapless tools, the knife at the throat of blameless white America. In casting African Americans as beyond the purview of polite and civilized society, in referring to them as a race of criminals, Moynihan joined the long tradition of black criminalization. In so doing, he undermined his own stated aims in writing "The Negro Family" in the first place. One does not build a safety net for a race of predators. One builds a cage.

Whatever the slings and arrows Moynihan suffered in the 1960s, his vision dominates liberal political discourse today. One hears Moynihan in Barack Obama's cultural critique of black fathers and black families. Strains of Moynihan's thinking ran through Bill Clinton's presidency. "We cannot . . . repair the American community and restore the American family until we provide the structure, the values, the discipline, and the reward that work gives," President Clinton told a group of black church leaders in Memphis

---

* Nicholas Lemann quotes this deeply unfortunate memo in his book *The Promised Land: The Great Black Migration and How It Changed America*.

in 1993. He argued for a policy initiative on three fronts—jobs, family, and crime—but the country's commitment to each of these propositions proved unequal. Incarceration soared during Clinton's two terms. There's very little evidence that it brought down crime—and abundant evidence that it hindered employment for black men, and accelerated the kind of family breakdown that Clinton and Moynihan both lamented. In their efforts to strengthen the black family, Clinton and Moynihan—and Obama, too—aspired to combine government social programs with cultural critiques of ghetto pathology (the "both/and" notion, as Obama has termed it), and they believed that Americans were capable of taking in critiques of black culture and white racism at once. But this underestimated the weight of the country's history.

For African Americans, unfreedom is the historical norm. Enslavement lasted for nearly 250 years. The 150 years that followed have encompassed debt peonage, convict lease-labor, and mass incarceration—a period that overlapped with Jim Crow. This provides a telling geographic comparison. Under Jim Crow, blacks in the South lived in a police state. Rates of incarceration were not that high—they didn't need to be, because state social control of blacks was nearly total. Then, as African Americans migrated north, a police state grew up around them there, too. In the cities of the North, "European immigrants' struggle" for the credential of whiteness gave them the motive to oppress blacks, writes Christopher Muller, a sociologist at Columbia who studies incarceration: "A central way European immigrants advanced politically in the years preceding the first Great Migration was by securing patronage positions in municipal services such as law enforcement." By 1900, the black incarceration rate in the North was about 600 per 100,000—slightly lower than the national incarceration rate today.

That early-twentieth-century rates of black imprisonment were lower in the South than in the North reveals how the carceral state functions as a system of control. Jim Crow applied the control in the South. Mass incarceration did it in the North. After the civil rights movement triumphed in the 1960s and toppled Jim Crow laws, the South adopted the tactics of the North, and its rates of imprisonment surged far past the North's. Mass incarceration became the national model of social control. Indeed, while the Gray Wastes have expanded their population, their most significant characteristic remains unchanged: In 1900, the black-white incarceration disparity in the North was seven to one—roughly the same disparity that exists today on a national scale.*

IX.
"NOW COMES THE PROPOSITION THAT THE NEGRO IS ENTITLED TO DAMAGES"

In his inaugural year as the governor of Texas, 1995, George W. Bush presided over a government that opened a new prison nearly every week. Under Bush, the state's prison budget rose from $1.4 billion to $2.4 billion, and the total number of prison beds went from about 118,000 to more than 166,000. Almost a decade later Bush, by then the president of the United States, decided that he, and the rest of the country, had made a mistake. "This year, some 600,000 inmates will be released from prison back into society," Bush said during his 2004 State of the Union address. "We know from long experience that if they can't find work, or a home, or help, they are much more likely to commit crime and return to prison."

As we enter the 2016 presidential-election cycle, candidates on both sides of the partisan divide are echoing Bush's call. From the Democratic Socialist Bernie Sanders ("To my mind, it makes eminently more sense to invest in jobs and education, rather than jails

---

* The historical numbers on mass incarceration come from Christopher Muller's 2012 article, "Northward Migration and the Rise of Racial Disparity in American Incarceration, 1880–1950."

and incarceration") to mainstream progressives like Hillary Clinton ("Without the mass incarceration that we currently practice, millions fewer people would be living in poverty") to right-wing Tea Party candidates like Ted Cruz ("Harsh mandatory minimum sentences for nonviolent drug crimes have contributed to prison overpopulation and are both unfair and ineffective"), there is now broad agreement that the sprawling carceral state must be dismantled. Longtime criminal-justice-reform activists who struggled through the tough-on-crime '90s are heartened to see the likes of Koch Industries, a conglomerate owned by patrons of the libertarian right, teaming up with the Center for American Progress, a liberal think tank, in service of decarceration.

But the task is Herculean. The changes needed to achieve an incarceration rate in line with the rest of the developed world are staggering. In 1972, the U.S. incarceration rate was 161 per 100,000—slightly higher than the English and Welsh incarceration rate today (148 per 100,000). To return to that 1972 level, America would have to cut its prison and jail population by some 80 percent. The popular notion that this can largely be accomplished by releasing nonviolent drug offenders is false—as of 2012, 54 percent of all inmates in state prisons had been sentenced for violent offenses. The myth is that "we have a lot of people in prison and a bunch of good guys, and we can easily see the difference between the good guys and the bad guys," says Marie Gottschalk, a political scientist at the University of Pennsylvania and the author of the recent book *Caught: The Prison State and the Lockdown of American Politics.* Her point is that it's often hard to tell a nonviolent offender from a violent offender. Is a marijuana dealer who brandishes a switchblade a violent criminal? How about the getaway driver in an armed robbery? And what if someone now serving time for a minor drug offense has a prior conviction for aggravated assault? One 2004 study found that the proportion of "unambiguously low-level drug offenders" could be less than 6 percent in state prisons and less than 2 percent in federal ones.

Decarceration raises a difficult question: What do we mean by violent crime, and how should it be punished? And what is the moral logic that allows forever banishing the Odell Newtons of America to the Gray Wastes? At the moment, that moral logic, as evidenced by the frequency with which the United States locks up people for life, remains peculiarly American. Some 50 out of every 100,000 Americans are serving a life sentence—which is, Gottschalk notes, a rate "comparable to the incarceration rate for *all* prisoners, including pretrial detainees, in Sweden and other Scandinavian countries." If one purpose of prison is to protect the public, then high rates of life imprisonment make little sense, because offenders, including those convicted of violent crimes, tend to age out of crime. Arguing for leniency toward violent criminals is not easy politically. In many European countries, a ten-year sentence even for a violent crime would seem harsh to citizens, but Gottschalk observes that the fact that American prisons are filled with "lifers and de facto lifers who will likely die in prison" makes the typical European sentence seem lenient to American politicians and their constituents. Thus the initial impediment to undoing mass incarceration in America is not that we don't have the answers for how to treat violent crime—it's that our politics seem allergic to the very question.

The Gray Wastes are a moral abomination for reasons beyond the sheer number of their tenants. In 1970 the national correctional system was much smaller than it is today, but even so, blacks were incarcerated at several times the rate of whites. There is no reason to assume that a smaller correctional system inevitably means a more equitable correctional system. Examining Minnesota's system, Richard S. Frase, a professor of criminal law at the University of Minnesota, found a state whose relatively sane justice policies give it one of the lowest incarceration rates in the country—and yet whose economic disparities give it one of the worst black-white incarceration ratios in the country. Changing criminal-justice policy did very little to change the fact that blacks committed crimes at a higher rate than whites in Minnesota. Why did blacks in Minnesota commit crimes at a higher rate than whites? Because the state's broad racial gulf in criminal offending mirrored another depressing gulf. "The black family poverty rate in Minnesota was over six times higher than the white poverty rate, whereas for the United States as a whole the black poverty rate was 3.4 times higher," Frase writes.*

The lesson of Minnesota is that the chasm in incarceration rates is deeply tied to the socioeconomic chasm between black and white America. The two are self-reinforcing—impoverished black people are more likely to end up in prison, and that experience breeds impoverishment. An array of laws, differing across the country but all emanating from our tendency toward punitive criminal justice—limiting or banning food stamps for drug felons; prohibiting ex-offenders from obtaining public housing—ensure this. So does the rampant discrimination against ex-offenders and black men in general. This, too, is self-reinforcing. The American population most discriminated against is also its most incarcerated—and the incarceration of so many African Americans, the mark of criminality, justifies everything they endure after.

Mass incarceration is, ultimately, a problem of troublesome entanglements. To war seriously against the disparity in unfreedom requires a war against a disparity in resources. And to war against a disparity in resources is to confront a history in which both the plunder and the mass incarceration of blacks are accepted commonplaces. Our current debate over criminal-justice reform pretends that it is possible to disentangle ourselves without significantly disturbing the other aspects of our lives, that one can extract the thread of mass incarceration from the larger tapestry of racist American policy.

---

* Frase published his findings in his 2009 research paper "What Explains Persistent Racial Disproportionality in Minnesota's Prison and Jail Populations?" I first encountered this article in Marie Gottschalk's book *Caught*.

Daniel Patrick Moynihan knew better. His 1965 report on "The Negro Family" was explosive for what it claimed about black mothers and black fathers—but if it had contained all of Moynihan's thinking on the subject, including his policy recommendations, it likely would have been politically nuclear. "Now comes the proposition that the Negro is entitled to damages as to unequal favored treatment—in order to compensate for past unequal treatment of an opposite kind," Moynihan wrote in 1964.* His point was simple, if impolitic: Blacks were suffering from the effects of centuries of ill treatment at the hands of white society. Ending that ill treatment would not be enough; the country would have to make amends for it. "It may be that without unequal treatment in the immediate future there is no way for [African Americans] to achieve anything like equal status in the long run," Moynihan wrote.

As we look ahead to what politicians are now saying will be the end of mass incarceration, we are confronted with the reality of what Moynihan observed in 1965, intensified and compounded by the past fifty years of the carceral state. What of the "damages" wrought by mass incarceration? What of the black men whose wages remained stagnant for decades largely due to our correctional policy? What of the twentieth-century wars on drugs repeatedly pursued on racist grounds, and their devastating effects on black communities? The post-civil-rights consensus aims for the termination of injury. Remedy is beyond our field of vision. When old wounds fester, quackery is prescribed and hoary old fears and insidious old concepts burble to the surface—"matriarchy"; "superpredators"; "bio-underclass." This, too, was part of Moynihan, but it wasn't all of him.

A serious reformation of our carceral policy—one seeking a smaller prison population, and a prison population that looks more

---

* Moynihan's thoughts on "unequal treatment" can be found in an April 20, 1964, outline of a memo to Labor Secretary W. Willard Wirtz.

like America—cannot concern itself merely with sentencing reform, cannot pretend as though the past fifty years of criminal-justice policy did not do real damage. And so it is not possible to truly reform our justice system without reforming the institutional structures, the communities, and the politics that surround it. Robert Sampson argues for "affirmative action for neighborhoods"—reform that would target investment in both persistently poor neighborhoods and the poor individuals living in those neighborhoods. One class of people suffers deprivation at levels above and beyond the rest of the country—the same group that so disproportionately fills our jails and prisons. To pull too energetically on one thread is to tug at the entire tapestry.

Moynihan may have left any recommendations as to "favored treatment" for blacks out of his report. But the question has not disappeared. In fact, it is more urgent than ever. The economic and political marginalization of black people virtually ensured that they would be the ones who would bear the weight of what one of President Nixon's own aides called his "bullshit" crime policy, and thus be fed into the maw of the Gray Wastes. And should crime rates rise again, there is no reason to believe that black people, black communities, black families will not be fed into the great maw again. Indeed, the experience of mass incarceration, the warehousing and deprivation of whole swaths of our country, the transformation of that deprivation into wealth transmitted through government jobs and private investment, the pursuit of the War on Drugs on nakedly racist grounds, have only intensified the ancient American dilemma's white-hot core—the problem of "past unequal treatment," the difficulty of "damages," the question of reparations.

8.

NOTES FROM
THE
EIGHTH YEAR

———

HE CAN'T WIN. THIS IS WHAT THE PRESIDENT OF THE UNITED States told me when we first spoke about Donald Trump. By then we'd spoken a few times off the record, always in groups. Just before *Between the World and Me* was published, I sent a galley through a mutual friend. Obama read it and then months later invited me to the White House for lunch. He was cordial, receptive, and pointed; he immediately fixed in on my critiques of his respectability politics. I told him I'd been raised around similar rhetoric and that I thought it did not always take into consideration the sensitivities and interior lives of black boys in particular. I spoke candidly about his Morehouse speech and why it rankled to see young black men on the day of their graduation being lectured to not make excuses. I do not think I convinced him of much. Still I was impressed that he'd been willing to actually hear me out, taking candor as well as he'd given it.

But what I remember most is the sense of impossibility with which Obama regarded the Trump presidency. I confess to basically feeling the same. It seemed to me that white people, if only out of an instinct for self-preservation, would reject Donald Trump. If there was a difference between me and the president, it was that I thought Trump wouldn't win, whereas Obama thought, categorically, that he couldn't. What amazes me thinking back on that day is the ease with which two people, knowing full well what this country is capable of, dismissed the possibility of a return to the old form.

But it's easy to understand Obama's dismissal. He saw America through both black and immigrant eyes. The country still was a place of wonder for him. His hero was Abraham Lincoln, a man who rose out of the Illinois backwater to become, if not an implacable foe of white supremacy, one worthy of being shot in the head over its defense.

I also felt a sense of wonder. Eight years prior, I'd been plucked by fate from the roiling sea. From dry land it is natural to look at the world around you, and maybe even the country around you, and credit it with something beyond its sins. It is not solely a romantic notion. As much I loved the culture of France, and I did, I knew that I was lucky not to have been born there. Their particular philosophy of merit, the intense focus on grades and tests, the rigid class stratification, would have made my story impossible. It is, I think, the very chaos of America that allowed me to prosper. I could come to New York and declare myself a writer, and while a degree from Harvard might have helped, it was not essential. The chaos of America, and perhaps more aptly the chaos of New York, made it seem that anything could happen. Often that meant the worst. But sometimes it meant the best. I suspect, though I do not know, that the lack of both ceilings and safety nets is how we got a black president. I suspect it is how, at least for these eight years, I came to thrive.

I had started in an unemployment office. I had started with the refuse of failure—a reporter's pad half-filled with notes on some soon-to-be-disgraced entertainer—had graduated to a blog written for the amusement of my father and myself, had assembled a horde of post-docs, nerds, and feminists to enlighten me, and on their wisdom had been throttled into this odd world of awards, fellowships, and praise. I do not mean to sound so passive. But my struggle is to remain conscious, to remember the gifts of so many out there, treading, drowning. And the praise will make you forget all that, will convince you of your own special nature, instead of reminding you that you had the great fortune of living and writing in the most incredible of eras—the era of a black president.

I am trying to record this story, and remember that it is only partially mine. I am trying to remember that the best can happen to you in one moment and the worst can happen to your country in the next, and even still you can allow yourself to forget, get lost in your own story and forget that this really is chaos. I think we all should have known better. Trump did not spring out of nothingness but from the eight years of crazy, from the hawking of Obama-waffles to shouts of "You lie," from WHITE SLAVERY banners to Obama-phone plots, from chimpanzee memes to watermelon-at-the-White-House jokes. The former speaker of the House John Boehner claimed Obama had "never had a real job"—and Boehner was said to be one of the sane ones. Newt Gingrich called Obama the "food-stamp president"—and he was said to be one of the smart ones. I can't say I knew white people would elect Donald Trump—and that is who did it—but I did not put it past them.

Among the many things I wanted to understand about Obama was why he did. For two years, before we'd met for lunch, I'd inquired about the possibility of interviewing him. We'd spoken only during the few off-the-record briefings he'd hosted. But as I looked to the end of his term, I hoped he'd entertain a longer conversation. As proud as I was of "Fear of a Black President," it had always bothered me that the piece was more a work of ideas than reporting, and whatever grounding it enjoyed did not come from the man it sought to analyze. There had always been two facets to my identity as a writer: an essayist and a features writer. In the first style I impose myself on the work—I drive the narrative. In the second, I follow the narrative through my subject. But features work best when you have access. Without it, I tended to float into the realm of essay. I thought I was at my best when I could combine the reporting and the essay. "The Case for Reparations" is, for that reason, the best piece in this volume to my mind. But the second-best piece, to me, is the article that follows—"My President Was Black"—because of the access the president eventually agreed to grant. This was not easily accomplished. Someone was going to write a big "Obama and race" story in that last year and there was some suspicion among people in his camp that, given my previous criticism, I was the wrong journalist for that story. But at the end of the lunch, he had told me he'd like to speak again, in some public forum, in the same way we'd spoken that afternoon. In his mind, this would be post-presidency. I was thinking a little sooner.

Obama agreed to be interviewed for "My President Was Black," a piece that felt to me not just like the end of an era for the president but also the end of one for me. *Between the World and Me* had made my personal invitation to the White House possible and thus made "My President Was Black" possible. The challenge here was not in the interviewing but in finding that quiet space I'd occupied to write all of my previous pieces. I needed to find some way to withdraw from the world, to ignore every critique of my writing I'd (mistakenly) read, and to not forget my own voice. This was very different from my days as a blogger, when I thrived amid the noise, when the interactions I'd had sharpened me. This was the first piece I'd written that was not crafted as a student in the crowd. It was not that I ended the process of criticism and conversation; I simply shrank that interaction down to people I directly knew and respected. Likely, I lost something in that shift. But I was coming to understand that losing things, too, was part of the journey.

At the same time, "My President Was Black" drew on all of

those earlier conversations I'd had on the blog and all the books I'd read springing from those interactions. In that sense, not everything was lost. And it was the first piece I wrote where I felt I was not engaging the questions that had so initially provoked me. I believed that the answer to the question of the color line was right in front of us. Rob a people generationally and there will be effects. I also understood why that answer, barring extreme external events, would never be accepted and reckoned with. It simply broke too much of America's sense of its own identity. So I felt after this last piece that I was done arguing. I was resigned. I was at peace.

When I think about what comes next, I think about fighting to remain in that place. I think of the freedom I felt writing "My President Was Black"—the chance to sit back and tell a story as it unfolded, as opposed to imposing myself and my opinions on my writing. True, a writer's opinions and subjectivity are always in the work—even for novelists and poets—but I think I prefer to have them in the background, operating as subtext. There's something inherently beautiful about a story, in its ability to make more powerful arguments than an explicit polemic. And there is something demeaning about repeatedly yelling "I am a human" in a world premised on denying that fact.

I don't ever want to lose sight of how short my time is here. And I don't ever want to forget that resistance must be its own reward, since resistance, at least within the life span of the resistors, almost always fails. I don't ever want to forget, even with whatever personal victories I achieve, even in the victories we achieve as a people or a nation, that the larger story of America and the world probably does not end well. Our story is a tragedy. I know it sounds odd, but that belief does not depress me. It focuses me. After all, I am an atheist and thus do not believe anything, even a strongly held belief, is destiny. And if tragedy is to be proven wrong, if there really is hope out there, I think it can only be made manifest by remembering the cost of it being proven right. No one—not our fathers, not our police, and not our gods—is coming to save us. The worst really is possible. My aim is to never be caught, as the rappers say, acting like it can't happen. And my ambition is to write both in defiance of tragedy and in blindness of its possibility, to keep screaming into the waves—just as my ancestors did.

MY PRESIDENT
WAS BLACK

"They're a rotten crowd," I shouted across the lawn.
"You're worth the whole damn bunch put together."
—F. SCOTT FITZGERALD, *The Great Gatsby*

I.
"LOVE WILL MAKE YOU DO WRONG"

IN THE WANING DAYS OF PRESIDENT BARACK OBAMA'S ADministration, he and his wife, Michelle, hosted a farewell party, the full import of which no one could then grasp. It was late October, Friday the 21st, and the president had spent many of the previous weeks, as he would spend the two subsequent weeks, campaigning for the Democratic presidential nominee, Hillary Clinton. Things were looking up. Polls in the crucial states of Virginia and Pennsylvania showed Clinton with solid advantages. The formidable GOP strongholds of Georgia and Texas were said to be under threat. The moment seemed to buoy Obama. He had been light on his feet in these last few weeks, cracking jokes at the expense of Republican opponents and laughing off hecklers. At a rally in Orlando on October 28, he greeted a student who would be introducing him by dancing toward her and then noting that the song playing over the loudspeakers—the Gap Band's "Outstanding"—was older than she was. "This is classic!" he said. Then he flashed the smile that had launched America's first black presidency, and started dancing again. Three months still remained before Inauguration Day, but staffers had already begun to count down the days. They did this with a mix of pride and longing—like college seniors in early May. They had no sense of the world they were graduating into. None of us did.

The farewell party, presented by BET (Black Entertainment Television), was the last in a series of concerts the first couple had hosted at the White House. Guests were asked to arrive at 5:30 P.M. By 6, two long lines stretched behind the Treasury Building, where the Secret Service was checking names. The people in these lines were, in the main, black, and their humor reflected it. The brisker queue was dubbed the "good-hair line" by one guest, and there was laughter at the prospect of the Secret Service subjecting us all to a "brown-paper-bag test." This did not come to pass, but security was tight. Several guests were told to stand in a makeshift pen and wait to have their backgrounds checked a second time.

Dave Chappelle was there. He coolly explained the peril and promise of comedy in what was then still only a remotely potential Donald Trump presidency: "I mean, we never had a guy have his own pussygate scandal." Everyone laughed. A few weeks later, he would be roundly criticized for telling a crowd at the Cutting Room, in New York, that he had voted for Clinton but did not feel good about it. "She's going to be on a coin someday," Chappelle said. "And her behavior has not been coinworthy." But on this crisp October night, everything felt inevitable and grand. There was a slight wind. It had been in the 80s for much of that week. Now, as the sun set, the season remembered its name. Women shivered in their cocktail dresses. Gentlemen chivalrously handed over their suit coats. But when Naomi Campbell strolled past the security pen in a sleeveless number, she seemed as invulnerable as ever.

Cellphones were confiscated to prevent surreptitious recordings from leaking out. (This effort was unsuccessful. The next day, a partygoer would tweet a video of the leader of the free world dancing to Drake's "Hotline Bling.") After withstanding the barrage of security, guests were welcomed into the East Wing of the White House, and then ushered back out into the night, where they boarded a succession of orange-and-green trolleys. The singer and actress Janelle Monáe, her famous and fantastic pompadour preceding her, stepped on board and joked with a companion about the historical import of "sitting in the back of the bus." She took a seat three rows from the front and hummed into the night. The trolley dropped the guests on the South Lawn, in front of a giant tent. The South Lawn's fountain was lit up with blue lights. The White House proper loomed like a ghost in the distance. I heard the band, inside, beginning to play Al Green's "Let's Stay Together."

"Well, you can tell what type of night this is," Obama said from the stage, opening the event. "Not the usual ruffles and flourishes!"

The crowd roared.

"This must be a BET event!"

The crowd roared louder still.

Obama placed the concert in the White House's musical tradition, noting that guests of the Kennedys had once done the twist at the residence—"the twerking of their time," he said, before adding, "There will be no twerking tonight. At least not by me."

The Obamas are fervent and eclectic music fans. In the past eight years, they have hosted performances at the White House by everyone from Mavis Staples to Bob Dylan to Tony Bennett to the Blind Boys of Alabama. After the rapper Common was invited to perform in 2011, a small fracas ensued in the right-wing media. He performed anyway—and was invited back again this glorious fall evening and almost stole the show. The crowd sang along to the hook for his hit ballad "The Light." And when he brought on the gospel singer Yolanda Adams to fill in for John Legend on the Oscar-winning song "Glory," glee turned to rapture.

De La Soul was there. The hip-hop trio had come of age as boyish B-boys with Gumby-style high-top fades. Now they moved across the stage with a lovely mix of lethargy and grace, like your favorite uncle making his way down the Soul Trainline, wary of throwing out a hip. I felt a sense of victory watching them rock the crowd, all while keeping it in the pocket. The victory belonged to hip-hop—an art form birthed in the burning Bronx and now standing full grown, at the White House, unbroken and unedited. Usher led the crowd in a call-and-response: "Say it loud, I'm black and I'm proud." Jill Scott showed off her operatic chops. Bell Biv DeVoe, contemporaries of De La, made history with their performance by surely becoming the first group to suggest to a presidential audience that one should "never trust a big butt and a smile."

The ties between the Obama White House and the hip-hop community are genuine. The Obamas are social with Beyoncé and Jay-Z. They hosted Chance the Rapper and Frank Ocean at a state dinner, and last year invited Swizz Beatz, Busta Rhymes, and Ludacris, among others, to discuss criminal-justice reform and other initiatives. Obama once stood in the Rose Garden passing large flash cards to the *Hamilton* creator and rapper Lin-Manuel Miranda, who then freestyled using each word on the cards. "Drop the beat," Obama said, inaugurating the session. At fifty-five, Obama is younger than pioneering hip-hop artists like Afrika Bambaataa, DJ Kool Herc, and Kurtis Blow. If Obama's enormous symbolic power draws primarily from being the country's first black president, it also draws from his membership in hip-hop's foundational generation.

That night, the men were sharp in their gray or black suits and optional ties. Those who were not in suits had chosen to make a statement, like the dark-skinned young man who strolled in, sockless, with blue jeans cuffed so as to accentuate his gorgeous black-suede loafers. Everything in his ensemble seemed to say, "My fellow Americans, do not try this at home." There were women in fur jackets and high heels; others with sculpted naturals, the sides shaved close, the tops blooming into curls; others still in gold bamboo earrings and long blond dreads. When the actor Jesse Williams took the stage, seemingly awed before such black excellence, before such black opulence, assembled just feet from where slaves had once toiled, he simply said, "Look where we are. Look where we are right now."

This would not happen again, and everyone knew it. It was not just that there might never be another African American president of the United States. It was the feeling that this particular black family, the Obamas, represented the best of black people, the ultimate credit to the race, incomparable in elegance and bearing. "There are no more," the comedian Sinbad joked back in 2010. "There are no black men raised in Kansas and Hawaii. That's the last one. Y'all better treat this one right. The next one gonna be from Cleveland. He gonna wear a perm. Then you gonna see what it's really like." Throughout their residency, the Obamas had refrained from showing America "what it's really like," and had instead followed the first lady's motto, "When they go low, we go high." This was the ideal—black and graceful under fire—saluted that evening. The president was lionized as "our crown jewel." The first lady was praised as the woman "who put the O in Obama."

Barack Obama's victories in 2008 and 2012 were dismissed by some of his critics as merely symbolic for African Americans. But there is nothing "mere" about symbols. The power embedded in the word *nigger* is also symbolic. Burning crosses do not literally raise the black poverty rate, and the Confederate flag does not directly expand the wealth gap.

Much as the unbroken ranks of forty-three white male presidents communicated that the highest office of government in the country—indeed, the most powerful political office in the world—was off-limits to black individuals, the election of Barack Obama communicated that the prohibition had been lifted. It communicated much more. Before Obama triumphed in 2008, the most famous depictions of black success tended to be entertainers or athletes. But Obama had shown that it was "possible to be smart and cool at the same damn time," as Jesse Williams put it at the BET party. Moreover, he had not embarrassed his people with a string of scandals. Against the specter of black pathology, against the narrow images of welfare moms and deadbeat dads, his time in the White House had been an eight-year showcase of a healthy and successful black family spanning three generations, with two dogs to boot. In short, he became a symbol of black people's everyday, extraordinary Americanness.

Whiteness in America is a different symbol—a badge of advantage. In a country of professed meritocratic competition, this badge has long ensured an unerring privilege, represented in a 220-year monopoly on the highest office in the land. For some not-insubstantial sector of the country, the elevation of Barack Obama communicated that the power of the badge had diminished. For eight long years, the badge-holders watched him. They saw footage of the president throwing bounce passes and shooting jumpers. They saw him enter a locker room, give a businesslike handshake to a white staffer, and then greet Kevin Durant with something more soulful. They saw his wife dancing with Jimmy Fallon and posing, resplendent, on the covers of magazines that had, only a decade earlier, been almost exclusively, if unofficially, reserved for ladies imbued with the great power of the badge.

For the preservation of the badge, insidious rumors were concocted to denigrate the first black White House. Obama gave free cellphones to disheveled welfare recipients. Obama went to Europe and complained that "ordinary men and women are too small-minded to govern their own affairs." Obama had inscribed an Arabic saying on his wedding ring, then stopped wearing the ring, in observance of Ramadan. He canceled the National Day of Prayer; refused to sign certificates for Eagle Scouts; faked his attendance at Columbia University; and used a teleprompter to address a group of elementary school students. The badge-holders fumed. They wanted their country back. And, though no one at the farewell party knew it, in a couple of weeks they would have it.

On this October night, though, the stage belonged to another America. At the end of the party, Obama looked out into the crowd, searching for Dave Chappelle. "Where's Dave?" he cried. And then, finding him, the president referenced Chappelle's legendary Brooklyn concert. "You got your block party. I got my block party." Then the band struck up Al Green's "Love and Happiness"—the evening's theme. The president danced in a line next to Ronnie DeVoe. Together they mouthed the lyrics: "Make you do right. Love will make you do wrong."

II.
HE WALKED ON ICE BUT NEVER FELL

Last spring, I went to the White House to meet the president for lunch. I arrived slightly early and sat in the waiting area. I was introduced to a deaf woman who worked as the president's receptionist, a black woman who worked in the press office, a Muslim woman in a head scarf who worked on the National Security Council, and an Iranian American woman who worked as a personal aide to the president. This receiving party represented a healthy cross section of the people Donald Trump had been mocking, and would continue to spend his campaign mocking. At the time, the president seemed untroubled by Trump. When I told Obama that I thought Trump's candidacy was an explicit reaction to the fact of a black president, he said he could see that, but then enumerated other explanations. When assessing Trump's chances, he was direct: He couldn't win.

This assessment was born out of the president's innate optimism and unwavering faith in the ultimate wisdom of the American people—the same traits that had propelled his unlikely five-year ascent from Illinois state senator to U.S. senator to leader of the free world. The speech that launched his rise, the keynote address at the 2004 Democratic National Convention, emerged right from this logic. He addressed himself to his "fellow Americans, Democrats, Republicans, independents," all of whom, he insisted, were more united than they had been led to believe. America was home to devout worshippers and Little League coaches in blue states, civil libertarians and "gay friends" in red states. The presumably white "counties around Chicago" did not want their taxes burned on welfare, but they didn't want them wasted on a bloated Pentagon budget either. Inner-city black families, no matter their perils, understood "that government alone can't teach our kids to learn . . . that children can't achieve unless we raise their expectations and turn off the television sets and eradicate the slander that says a black youth with a book is acting white."

Perceived differences were the work of "spinmasters and negative-ad peddlers who embrace the politics of 'anything goes.'" Real America had no use for such categorizations. By Obama's lights, there was no liberal America, no conservative America, no black America, no white America, no Latino America, no Asian America, only "the United States of America." All these disparate strands of the American experience were bound together by a common hope:

> It's the hope of slaves sitting around a fire singing freedom songs; the hope of immigrants setting out for distant shores; the hope of a young naval lieutenant bravely patrolling the Mekong Delta; the hope of a mill worker's son who dares to defy the odds; the hope of a skinny kid with a funny name who believes that America has a place for him, too.

This speech ran counter to the history of the people it sought to address. Some of those same immigrants had firebombed the homes of the children of those same slaves. That young naval lieutenant was an imperial agent for a failed, immoral war. American division was real. In 2004, John Kerry did not win a single southern state. But Obama appealed to a belief in innocence—in particular a white innocence—that ascribed the country's historical errors more to misunderstanding and the work of a small cabal than to any deliberate malevolence or widespread racism. America was good. America was great.

Over the next twelve years, I came to regard Obama as a skilled politician, a deeply moral human being, and one of the greatest presidents in American history. He was phenomenal—the most agile interpreter and navigator of the color line I had ever seen. He had an ability to emote a deep and sincere connection to the hearts of black people, while never doubting the hearts of white people. This was the core of his 2004 keynote, and it marked his historic race speech during the 2008 campaign at Philadelphia's National Constitution Center—and blinded him to the appeal of Trump. ("As a general proposition, it's hard to run for president by telling people how terrible things are," Obama once said to me.)

But if the president's inability to cement his legacy in the form of Hillary Clinton proved the limits of his optimism, it also revealed the exceptional nature of his presidential victories. For eight years Barack Obama walked on ice and never fell. Nothing in that time suggested that straight talk on the facts of racism in American life would have given him surer footing.

I HAD MET THE PRESIDENT a few times before. In his second term, I'd written articles criticizing him for his overriding trust in colorblind policy and his embrace of "personal responsibility" rhetoric when speaking to African Americans. I saw him as playing both sides. He would invoke his identity as a president of all people to decline to advocate for black policy—and then invoke his black identity to lecture black people for continuing to "make bad choices." In response, Obama had invited me, along with other journalists, to the White House for off-the-record conversations. I attempted to press my points in these sessions. My efforts were laughable and ineffective. I was always inappropriately dressed, and inappropriately calibrated in tone: In one instance, I was too deferential; in another, too bellicose. I was discombobulated by fear—not by fear of the power of his office (though that is a fearsome and impressive thing) but by fear of his obvious brilliance. It is said that Obama speaks "professorially," a fact that understates the quickness and agility of his mind. These were not like press conferences—the president would speak in depth and with great familiarity about a range of subjects. Once, I watched him effortlessly reply to queries covering everything from electoral politics to the American economy to environmental policy. And then he turned to me. I thought of George Foreman, who once booked an exhibition with multiple opponents in which he pounded five straight journeymen—and I suddenly had some idea of how it felt to be the last of them.

Last spring, we had a light lunch. We talked casually and candidly. He talked about the brilliance of LeBron James and Stephen Curry—not as basketball talents but as grounded individuals. I asked him whether he was angry at his father, who had abandoned him at a young age to move back to Kenya, and whether that motivated any of his rhetoric. He said it did not, and he credited the attitude of his mother and grandparents for this. Then it was my turn to be autobiographical. I told him that I had heard the kind of "straighten up" talk he had been giving to black youth, for instance in his 2013 Morehouse commencement address, all my life. I told him that I thought it was not sensitive to the inner turmoil that can be obscured by the hardness kids often evince. I told him I thought this because I had once been one of those kids. He seemed to concede this point, but I couldn't tell whether it mattered to him. Nonetheless, he agreed to a series of more formal conversations on this and other topics.

The improbability of a black president had once been so strong that its most vivid representations were comedic. Witness Dave Chappelle's profane Black Bush from the early 2000s ("This nigger very possibly has weapons of mass destruction! I can't sleep on that!") or Richard Pryor's black president in the 1970s promising black astronauts and black quarterbacks ("Ever since the Rams got rid of James Harris, my jaw's been uptight!"). In this model, so potent is the force of blackness that the presidency is forced to conform to it. But once the notion advanced out of comedy and into reality, the opposite proved to be true.

Obama's DNC speech is the key. It does not belong to the literature of "the struggle"; it belongs to the literature of prospective presidents—men (as it turns out) who speak not to gravity and reality, but to aspirations and dreams. When Lincoln invoked the dream of a nation "conceived in liberty" and pledged to the ideal that "all men are created equal," he erased the near-extermination of one people and the enslavement of another. When Roosevelt told the country that "the only thing we have to fear is fear itself," he invoked the dream of American omnipotence and boundless capability. But black people, then living under a campaign of terror for more than half a century, had quite a bit to fear, and Roosevelt could not save them. The dream Ronald Reagan invoked in 1984— that "it's morning again in America"—meant nothing to the inner cities, besieged as they were by decades of redlining policies, not to mention crack and Saturday night specials. Likewise, Obama's keynote address conflated the slave and the nation of immigrants who profited from him. To reinforce the majoritarian dream, the nightmare endured by the minority is erased. That is the tradition to which the "skinny kid with a funny name" who would be president belonged. It is also the only tradition in existence that could have possibly put a black person in the White House.

Obama's embrace of white innocence was demonstrably necessary as a matter of political survival. Whenever he attempted to buck this directive, he was disciplined. His mild objection to the arrest of Henry Louis Gates Jr. in 2009 contributed to his declining favorability numbers among whites—still a majority of voters. His comments after the killing of Trayvon Martin—"If I had a son, he'd look like Trayvon"—helped make that tragedy a rallying point for people who did not care about Martin's killer as much as they cared about finding ways to oppose the president. Michael Tesler, a political science professor at UC Irvine, has studied the effect of Obama's race on the American electorate. "No other factor, in fact, came close to dividing the Democratic primary electorate as powerfully as their feelings about African Americans," he and his co-author, David O. Sears, concluded in their book *Obama's Race: The 2008 Election and the Dream of a Post-Racial America.* "The impact of racial attitudes on individual vote decisions . . . was so strong that it appears to have even outstripped the substantive impact of racial attitudes on Jesse Jackson's more racially charged campaign for the nomination in 1988." When Tesler looked at the 2012 campaign in his second book, *Post-Racial or Most-Racial? Race and Politics in the Obama Era,* very little had improved. Analyzing the extent to which racial attitudes affected people associated with Obama during the 2012 election, Tesler concluded that "racial attitudes spilled over from Barack Obama into mass assessments of Mitt Romney, Joe Biden, Hillary Clinton, Charlie Crist, and even the Obama family's dog Bo."

Yet despite this entrenched racial resentment, and in the face of complete resistance by congressional Republicans, overtly launched from the moment Obama arrived in the White House, the president accomplished major feats. He remade the nation's healthcare system. He revitalized a Justice Department that vigorously investigated police brutality and discrimination, and he began dismantling the private-prison system for federal inmates. Obama nominated the first Latina justice to the Supreme Court, gave presidential support to marriage equality, and ended the U.S. military's Don't Ask, Don't Tell policy, thus honoring the civil rights tradition that had inspired him. And if his very existence inflamed America's racist conscience, it also expanded the country's antiracist imagination. Millions of young people now know their only president to have been an African American. Writing for *The New*

Yorker, Jelani Cobb once noted that "until there was a black Presidency it was impossible to conceive of the limitations of one." This is just as true of the possibilities. In 2014, the Obama administration committed itself to reversing the War on Drugs through the power of presidential commutation. The administration said that it could commute the sentences of as many as ten thousand prisoners. As of November, the president had commuted only 944 sentences. By any measure, Obama's effort fell woefully short, except for this small one: the measure of almost every other modern president who preceded him. Obama's 944 commutations are the most in nearly a century—and more than the past eleven presidents' combined.

Obama was born into a country where laws barring his very conception—let alone his ascendancy to the presidency—had long stood in force. A black president would always be a contradiction for a government that, throughout most of its history, had oppressed black people. The attempt to resolve this contradiction through Obama—a black man with deep roots in the white world—was remarkable. The price it exacted, incredible. The world it gave way to, unthinkable.

III.
"I DECIDED TO BECOME PART OF THAT WORLD"

When Barack Obama was ten, his father gave him a basketball, a gift that connected the two directly. Obama was born in 1961 in Hawaii and raised by his mother, Ann Dunham, who was white, and her parents, Stanley and Madelyn. They loved him ferociously, supported him emotionally, and encouraged him intellectually. They also told him he was black. Ann gave him books to read about famous black people. When Obama's mother had begun dating his father, the news had not been greeted with the threat of lynching (as it might have been in various parts of the continental United

States), and Obama's grandparents always spoke positively of his father. This biography makes Obama nearly unique among black people of his era.

In the president's memoir *Dreams from My Father,* he says he was not an especially talented basketball player, but he played with a consuming passion. That passion was directed at something more than just the mastering of the pick-and-roll or the perfecting of his jump shot. Obama came of age during the time of the University of Hawaii basketball team's "Fabulous Five"—a name given to its all-black starting five, two decades before it would be resurrected at the University of Michigan by the likes of Chris Webber and Jalen Rose. In his memoir, Obama writes that he would watch the University of Hawaii players laughing at "some inside joke," winking "at the girls on the sidelines," or "casually flipping lay-ups." What Obama saw in the Fabulous Five was not just game, but a culture he found attractive:

> By the time I reached high school, I was playing on Punahou's teams, and could take my game to the university courts, where a handful of black men, mostly gym rats and has-beens, would teach me an attitude that didn't just have to do with the sport. That respect came from what you did and not who your daddy was. That you could talk stuff to rattle an opponent, but that you should shut the hell up if you couldn't back it up. That you didn't let anyone sneak up behind you to see emotions—like hurt or fear—you didn't want them to see.

These are lessons, particularly the last one, that for black people apply as much on the street as they do on the court. Basketball was a link for Obama, a medium for downloading black culture from the mainland that birthed the Fabulous Five. Assessing his own thought process at the time, Obama writes, "I decided to become part of that world." This is one of the most incredible sentences ever written in the long, decorated history of black memoir, if only because very few black people have ever enjoyed enough power to write it.

Historically, in black autobiography, to be remanded into the black race has meant exposure to a myriad of traumas, often commencing in childhood. Frederick Douglass is separated from his grandmother. The enslaved Harriet Ann Jacobs must constantly cope with the threat of rape before she escapes. After telling his teacher he wants to be a lawyer, Malcolm X is told that the job isn't for "niggers." Black culture often serves as the balm for such traumas, or even the means to resist them. Douglass finds the courage to face the "slave-breaker" Edward Covey after being given an allegedly enchanted root by "a genuine African" possessing powers from "the eastern nations." Malcolm X's dancing connects him to his "long-suppressed African instincts." If black racial identity speaks to all the things done to people of recent African ancestry, black cultural identity was created in response to them. The division is not neat; the two are linked, and it is incredibly hard to be a full participant in the world of cultural identity without experiencing the trauma of racial identity.

Obama is somewhat different. He writes of bloodying the nose of a white kid who called him a "coon," and of chafing at racist remarks from a tennis coach, and of feeling offended after a white woman in his apartment building told the manager that he was following her. But the kinds of traumas that marked African Americans of his generation—beatings at the hands of racist police, being herded into poor schools, grinding out a life in a tenement building—were mostly abstract for him. Moreover, the kind of spatial restriction that most black people feel at an early age—having rocks thrown at you for being on the wrong side of the tracks, for instance—was largely absent from his life. In its place, Obama was gifted with a well-stamped passport and admittance to elite private schools—all of which spoke of other identities, other lives and other worlds where the color line was neither determinative nor especially relevant. Obama could have grown into a raceless cosmopolitan. Surely he would have lived in a world of problems, but problems not embodied by him.

Instead, he decided to enter this world.

"I always felt as if being black was cool," Obama told me while traveling to a campaign event. He was sitting on Air Force One, his tie loosened, his shirtsleeves rolled up. "[Being black] was not something to run away from but something to embrace. Why that is, I think, is complicated. Part of it is I think that my mother thought black folks were cool, and if your mother loves you and is praising you—and says you look good, are smart—as you are, then you don't kind of think in terms of *How can I avoid this?* You feel pretty good about it."

As a child, Obama's embrace of blackness was facilitated, not impeded, by white people. Obama's mother pointed him toward the history and culture of African Americans. Stanley, his grandfather, who came originally from Kansas, took him to basketball games at the University of Hawaii, as well as to black bars. Stanley introduced him to the black writer Frank Marshall Davis. The facilitation was as much indirect as direct. Obama recalls watching his grandfather at those black bars and understanding that "most of the people in the bar weren't there out of choice," and that "our presence there felt forced." From his mother's life of extensive travel, he learned to value the significance of having a home.

That suspicion of rootlessness extends throughout *Dreams from My Father*. He describes integration as a "one-way street" on which black people are asked to abandon themselves to fully experience America's benefits. Confronted with a woman named Joyce, a mixed-race, green-eyed college classmate who insists that she is not "black" but "multiracial," Obama is scornful. "That was the problem with people like Joyce," he writes. "They talked about the richness of their multicultural heritage and it sounded real good, until you noticed that they avoided black people." Later in the memoir, Obama tells the story of falling in love with a white woman. During a visit to her family's country house, he found himself in the library, which was filled with pictures of the woman's illustrious relations. But instead of being in awe, Obama realized that he and the woman lived in different worlds. "And I knew that if we stayed together, I'd eventually live in hers," he writes. "Between the two of us, I was the one who knew how to live as an outsider."

After college, Obama found a home, as well as a sense of himself, working on the South Side of Chicago as a community organizer. "When I started doing that work, my story merges with a larger story. That happens naturally for a John Lewis," he told me, referring to the civil rights hero and Democratic congressman. "That happens more naturally for you. It was less obvious to me. How do I pull all these different strains together: Kenya and Hawaii and Kansas, and white and black and Asian—how does that fit? And through action, through work, I suddenly see myself as part of the bigger process for, yes, delivering justice for the [African American community] and specifically the South Side community, the low-income people—justice on behalf of the African American community. But also thereby promoting my ideas of justice and equality and empathy that my mother taught me were universal. So I'm in a position to understand those essential parts of me not as separate and apart from any particular community but connected to every community. And I can fit the African American struggle for freedom and justice in the context of the universal aspiration for freedom and justice."

Throughout Obama's 2008 campaign and into his presidency, this attitude proved key to his deep support in the black community. African Americans, weary of high achievers who distanced themselves from their black roots, understood that Obama had paid a price for checking "black" on his census form, and for living black, for hosting Common, for brushing dirt off his shoulder during the primaries, for marrying a woman who looked like Michelle Obama. If women, as a gender, must suffer the constant evaluations and denigrations of men, black women must suffer that, plus a broad dismissal from the realm of what American society deems to be beautiful. But Michelle Obama is beautiful in the way that black people know themselves to be. Her prominence as first lady directly attacks a poison that diminishes black girls from the moment they are capable of opening a magazine or turning on a television.

The South Side of Chicago, where Obama began his political career, is home to arguably the most prominent and storied black political establishment in the country. In addition to Oscar Stanton De Priest, the first African American elected to Congress in the twentieth century, the South Side produced the city's first black mayor, Harold Washington; Jesse Jackson, who twice ran for president; and Carol Moseley Braun, the first African American woman to win a Senate race. These victories helped give rise to Obama's own. Harold Washington served as an inspiration to Obama and looms heavily over the Chicago section of *Dreams from My Father*.

Washington forged the kind of broad coalition that Obama would later assemble nationally. But Washington did this in the mid-1980s in segregated Chicago, and he had not had the luxury, as Obama did, of becoming black with minimal trauma. "There was an edge to Harold that frightened some white voters," David Axelrod, who worked for both Washington and Obama, told me recently. Axelrod recalled sitting around a conference table with Washington after he had won the Democratic primary for his reelection in 1987, just as the mayor was about to hold a press conference. Washington asked what percentage of Chicago's white vote he'd received. "And someone said, 'Well, you got 21 percent. And that's really good because last time' "—in his successful 1983 mayoral campaign—" 'you only got 8,' " Axelrod recalled. "And he kind of smiled, sadly, and said, 'You know, I probably spent 70 percent of my time in those white neighborhoods, and I think I've been a good mayor for everybody, and I got 21 percent of the white vote and we think it's good.' And he just kind of shook his head and said, 'Ain't it a bitch to be a black man in the land of the free and the home of the brave?'

"That was Harold. He felt those things. He had fought in an all-black unit in World War II. He had come up in times—and that and the sort of indignities of what you had to do to come up through the machine really seared him." During his 1983 mayoral campaign, Washington was loudly booed outside a church in northwest Chicago by middle-class Poles, Italians, and Irish, who feared blacks would uproot them. "It was as vicious and ugly as anything you would have seen in the old South," Axelrod said.

Obama's ties to the South Side tradition that Washington represented were complicated. Like Washington, Obama attempted to forge a coalition between black South Siders and the broader community. But Obama, despite his adherence to black cultural mores, was, with his Kansan and Hawaiian roots, his Ivy League pedigree, and his ties to the University of Chicago, still an exotic out-of-towner. "They were a bit skeptical of him," says Salim Muwakkil, a journalist who has covered Obama since before his days in the Illinois state Senate. "Chicago is a very insular community, and he came from nowhere, seemingly."

Obama compounded people's suspicions by refusing to humble himself and go along with the political currents of the South Side. "A lot of the politicians, especially the black ones, were just leery of him," Kaye Wilson, the godmother to Obama's children and one of the president's earliest political supporters, told me recently.

But even as many in the black political community were skeptical of Obama, others encouraged him—sometimes when they voted against him. When Obama lost the 2000 Democratic primary race against Bobby Rush, the African American incumbent congressman representing Illinois' First Congressional District, the then-still-obscure future president experienced the defeat as having to do more with his age than his exoticism. "I'd go meet people and I'd knock on doors and stuff, and some of the grandmothers who were the folks I'd been organizing and working with doing community stuff, they weren't parroting back some notion of 'You're too Harvard,' or 'You're too Hyde Park,' or what have you,"

Obama told me. "They'd say, 'You're a wonderful young man, you're going to do great things. You just have to be patient.' So I didn't feel the loss as a rejection by black people. I felt the loss as 'politics anywhere is tough.' Politics in Chicago is especially tough. And being able to break through in the African American community is difficult because of the enormous loyalty that people feel towards anybody who has been around awhile."

There was no one around to compete for loyalty when Obama ran for the Senate in 2004, or for president in 2008. He was no longer competing against other African Americans; he was representing them. "He had that hybridity which told the 'do-gooders'—in Chicago they call the reformers the do-gooders—that he was acceptable," Muwakkil told me.

Obama ran for the Senate two decades after the death of Harold Washington. Axelrod checked in on the precinct where Washington had been so loudly booed by white Chicagoans. "Obama carried, against seven candidates for the Senate, almost the entire northwest side and that precinct," he said. "And I told him, 'Harold's smiling down on us tonight.'"

Obama believes that his statewide victory for the Illinois Senate seat held particular portent for the events of 2008. "Illinois is the most demographically representative state in the country," he told me. "If you took all the percentages of black, white, Latino; rural, urban; agricultural, manufacturing—[if] you took that cross section across the country and you shrank it, it would be Illinois."

Illinois effectively allowed Obama to play a scrimmage before the big national game in 2008. "When I ran for the Senate I had to go into southern Illinois, downstate Illinois, farming communities— some with very tough racial histories, some areas where there just were no African Americans of any number," Obama told me. "And when we won that race, not just an African American from Chicago, but an African American with an exotic history and [the] name Barack Hussein Obama, [it showed that I] could connect with and appeal to a much broader audience."

The mix of Obama's "hybridity" and the changing times allowed him to extend his appeal beyond the white ethnic corners of Chicago, past the downstate portions of Illinois, and out into the country at large. "Ben Nelson, one of the most conservative Democrats in the Senate, from Nebraska, would only bring in one national Democrat to campaign for him," Obama recalls. "And it was me. And so part of the reason I was willing to run [for president in 2008] was that I had had two years in which we were generating enormous crowds all across the country—and the majority of those crowds were not African American; and they were in pretty remote places, or unlikely places. They weren't just big cities or they weren't just liberal enclaves. So what that told me was, it was possible."

What those crowds saw was a black candidate unlike any other before him. To simply point to Obama's white mother, or to his African father, or even to his rearing in Hawaii, is to miss the point. For most African Americans, white people exist either as a direct or an indirect force for bad in their lives. Biraciality is no shield against this; often it just intensifies the problem. What proved key for Barack Obama was not that he was born to a black man and a white woman, but that his white family approved of the union, and approved of the child who came from it. They did this in 1961— a time when sex between black men and white women, in large swaths of the country, was not just illegal but fraught with mortal danger. But that danger is not part of Obama's story. The first white people he ever knew, the ones who raised him, were decent in a way that very few black people of that era experienced.

I asked Obama what he made of his grandparents' impressively civilized reception of his father. "It wasn't Harry Belafonte," Obama said laughingly of his father. "This was like an *African* African. And he was like a blue-black brother. Nilotic. And so, yeah, I will always give my grandparents credit for that. I'm not saying they were happy about it. I'm not saying that they were not, after the guy leaves, looking at each other like, 'What the heck?' But whatever misgivings they had, they never expressed to me, never spilled over into how they interacted with me.

"Now, part of it, as I say in my book, was we were in this unique environment in Hawaii where I think it was much easier. I don't know if it would have been as easy for them if they were living in Chicago at the time, because the lines just weren't as sharply drawn in Hawaii as they were on the mainland."

Obama's early positive interactions with his white family members gave him a fundamentally different outlook toward the wider world than most blacks of the 1960s had. Obama told me he rarely had "the working assumption of discrimination, the working assumption that white people would not treat me right or give me an opportunity or judge me [other than] on the basis of merit." He continued, "The kind of working assumption" that white people would discriminate against him or treat him poorly "is less embedded in my psyche than it is, say, with Michelle."

In this, the first lady is more representative of black America than her husband is. African Americans typically raise their children to protect themselves against a presumed hostility from white teachers, white police officers, white supervisors, and white co-workers. The need for that defense is, more often than not, reinforced either directly by actual encounters or indirectly by observing the vast differences between one's own experience and those across the color line. Marty Nesbitt, the president's longtime best friend, who, like Obama, had positive interactions with whites at a relatively early age, told me that when he and his wife went to buy their first car, she was insistent on buying from a black salesperson. "I'm like, 'We've got to find a salesman,'" Nesbitt said. "She's like, 'No, no, no. We're waiting for the brother.' And I'm like, 'He's with a customer.' They were filling out documents and she was like, 'We're going to stay around.' And a white guy came up to us. 'Can I help you?' 'Nope.'" Nesbitt was not out to condemn anyone with this story. He was asserting that "the willingness of African Americans [in Chicago] to help lift each other up is powerful."

But that willingness to help is also a defense, produced by decades of discrimination. Obama sees race through a different lens, Kaye Wilson told me. "It's just very different from ours," she explained. "He's got buddies that are white, and they're his buddies, and they love him. And I don't think they love him just because he's the president. They love him because they're his friends from Hawaii, some from college and all.

"So I think he's got that, whereas I think growing up in the racist United States, we enter this thing with, you know, 'I'm looking at you. I'm not trusting you to be one hundred with me.' And I think he grew up in a way that he had to trust [white people]— how can you live under the roof with people and think that they don't love you? He needs that frame of reference. He needs that lens. If he didn't have it, it would be . . . a Jesse Jackson, you know? Or Al Sharpton. Different lens."

That lens, born of literally relating to whites, allowed Obama to imagine that he could be the country's first black president. "If I walked into a room and it's a bunch of white farmers, trade unionists, middle age—I'm not walking in thinking, *Man, I've got to show them that I'm normal,*" Obama explained. "I walk in there, I think, with a set of assumptions: like, these people look just like my grandparents. And I see the same Jell-O mold that my grandmother served, and they've got the same, you know, little stuff on their mantelpieces. And so I am maybe disarming them by just assuming that we're okay."

What Obama was able to offer white America is something very few African Americans could—trust. The vast majority of us are, necessarily, too crippled by our defenses to ever consider such a proposition. But Obama, through a mixture of ancestral connections and distance from the poisons of Jim Crow, can credibly and sincerely trust the majority population of this country. That trust is reinforced, not contradicted, by his blackness. Obama isn't shuffling before white power (Herman Cain's "shucky ducky" act) or flattering white ego (O. J. Simpson's listing not being seen as black as a great accomplishment). That, too, is defensive, and deep down, I suspect, white people know it. He stands firm in his own cultural traditions and says to the country something virtually no black person can, but every president must: "I believe you."

IV.
"YOU STILL GOTTA GO BACK TO THE HOOD"

Just after Columbus Day, I accompanied the president and his formidable entourage on a visit to North Carolina A&T State University, in Greensboro. Four days earlier, *The Washington Post* had published an old audio clip that featured Donald Trump lamenting a failed sexual conquest and exhorting the virtues of sexual assault. The next day, Trump claimed that this was "locker room" talk. As we flew to North Carolina, the president was in a state of bemused disbelief. He plopped down in a chair in the staff cabin of Air Force One and said, "I've been in a lot of locker rooms. I don't think I've ever heard that one before." He was casual and relaxed. A feeling of cautious inevitability emanated from his staff, and why not? Every day seemed to bring a new, more shocking revelation or piece of evidence showing Trump to be unfit for the presidency: He had lost nearly $1 billion in a single year. He had likely not paid taxes in eighteen years. He was running a "university," for which he was under formal legal investigation. He had trampled on his own campaign's messaging by engaging in a Twitter crusade against a former beauty-pageant contestant. He had been denounced by leadership in his own party, and the trickle of prominent Republicans—both in and out of office—who had publicly repudiated him threatened to become a geyser. At this moment, the idea that a campaign so saturated in open bigotry, misogyny, chaos, and possible corruption could win a national election was ludicrous. This was America.

The president was going to North Carolina to keynote a campaign rally for Clinton, but first he was scheduled for a conversation about My Brother's Keeper, his initiative on behalf of disadvantaged youth. Announcing My Brother's Keeper—or MBK, as it's come to be called—in 2014, the president had sought to avoid giving the program a partisan valence, noting that it was "not some big new government program." Instead, it would involve the government in concert with the nonprofit and business sectors to intervene in the lives of young men of color who were "at risk." MBK serves as a kind of network for those elements of federal, state, and local government that might already have a presence in the lives of these young men. It is a quintessentially Obama program—conservative in scope, with impacts that are measurable.

"It comes right out of his own life," Broderick Johnson, the cabinet secretary and an assistant to the president, who heads MBK, told me recently. "I have heard him say, 'I don't want us to have a bunch of forums on race.' He reminds people, 'Yeah, we can talk about this. But what are we going to do?'" On this afternoon in North Carolina, what Obama did was sit with a group of young men who'd turned their lives around in part because of MBK. They told stories of being in the street, of choosing quick money over school, of their homes being shot up, and—through the help of mentoring or job programs brokered by MBK—transitioning into college or a job. Obama listened solemnly and empathetically to each of them. "It doesn't take that much," he told them. "It just takes someone laying hands on you and saying, 'Hey, man, you count.'"

When he asked the young men whether they had a message he should take back to policy makers in Washington, D.C., one observed that despite their best individual efforts, they still had to go back to the very same deprived neighborhoods that had been the sources of trouble for them. "It's your environment," the young man said. "You can do what you want, but you still gotta go back to the hood."

He was correct. The ghettos of America are the direct result of decades of public-policy decisions: the redlining of real-estate zoning maps, the expanded authority given to prosecutors, the increased funding given to prisons. And all of this was done on the backs of people still reeling from the 250-year legacy of slavery. The results of this negative investment are clear—African Americans rank at the bottom of nearly every major socioeconomic measure in the country.

Obama's formula for closing this chasm between black and white America, like that of many progressive politicians today, proceeded from policy designed for all of America. Blacks disproportionately benefit from this effort, since they are disproportionately in need. The Affordable Care Act, which cut the uninsured rate in the black community by at least a third, was Obama's most prominent example. Its full benefit has yet to be felt by African Americans, because several states in the South have declined to expand Medicaid. But when the president and I were meeting, the ACA's advocates believed that pressure on state budgets would force expansion, and there was evidence to support this: Louisiana had expanded Medicaid earlier in 2016, and advocates were gearing up for wars to be waged in Georgia and Virginia.

Obama also emphasized the need for a strong Justice Department with a deep commitment to nondiscrimination. When Obama moved into the White House in 2009, the Justice Department's Civil Rights Division "was in shambles," former Attorney General Eric Holder told me recently. "I mean, I had been there for twelve years as a line guy. I started out in '76, so I served under Republicans and Democrats. And what the [George W.] Bush administration, what the Bush DOJ did, was unlike anything that had ever happened before in terms of politicized hiring." The career civil servants below the political appointees, Holder said, were not even invited to the meetings in which the key hiring and policy decisions were made. After Obama's inauguration, Holder told me, "I remember going to tell all the folks at the Civil Rights Division, 'The Civil Rights Division is open for business again.' The president gave me additional funds to hire people."

The political press developed a narrative that because Obama felt he had to modulate his rhetoric on race, Holder was the administration's true, and thus blacker, conscience. Holder is certainly blunter, and this worried some of the White House staff. Early in Obama's first term, Holder gave a speech on race in which he said the United States had been a "nation of cowards" on the subject. But positioning the two men as opposites elides an important fact: Holder was appointed by the president, and went only as far as the president allowed. I asked Holder whether he had toned down his rhetoric after that controversial speech. "Nope," he said. Reflecting on his relationship with the president, Holder said, "We were also kind of different people, you know? He is the Zen guy. And I'm kind of the hot-blooded West Indian. And I thought we made a good team, but there's nothing that I ever did or said that I don't think he would have said, 'I support him 100 percent.'

"Now, the 'nation of cowards' speech, the president might have used a different phrase—maybe, probably. But he and I share a worldview, you know? And when I hear people say, 'Well, you are blacker than him' or something like that, I think, *What are you all talking about?*"

For much of his presidency, a standard portion of Obama's speeches about race riffed on black people's need to turn off the television, stop eating junk food, and stop blaming white people for their problems. Obama would deliver this lecture to any black audience, regardless of context. It was bizarre, for instance, to see the president warning young men who'd just graduated from Morehouse College, one of the most storied black colleges in the country, about making "excuses" and blaming whites.

This part of the Obama formula is the most troubling, and least thought out. This judgment emerges from my own biography. I am the product of black parents who encouraged me to read, of black teachers who felt my work ethic did not match my potential, of black college professors who taught me intellectual rigor. And they did this in a world that every day insulted their humanity. It was not so much that the black layabouts and deadbeats Obama invoked in his speeches were unrecognizable. I had seen those people too. But I'd also seen the same among white people. If black men were overrepresented among drug dealers and absentee dads of the world, it was directly related to their being underrepresented among the Bernie Madoffs and Kenneth Lays of the world. Power was what mattered, and what characterized the differences between black and white America was not a difference in work ethic, but a system engineered to place one on top of the other.

The mark of that system is visible at every level of American society, regardless of the quality of one's choices. For instance, the unemployment rate among black college graduates (4.1 percent) is almost the same as the unemployment rate among white high-school graduates (4.6 percent). But that college degree is generally purchased at a higher price by blacks than by whites. According to research by the Brookings Institution, African Americans tend to carry more student debt four years after graduation ($53,000 versus $28,000) and suffer from a higher default rate on their loans (7.6 percent versus 2.4 percent) than white Americans. This is both the result and the perpetuator of a sprawling wealth gap between the races. White households, on average, hold seven times as much wealth as black households—a difference so large as to make comparing the "black middle class" and "white middle class" meaningless; they're simply not comparable. According to Patrick Sharkey, a sociologist at New York University who studies economic mobility, black families making $100,000 a year or more live in more disadvantaged neighborhoods than white families making less than $30,000. This gap didn't just appear by magic; it's the result of the government's effort over many decades to create a pigmentocracy—one that will continue without explicit intervention.

Obama had been on the record as opposing reparations. But now, late in his presidency, he seemed more open to the idea—in theory, at least, if not in practice.

"Theoretically, you can make obviously a powerful argument

that centuries of slavery, Jim Crow, discrimination are the primary cause for all those gaps," Obama said, referencing the gulf in education, wealth, and employment that separates black and white America. "That those were wrongs to the black community as a whole, and black families specifically, and that in order to close that gap, a society has a moral obligation to make a large, aggressive investment, even if it's not in the form of individual reparations checks but in the form of a Marshall Plan."

The political problems with turning the argument for reparations into reality are manifold, Obama said. "If you look at countries like South Africa, where you had a black majority, there have been efforts to tax and help that black majority, but it hasn't come in the form of a formal reparations program. You have countries like India that have tried to help untouchables, with essentially affirmative-action programs, but it hasn't fundamentally changed the structure of their societies. So the bottom line is that it's hard to find a model in which you can practically administer and sustain political support for those kinds of efforts."

Obama went on to say that it would be better, and more realistic, to get the country to rally behind a robust liberal agenda and build on the enormous progress that's been made toward getting white Americans to accept nondiscrimination as a basic operating premise. But the progress toward nondiscrimination did not appear overnight. It was achieved by people willing to make an unpopular argument and live on the frontier of public opinion. I asked him whether it wasn't—despite the practical obstacles—worth arguing that the state has a collective responsibility not only for its achievements but for its sins.

"I want my children—I want Malia and Sasha—to understand that they've got responsibilities beyond just what they themselves have done," Obama said. "That they have a responsibility to the larger community and the larger nation, that they should be sensitive to and extra thoughtful about the plight of people who have been oppressed in the past, are oppressed currently. So that's a wisdom that I want to transmit to my kids. . . . But I would say that's a high level of enlightenment that you're looking to have from a majority of the society. And it may be something that future generations are more open to, but I am pretty confident that for the foreseeable future, using the argument of nondiscrimination, and 'Let's get it right for the kids who are here right now,' and giving them the best chance possible, is going to be a more persuasive argument."

Obama is unfailingly optimistic about the empathy and capabilities of the American people. His job necessitates this: "At some level what the people want to feel is that the person leading them sees the best in them," he told me. But I found it interesting that that optimism does not extend to the possibility of the public's accepting wisdoms—such as the moral logic of reparations—that the president, by his own account, has accepted for himself and is willing to teach his children. Obama says he always tells his staff that "better is good." The notion that a president would attempt to achieve change within the boundaries of the accepted consensus is appropriate. But Obama is almost constitutionally skeptical of those who seek to achieve change outside that consensus.

EARLY IN 2016, OBAMA invited a group of African American leaders to meet with him at the White House. When some of the activists affiliated with Black Lives Matter refused to attend, Obama began calling them out in speeches. "You can't refuse to meet because that might compromise the purity of your position," he said. "The value of social movements and activism is to get you at the table, get you in the room, and then start trying to figure out how is this problem going to be solved. You then have a responsibility to prepare an agenda that is achievable—that can institutionalize the changes you seek—and to engage the other side."

Opal Tometi, a Nigerian American community activist who is

one of the three founders of Black Lives Matter, explained to me that the group has a more diffuse structure than most civil rights organizations. One reason for this is to avoid the cult of personality that has plagued black organizations in the past. So the founders asked its membership in Chicago, the president's hometown, whether they should meet with Obama. "They felt—and I think many of our members felt—there wouldn't be the depth of discussion that they wanted to have," Tometi told me. "And if there wasn't that space to have a real heart-to-heart, and if it was just surface level, that it would be more of a disservice to the movement."

Tometi noted that some other activists allied with Black Lives Matter had been planning to attend the meeting, so they felt their views would be represented. Nevertheless, Black Lives Matter sees itself as engaged in a protest against the treatment of black people by the American state, and so Tometi and much of the group's leadership, concerned about being used for a photo op by the very body they were protesting, opted not to go.

When I asked Obama about this perspective, he fluctuated between understanding where the activists were coming from and being hurt by such brush-offs. "I think that where I've gotten frustrated during the course of my presidency has never been because I was getting pushed too hard by activists to see the justness of a cause or the essence of an issue," he said. "I think where I got frustrated at times was the belief that the president can do anything if he just decides he wants to do it. And that sort of lack of awareness on the part of an activist about the constraints of our political system and the constraints on this office, I think, sometimes would leave me to mutter under my breath. Very rarely did I lose it publicly. Usually I'd just smile."

He laughed, then continued, "The reason I say that is because those are the times where sometimes you feel actually a little bit hurt. Because you feel like saying to these folks, '[Don't] you think if I could do it, I [would] have just done it? Do you think that the only problem is that I don't care enough about the plight of poor people, or gay people?' "

I asked Obama whether he thought that perhaps protesters' distrust of the powers that be could ultimately be healthy. "Yes," he said. "Which is why I don't get too hurt. I mean, I think there is a benefit to wanting to hold power's feet to the fire until you actually see the goods. I get that. And I think it is important. And frankly, sometimes it's useful for activists just to be out there to keep you mindful and not get complacent, even if ultimately you think some of their criticism is misguided."

Obama himself was an activist and a community organizer, albeit for only two years—but he is not, by temperament, a protester. He is a consensus-builder; consensus, he believes, ultimately drives what gets done. He understands the emotional power of protest, the need to vent before authority—but that kind of approach does not come naturally to him. Regarding reparations, he said, "Sometimes I wonder how much of these debates have to do with the desire, the legitimate desire, for that history to be recognized. Because there is a psychic power to the recognition that is not satisfied with a universal program; it's not satisfied by the Affordable Care Act, or an expansion of Pell Grants, or an expansion of the earned-income tax credit." These kinds of programs, effective and disproportionately beneficial to black people though they may be, don't "speak to the hurt, and the sense of injustice, and the self-doubt that arises out of the fact that [African Americans] are behind now, and it makes us sometimes feel as if there must be something wrong with us—unless you're able to see the history and say, 'It's amazing we got this far given what we went through.'

"So in part, I think the argument sometimes that I've had with folks who are much more interested in sort of race-specific programs is less an argument about what is practically achievable and sometimes maybe more an argument of 'We want society to see what's happened and internalize it and answer it in demonstrable ways.' And those impulses I very much understand—but my hope would be that as we're moving through the world right now, we're able to get that psychological or emotional peace by seeing very concretely our kids doing better and being more hopeful and having greater opportunities."

Obama saw—at least at that moment, before the election of Donald Trump—a straight path to that world. "Just play this out as a thought experiment," he said. "Imagine if you had genuine, high-quality early-childhood education for every child, and suddenly every black child in America—but also every poor white child or Latino [child], but just stick with every black child in America—is getting a really good education. And they're graduating from high school at the same rates that whites are, and they are going to college at the same rates that whites are, and they are able to afford college at the same rates because the government has universal programs that say that you're not going to be barred from school just because of how much money your parents have.

"So now they're all graduating. And let's also say that the Justice Department and the courts are making sure, as I've said in a speech before, that when Jamal sends his résumé in, he's getting treated the same as when Johnny sends his résumé in. Now, are we going to have suddenly the same number of CEOs, billionaires, etc., as the white community? In ten years? Probably not, maybe not even in twenty years.

"But I guarantee you that we would be thriving, we would be succeeding. We wouldn't have huge numbers of young African American men in jail. We'd have more family formation as college-graduated girls are meeting boys who are their peers, which then in turn means the next generation of kids are growing up that much better. And suddenly you've got a whole generation that's in a position to start using the incredible creativity that we see in music, and sports, and frankly even on the streets, channeled into starting all kinds of businesses. I feel pretty good about our odds in that situation."

The thought experiment doesn't hold up. The programs Obama favored would advance white America too—and without a specific commitment to equality, there is no guarantee that the programs would eschew discrimination. Obama's solution relies on a good-will that his own personal history tells him exists in the larger country. My own history tells me something different. The large numbers of black men in jail, for instance, are not just the result of poor policy, but of not seeing those men as human.

When President Obama and I had this conversation, the target he was aiming to reach seemed to me to be many generations away, and now—as President-Elect Trump prepares for office—seems even many more generations off. Obama's accomplishments were real: a $1 billion settlement on behalf of black farmers, a Justice Department that exposed Ferguson's municipal plunder, the increased availability of Pell Grants (and their availability to some prisoners), and the slashing of the crack/cocaine disparity in sentencing guidelines, to name just a few. Obama was also the first sitting president to visit a federal prison. There was a feeling that he'd erected a foundation upon which further progressive policy could be built. It's tempting to say that foundation is now endangered. The truth is, it was never safe.

V.
"THEY RODE THE TIGER"

Obama's greatest misstep was born directly out of his greatest insight. Only Obama, a black man who emerged from the best of white America, and thus could sincerely trust white America, could be so certain that he could achieve broad national appeal. And yet only a black man with that same biography could underestimate his opposition's resolve to destroy him. In some sense an Obama presidency could never have succeeded along the normal presidential lines; he needed a partner, or partners, in Congress who could put governance above party. But he struggled to win over even some of his own allies. Ben Nelson, the Democratic senator from Nebraska whom Obama helped elect, became an obstacle to healthcare reform. Joe Lieberman, whom Obama saved from retribution at the hands of Senate Democrats after Lieberman campaigned for Obama's 2008 opponent, John McCain, similarly obstructed Obamacare. Among Republicans, senators who had seemed amenable to Obama's agenda—Chuck Grassley, Susan Collins, Richard Lugar, Olympia Snowe—rebuffed him repeatedly.

The obstruction grew out of narrow political incentives. "If Republicans didn't cooperate," Obama told me, "and there was not a portrait of bipartisan cooperation and a functional federal government, then the party in power would pay the price and they could win back the Senate and/or the House. That wasn't an inaccurate political calculation."

Obama is not sure of the degree to which individual racism played into this calculation. "I do remember watching Bill Clinton get impeached and Hillary Clinton being accused of killing Vince Foster," he said. "And if you ask them, I'm sure they would say, 'No, actually what you're experiencing is not because you're black, it's because you're a Democrat.' "

But personal animus is just one manifestation of racism; arguably the more profound animosity occurs at the level of interests. The most recent Congress boasted 138 members from the states that comprised the old Confederacy. Of the 101 Republicans in that group, 96 are white and one is black. Of the 37 Democrats, 18 are black and 15 are white. There are no white congressional Democrats in the Deep South. Exit polls in Mississippi in 2008 found that 96 percent of voters who described themselves as Republicans were white. The Republican Party is not simply the party of whites, but the preferred party of whites who identify their interest as defending the historical privileges of whiteness. The researchers Josh Pasek, Jon A. Krosnick, and Trevor Tompson found that in 2012, 32 percent of Democrats held antiblack views, while 79 percent of Republicans did. These attitudes could even spill over to white Democratic politicians, because they are seen as representing the party of blacks. Studying the 2016 election, the political scientist Philip Klinkner found that the most predictive question for understanding whether a voter favored Hillary Clinton or Donald Trump was "Is Barack Obama a Muslim?"

In our conversations, Obama said he didn't doubt that there was a sincerely nonracist states-rights contingent of the GOP. And yet he suspected that there might be more to it. "A rudimentary knowledge of American history tells you that the relationship between the federal government and the states was very much mixed up with attitudes towards slavery, attitudes towards Jim Crow, attitudes towards antipoverty programs and who benefited and who didn't," he said.

"And so I'm careful not to attribute any particular resistance or slight or opposition to race. But what I do believe is that if somebody didn't have a problem with their daddy being employed by the federal government, and didn't have a problem with the Tennessee Valley Authority electrifying certain communities, and didn't have a problem with the interstate highway system being built, and didn't have a problem with the GI Bill, and didn't have a problem with the [Federal Housing Administration] subsidizing the suburbanization of America, and that all helped you build wealth and create a middle class—and then suddenly as soon as African Americans or Latinos are interested in availing themselves of those same mechanisms as ladders into the middle class, you now have a violent opposition to them—then I think you at least have to ask yourself the question of how consistent you are, and what's different, and what's changed."

Racism greeted Obama in both his primary and general election campaigns in 2008. Photos were circulated of him in Somali garb. Rush Limbaugh dubbed him "Barack the Magic Negro." Roger Stone, who would go on to advise the Trump campaign, claimed that Michelle Obama could be heard on tape yelling "Whitey." Detractors circulated emails claiming that the future first lady had written a racist senior thesis while at Princeton. A fifth of all West Virginia Democratic primary voters in 2008 openly admitted that race had influenced their vote. Hillary Clinton trounced him 67 to 26 percent.

After Obama won the presidency in defiance of these racial headwinds, traffic to the white-supremacist website Stormfront increased sixfold. Before the election, in August, just before the Democratic National Convention, the FBI uncovered an assassination plot hatched by white supremacists in Denver. Mainstream conservative publications floated the notion that Obama's memoir was too "stylish and penetrating" to have been written by the candidate, and found a plausible ghostwriter in the radical (and white) former Weatherman Bill Ayers. A Republican women's club in California dispensed "Obama Bucks" featuring slices of watermelon, ribs, and fried chicken. At the Values Voter Summit that year, conventioneers hawked "Obama Waffles," a waffle mix whose box featured a bug-eyed caricature of the candidate. Fake hip-hop lyrics were scrawled on the side ("Barry's Bling Bling Waffle Ring") and on the top, the same caricature was granted a turban and tagged with the instructions "Point box toward Mecca for tastier waffles." The display was denounced by the summit's sponsor, the Family Research Council. One would be forgiven for meeting this denunciation with guffaws: The council's president, Tony Perkins, had once addressed the white supremacist Council of Conservative Citizens with a Confederate flag draped behind him. By 2015, Perkins had deemed the debate over Obama's birth certificate "legitimate" and was saying that it "makes sense" to conclude that Obama was actually a Muslim.

By then, birtherism—inflamed in large part by a real-estate mogul and reality TV star named Donald Trump—had overtaken the Republican rank and file. In 2015, one poll found that 54 percent of GOP voters thought Obama was a Muslim. Only 29 percent believed he'd been born in America.

Still, in 2008, Obama had been elected. His supporters rejoiced. As Jay-Z commemorated the occasion:

> My president is black, in fact he's half-white,
> So even in a racist mind, he's half-right.

Not quite. A month after Obama entered the White House, a CNBC personality named Rick Santelli took to the trading floor of the Chicago Mercantile Exchange and denounced the president's efforts to help homeowners endangered by the housing crisis. "How many of you people want to pay for your neighbor's mort-gage that has an extra bathroom and can't pay their bills?" Santelli asked the assembled traders. He asserted that Obama should "re-ward people that could carry the water" as opposed to those who "drink the water," and denounced those in danger of foreclosure as "losers." Race was implicit in Santelli's harangue—the housing cri-sis and predatory lending had devastated black communities and expanded the wealth gap—and it culminated with a call for a "Tea Party" to resist the Obama presidency. In fact, right-wing ideo-logues had been planning just such a resistance for decades. They would eagerly answer Santelli's call.

ONE OF THE INTELLECTUAL forerunners of the Tea Party is said to be Ron Paul, the heterodox two-time Republican presidential can-didate, who opposed the war in Iraq and championed civil liberties. On other matters, Paul was more traditional. Throughout the '90s, he published a series of racist newsletters that referred to New York City as "Welfaria," called Martin Luther King Jr. Day "Hate Whitey Day," and asserted that 95 percent of black males in Wash-ington, D.C., were either "semi-criminal or entirely criminal." Paul's apologists have claimed that he had no real connection to the newsletters, even though virtually all of them were published in his name ("The Ron Paul Survival Report," "Ron Paul Political Report," "Dr. Ron Paul's Freedom Report") and written in his voice. Either way, the views of the newsletters have found their expression in his ideological comrades. Throughout Obama's first term, Tea Party activists voiced their complaints in racist terms. Activists brandished signs warning that Obama would implement "white slavery," waved the Confederate flag, depicted Obama as a witch doctor, and issued calls for him to "go back to Kenya." Tea Party supporters wrote "satirical" letters in the name of "We Colored People" and stoked the flames of birtherism. One of the Tea Party's most prominent sympathizers, the radio host Laura Ingraham, wrote a racist tract depicting Michelle Obama gorging herself on ribs, while Glenn Beck said the president was a "racist" with a "deep-seated hatred for white people." The Tea Party's leading exponent, Andrew Breitbart, engineered the smearing of Shirley Sherrod, the U.S. Department of Agriculture's director of rural development for Georgia, publishing egregiously misleading videos that wrongly made her appear to be engaging in antiwhite racist invective, which led to her dismissal. (In a rare act of cowardice, the Obama administration cravenly submitted to this effort.)

In those rare moments when Obama made any sort of comment attacking racism, firestorms threatened to consume his governing agenda. When, in July 2009, the president objected to the arrest of the eminent Harvard professor Henry Louis Gates Jr. while he was trying to get into his own house, pointing out that the officer had "acted stupidly," a third of whites said the remark made them feel less favorably toward the president, and nearly two-thirds claimed that Obama had "acted stupidly" by commenting. A chastened Obama then determined to make sure his public statements on race were no longer mere riffs but were designed to have an achievable effect. This was smart, but still the invective came. During Obama's 2009 address on health care before a joint session of Congress, Joe Wilson, a Republican congressman from South Carolina, incredibly, and in defiance of precedent and decorum, disrupted the proceedings by crying out "You lie!" A Missouri congressman equated

Obama with a monkey. A California GOP official took up the theme and emailed her friends an image depicting Obama as a chimp, with the accompanying text explaining, "Now you know why [there's] no birth certificate!" Former vice presidential candidate Sarah Palin assessed the president's foreign policy as a "shuck and jive shtick." Newt Gingrich dubbed him the "food-stamp president." The rhetorical attacks on Obama were matched by a very real attack on his political base—in 2011 and 2012, nineteen states enacted voting restrictions that made it harder for African Americans to vote.

Yet in 2012, as in 2008, Obama won anyway. Prior to the election, Obama, ever the optimist, had claimed that intransigent Republicans would decide to work with him to advance the country. No such collaboration was in the offing. Instead, legislation ground to a halt and familiar themes resurfaced. An Idaho GOP official posted a photo on Facebook depicting a trap waiting for Obama. The bait was a slice of watermelon. The caption read, "Breaking: The secret service just uncovered a plot to kidnap the president. More details as we get them. . . ." In 2014, conservatives assembled in support of Cliven Bundy's armed protest against federal grazing fees. As reporters descended on the Bundy ranch in Nevada, Bundy offered his opinions on "the Negro." "They abort their young children, they put their young men in jail, because they never learned how to pick cotton," Bundy explained. "And I've often wondered, are they better off as slaves, picking cotton and having a family life and doing things, or are they better off under government subsidy? They didn't get no more freedom. They got less freedom."

That same year, in the wake of Michael Brown's death, the Justice Department opened an investigation into the police department in Ferguson, Missouri. It found a city that, through racial profiling, arbitrary fines, and wanton harassment, had exploited law enforcement for the purposes of municipal plunder. The plunder was sanctified by racist humor dispensed via internal emails among the police that later came to light. The president of the United States, who during his first year in office had reportedly received three times the number of death threats of any of his predecessors, was a repeat target.

Much ink has been spilled in an attempt to understand the Tea Party protests, and the 2016 presidential candidacy of Donald Trump, which ultimately emerged out of them. One theory popular among (primarily) white intellectuals of varying political persuasions held that this response was largely the discontented rumblings of a white working class threatened by the menace of globalization and crony capitalism. Dismissing these rumblings as racism was said to condescend to this proletariat, which had long suffered the slings and arrows of coastal elites, heartless technocrats, and reformist snobs. Racism was not something to be coolly and empirically assessed but a slander upon the working man. Deindustrialization, globalization, and broad income inequality are real. And they have landed with at least as great a force upon black and Latino people in our country as upon white people. And yet these groups were strangely unrepresented in this new populism.

Christopher S. Parker and Matt A. Barreto, political scientists at the University of Washington and UCLA, respectively, have found a relatively strong relationship between racism and Tea Party membership. "Whites are less likely to be drawn to the Tea Party for material reasons, suggesting that, relative to other groups, it's really more about social prestige," they say. The notion that the Tea Party represented the righteous, if unfocused, anger of an aggrieved class allowed everyone from leftists to neoliberals to white nationalists to avoid a horrifying and simple reality: A significant swath of this country did not like the fact that their president was black, and that swath was not composed of those most damaged by an unquestioned faith in the markets. Far better to imagine the grievance put upon the president as the ghost of shambling factories and defunct union halls, as opposed to what it really was—a movement inaugurated by ardent and frightened white capitalists, raging from the commodities trading floor of one of the great financial centers of the world.

That movement came into full bloom in the summer of 2015, with the candidacy of Donald Trump, a man who'd risen to political prominence by peddling the racist myth that the president was not American. It was birtherism—not trade, not jobs, not isolationism—that launched Trump's foray into electoral politics. Having risen unexpectedly on this basis into the stratosphere of Republican politics, Trump spent the campaign freely and liberally trafficking in misogyny, Islamophobia, and xenophobia. And on November 8, 2016, he won election to the presidency. Historians will spend the next century analyzing how a country with such allegedly grand democratic traditions was, so swiftly and so easily, brought to the brink of fascism. But one needn't stretch too far to conclude that an eight-year campaign of consistent and open racism aimed at the leader of the free world helped clear the way.

"They rode the tiger. And now the tiger is eating them," David Axelrod, speaking of the Republican Party, told me. That was in October. His words proved too optimistic. The tiger would devour us all.

VI.
"WHEN YOU LEFT, YOU TOOK ALL OF ME WITH YOU"

One Saturday morning last May, I joined the presidential motorcade as it slipped out of the southern gate of the White House. A mostly white crowd had assembled. As the motorcade drove by, people cheered, held up their smartphones to record the procession, and waved American flags. To be within feet of the president seemed like the thrill of their lives. I was astounded. An old euphoria, which I could not immediately place, gathered up in me. And then I remembered, it was what I felt through much of 2008, as I watched Barack Obama's star shoot across the political sky. I had never seen so many white people cheer on a black man who was neither an athlete nor an entertainer. And it seemed that they loved him for this, and I thought in those days, which now feel so long ago, that they might then love me, too, and love my wife, and love my child, and love us all in the manner that the God they so fervently cited had commanded. I had been raised amid a people who wanted badly to believe in the possibility of a Barack Obama, even as their very lives argued against that possibility. So they would praise Martin Luther King Jr. in one breath and curse the white man, "the Great Deceiver," in the next. Then came Obama and the Obama family, and they were black and beautiful in all the ways we aspired to be, and all that love was showered upon them. But as Obama's motorcade approached its destination—Howard University, where he would give the commencement address—the complexion of the crowd darkened, and I understood that the love was specific, that even if it allowed Barack Obama, even if it allowed the luckiest of us, to defy the boundaries, then the masses of us, in cities like this one, would still enjoy no such feat.

These were our fitful, spasmodic years.

We were launched into the Obama era with no notion of what to expect, if only because a black presidency had seemed such a dubious proposition. There was no preparation, because it would have meant preparing for the impossible. There were few assessments of its potential import, because such assessments were regarded as speculative fiction. In retrospect it all makes sense, and one can see a jagged but real political lineage running through black Chicago. It originates in Oscar Stanton De Priest; continues through Congressman William Dawson, who, under Roosevelt, switched from the Republican to the Democratic Party; crescendos with the legendary Harold Washington; rises still with Jesse Jackson's 1988 victory in Michigan's Democratic caucuses; rises again with Carol Moseley Braun's triumph; and reaches its recent apex with the election of Barack Obama. If the lineage is apparent in hindsight, so are the limits of presidential power. For a century after emancipation, quasi-slavery haunted the South. And more than half a century after *Brown v. Board of Education,* schools throughout much of this country remain segregated.

There are no clean victories for black people, nor, perhaps, for any people. The presidency of Barack Obama is no different. One can now say that an African American individual can rise to the same level as a white individual, and yet also say that the number of black individuals who actually qualify for that status will be small. One thinks of Serena Williams, whose dominance and stunning achievements can't, in and of themselves, ensure equal access to tennis facilities for young black girls. The gate is open and yet so very far away.

I felt a mix of pride and amazement walking onto Howard's campus that day. Howard alumni, of which I am one, are an obnoxious fraternity, known for yelling the school chant across city blocks, sneering at other historically black colleges and universities, and condescending to black graduates of predominantly white institutions. I like to think I am more reserved, but I felt an immense satisfaction in being in the library where I had once found my history, and now found myself with the first black president of the United States. It seemed providential that he would give the commencement address here in his last year. The same pride I felt radiated out across the Yard, the large green patch in the main area of the campus where the ceremony would take place. When Obama walked out, the audience exploded, and when the time came for the color guard to present arms, a chant arose: "O-Ba-Ma! O-Ba-Ma! O-Ba-Ma!"

He gave a good speech that day, paying heed to Howard's rituals, calling out its famous alumni, shouting out the university's various dormitories, and urging young people to vote. (His usual riff on respectability politics was missing.) But I think he could have stood before that crowd, smiled, and said "Good luck," and they would have loved him anyway. He was their champion, and this was evident in the smallest of things. The national anthem was played first, but then came the black national anthem, "Lift Every Voice and Sing." As the lyrics rang out over the crowd, the students held up the Black Power fist—a symbol of defiance before power. And yet here, in the face of a black man in his last year in power, it scanned not as a protest, but as a salute.

Six months later the awful price of a black presidency would be known to those students, even as the country seemed determined not to acknowledge it. In the days after Donald Trump's victory, there would be an insistence that something as "simple" as racism could not explain it. As if enslavement had nothing to do with global economics, or as if lynchings said nothing about the idea of women as property. As though the past four hundred years could be reduced to the irrational resentment of full lips. No. Racism is never simple. And there was nothing simple about what was coming, or about Obama, the man who had unwittingly summoned this future into being.

It was said that the Americans who'd supported Trump were victims of liberal condescension. The word *racist* would be dismissed as a profane slur put upon the common man, as opposed to an accurate description of actual men. "We simply don't yet know how much racism or misogyny motivated Trump voters," David Brooks would write in *The New York Times*. "If you were stuck in a jobless town, watching your friends OD on opiates, scrambling every month to pay the electric bill, and then along came a guy who seemed able to fix your problems and hear your voice, maybe you would stomach some ugliness, too." This strikes me as perfectly logical. Indeed, it could apply just as well to Louis Farrakhan's appeal to the black poor and working class. But whereas the followers of an Islamophobic white nationalist enjoy the sympathy that must always greet the salt of the earth, the followers of an anti-Semitic black nationalist endure the scorn that must ever greet the children of the enslaved.

Much would be made of blue-collar voters in Wisconsin, Pennsylvania, and Michigan who'd pulled the lever for Obama in 2008 and 2012 and then for Trump in 2016. Surely these voters disproved racism as an explanatory force. It's still not clear how many individual voters actually flipped. But the underlying presumption—that Hillary Clinton and Barack Obama could be swapped in for each other—exhibited a problem. Clinton was a candidate who'd won one competitive political race in her life, whose political instincts were questioned by her own advisers, who took more than half a million dollars in speaking fees from an investment bank because it was "what they offered," who proposed to bring back to the White House a former president dogged by allegations of rape and sexual harassment. Obama was a candidate who'd become only the third black senator in the modern era; who'd twice been elected president, each time flipping red and purple states; who'd run one of the most scandal-free administrations in recent memory. Imagine an African American facsimile of Hillary Clinton: She would never be the nominee of a major political party and likely would not be in national politics at all.

Pointing to citizens who voted for both Obama and Trump does not disprove racism; it evinces it. To secure the White House, Obama needed to be a Harvard-trained lawyer with a decade of political experience and an incredible gift for speaking to cross sections of the country; Donald Trump needed only money and white bluster.

In the week after the election, I was a mess. I had not seen my wife in two weeks. I was on deadline for this article. My son was struggling in school. The house was in disarray. I played Marvin Gaye endlessly—"When you left, you took all of me with you." Friends began to darkly recall the ghosts of post-Reconstruction. The election of Donald Trump confirmed everything I knew of my country and none of what I could accept. The idea that America would follow its first black president with Donald Trump accorded with its history. I was shocked at my own shock. I had wanted Obama to be right.

I still want Obama to be right. I still would like to fold myself into the dream. This will not be possible.

By some cosmic coincidence, a week after the election I received a portion of my father's FBI file.* My father had grown up poor in Philadelphia. His father was struck dead on the street. His grandfather was crushed to death in a meatpacking plant. He'd served his country in Vietnam, gotten radicalized there, and joined the Black Panther Party, which brought him to the attention of J. Edgar Hoover. A memo written to the FBI director was "submitted aimed at discrediting WILLIAM PAUL COATES, Acting Captain of the BPP, Baltimore." The memo proposed that a fake letter be sent to the Panthers' co-founder Huey P. Newton. The fake letter accused my father of being an informant and concluded, "I want somethin done with this bootlikin facist pig nigger and I want it done now." The words *somethin done* need little interpretation. The Panthers were eventually consumed by an internecine war instigated by the FBI, one in which being labeled a police informant was a death sentence.

A few hours after I saw this file, I had my last conversation with the president. I asked him how his optimism was holding up, given Trump's victory. He confessed to being surprised at the outcome but said that it was tough to "draw a grand theory from it, because there were some very unusual circumstances." He pointed to both candidates' high negatives, the media coverage, and a "dispirited" electorate. But he said that his general optimism about the shape of American history remained unchanged. "To be optimistic about the long-term trends of the United States doesn't mean that everything is going to go in a smooth, direct, straight line," he said. "It goes forward sometimes, sometimes it goes back, sometimes it goes sideways, sometimes it zigs and zags."

---

* I was made aware of the FBI file by the diligent work of researchers from the show *Finding Your Roots*. I was taping an episode on my family the day of my last interview with the president.

I thought of Hoover's FBI, which harassed three generations of black activists, from Marcus Garvey's black nationalists to Martin Luther King Jr.'s integrationists to Huey Newton's Black Panthers, including my father. And I thought of the enormous power accrued to the presidency in the post-9/11 era—the power to obtain American citizens' phone records en masse, to access their emails, to detain them indefinitely. I asked the president whether it was all worth it. Whether this generation of black activists and their allies should be afraid.

"Keep in mind that the capacity of the NSA, or other surveillance tools, are specifically prohibited from being applied to U.S. citizens or U.S. persons without specific evidence of links to terrorist activity or, you know, other foreign-related activity," he said. "So, you know, I think this whole story line that somehow Big Brother has massively expanded and now that a new president is in place it's this loaded gun ready to be used on domestic dissent is just not accurate."

He counseled vigilance, "because the possibility of abuse by government officials always exists. The issue is not going to be that there are new tools available; the issue is making sure that the incoming administration, like my administration, takes the constraints on how we deal with U.S. citizens and persons seriously." This answer did not fill me with confidence. The next day, President-Elect Trump offered Lieutenant General Michael Flynn the post of national security adviser and picked Senator Jeff Sessions of Alabama as his nominee for attorney general. Last February, Flynn tweeted, "Fear of Muslims is RATIONAL" and linked to a YouTube video that declared followers of Islam want "80 percent of humanity enslaved or exterminated." Sessions had once been accused of calling a black lawyer "boy," claiming that a white lawyer who represented black clients was a disgrace to his race, and joking that he thought the Ku Klux Klan "was okay until I found out they smoked pot." I felt then that I knew what was coming—more Freddie Grays, more

Rekia Boyds, more informants and undercover officers sent to infiltrate mosques.

And I also knew that the man who could not countenance such a thing in his America had been responsible for the only time in my life when I felt, as the first lady had once said, proud of my country, and I knew that it was his very lack of countenance, his incredible faith, his improbable trust in his countrymen, that had made that feeling possible. The feeling was that little black boy touching the president's hair. It was watching Obama on the campaign trail, always expecting the worst and amazed that the worst never happened. It was how I'd felt seeing Barack and Michelle during the inauguration, the car slow-dragging down Pennsylvania Avenue, the crowd cheering, and then the two of them rising up out of the limo, rising up from fear, smiling, waving, defying despair, defying history, defying gravity.

EPILOGUE

THE FIRST WHITE PRESIDENT

Their "honor" became a vast and awful thing.

—W.E.B. DU BOIS, *Black Reconstruction*

I

IT IS INSUFFICIENT TO STATE THE OBVIOUS OF DONALD TRUMP: that he is a white man who would not be president were it not for this fact. With one immediate exception, Trump's predecessors made their way to high office through the passive power of whiteness—that bloody heirloom which cannot ensure mastery of all events but can conjure a tailwind for most of them. Land theft and human plunder cleared the grounds for Trump's forefathers and barred it for others. Once upon the field, these men became soldiers, statesmen, and scholars, held court in Paris, presided at Princeton, advanced into the Wilderness and then into the White House. Their individual triumphs made this exclusive party seem above America's founding sins, and it was forgotten that the former was in fact bound to the latter, that all their victories had transpired on cleared grounds. No such elegant detachment can be attributed to Donald Trump—a president who, more than any other, has made the awful inheritance explicit.

His political career began in advocacy of birtherism, that modern recasting of the old American precept that black people are not fit to be citizens of the country they built. But long before birtherism, Trump had made his worldview clear. He fought to keep blacks out of his buildings, called for the death penalty for the eventually exonerated Central Park Five, and railed against "lazy" black employees. "Black guys counting my money! I hate it," Trump was once quoted as saying. "The only kind of people I want counting my money are short guys that wear yarmulkes every day." After his cabal of conspiracy theorists forced President Obama to present his birth certificate, Trump then demanded the president's college grades (offering $5 million in exchange for them), insisting that Obama was not intelligent enough to have gone to an Ivy League university, and that his acclaimed memoir *Dreams from My Father* had been ghostwritten by a white man, Bill Ayers. While running for president Trump vented his displeasure at a judge presiding over a pair of cases in which he was a defendant. "He's a Mexican," Trump protested.

It is often said that Trump has no real ideology, which is not true—his ideology is white supremacy in all of its truculent and sanctimonious power. Trump inaugurated his campaign by casting himself as the defender of white maidenhood against Mexican "rapists," only to be later revealed as a proud violator. White supremacy has always had a perverse sexual tint. It is thus appropriate that Trump's rise was shepherded by Steve Bannon, a man who mocks his white male opponents as "cucks." The word, derived from *cuckold,* is specifically meant to debase by fear/fantasy—the target is so weak that he would submit to the humiliation of having his white wife lie with black men. That the slur *cuck* casts white men as victims aligns with the dictums of whiteness, which seek to alchemize one's profligate sins into virtue. So it was with Virginia slaveholders claiming that Britain sought to make slaves of them. So it was with rapacious Klansmen organized against alleged outrages. So it was with a candidate who called for a foreign power to hack his opponent's email and a president now claiming to be the victim of "the single greatest witch hunt of a politician in American history."

In Trump, white supremacists see one of their own. He denounced David Duke and the Ku Klux Klan, grudgingly. Bannon bragged that Breitbart News, the site he once published, was the preferred "platform" for the white supremacist "alt-right" movement. The alt-right's preferred actual home is Russia, which its leaders hail as "the great white power" and the specific power that helped ensure the election of Donald Trump.

To Trump whiteness is neither notional nor symbolic but is the very core of his power. In this, Trump is not singular. But whereas his forebears carried whiteness like an ancestral talisman, Trump cracked the glowing amulet open, releasing its eldritch energies. The repercussions are striking: Trump is the first president to have served in no public capacity before ascending to his perch. Perhaps more important, Trump is the first president to have publicly affirmed that his daughter is a "piece of ass." The mind seizes trying to imagine a black man extolling the virtues of sexual assault on tape ("And when you're a star, they let you do it"), fending off multiple accusations of said assaults, becoming immersed in multiple lawsuits for allegedly fraudulent business dealings, exhorting his followers to violence, and then strolling into the White House. But that is the point of white supremacy—to ensure that that which all others achieve with maximal effort, white people (and particularly white men) achieve with minimal qualification. Barack Obama delivered to black people the hoary message that in working twice as hard as white people, anything is possible. But Trump's counter is persuasive—work half as hard as black people and even more is possible.

A relationship between these two notions is as necessary as the relationship between these two men. It is almost as if the fact of

Obama, the fact of a black president, insulted Trump personally. The insult redoubled when Obama and Seth Meyers publicly humiliated Trump at the White House Correspondents' Dinner in 2011. But the bloody heirloom ensures the last laugh. Replacing Obama is not enough—Trump has made the negation of Obama's legacy the foundation of his own. And this too is whiteness. "Race is an idea, not a fact," writes the historian Nell Irvin Painter, and essential to the construct of a "white race" is the idea of not being a nigger. Before Barack Obama, niggers could be manufactured out of Sister Souljahs, Willie Hortons, Dusky Sallys, and Miscegenation Balls. But Donald Trump arrived in the wake of something more potent—an entire nigger presidency with nigger health care, nigger climate accords, nigger justice reform that could be targeted for destruction, that could be targeted for redemption, thus reifying the idea of being white. Trump truly is something new—the first president whose entire political existence hinges on the fact of a black president. And so it will not suffice to say Trump is a white man like all the others who rose to become president. He must be called by his correct name and rightful honorific—America's first white president.

II

The scope of Trump's commitment to whiteness is matched only by the depth of popular intellectual disbelief in it. We are now being told that support for Trump's "Muslim ban," his scapegoating of immigrants, his defenses of police brutality are somehow the natural outgrowth of the cultural and economic gap between Lena Dunham's America and Jeff Foxworthy's. The collective verdict holds that the Democratic Party lost its way when it abandoned commonsense everyday economic issues like job creation for the softer fare of social justice. The indictment continues: To their neoliberal economics, Democrats, and liberals at large, have married a condescending elitist affect that sneers at blue-collar culture and mocks white men as history's greatest monster and prime time television's biggest doofus. In this rendition, Donald Trump is not the product of white supremacy so much as the product of a backlash against contempt for white working people.

"We so obviously despise them, we so obviously condescend to them," Charles Murray, a conservative social scientist who cowrote *The Bell Curve,* recently told *The New Yorker's* George Packer. "The only slur you can use at a dinner party and get away with is to call somebody a redneck—that won't give you any problems in Manhattan."

"The utter contempt with which privileged Eastern liberals such as myself discuss red-state, gun-country, working-class America as ridiculous and morons and rubes," charged Anthony Bourdain, "is largely responsible for the upswell of rage and contempt and desire to pull down the temple that we're seeing now."

That black people who've lived under centuries of such derision and condescension have not yet been driven into the arms of Trump does not trouble these theoreticians. After all, in this analysis Trump's racism and the racism of his supporters are incidental to his rise. Indeed, the alleged glee with which liberals call out Trump's bigotry is assigned even more power than the bigotry itself. Ostensibly assaulted by campus protests, battered by theories of intersectionality, throttled by bathroom rights, a blameless white working class did the only thing any reasonable polity might: elect an orcish reality television star who insists on taking his intelligence briefings in picture-book form.

That Trump's rise was primarily powered by cultural resentment and economic reversal has become de rigueur among white pundits and thought leaders. But evidence for economic decline as a driving force among Trump's supporters is, at best, mixed. In a study of polling data, Gallup researchers Jonathan T. Rothwell and Pablo Diego-Rosell found that "people living in areas with diminished economic opportunity" were "somewhat more likely to support Trump." But the researchers also found that voters in their study who supported Trump generally had higher mean household incomes ($81,898) than those who did not ($77,046). Those who approved of Trump were "less likely to be unemployed and less likely to be employed part-time" than those who did not. They also tended to be from areas that were very white: "The racial and ethnic isolation of whites at the zip code level is one of the strongest predictors of Trump support."

An analysis of exit polls conducted during the presidential primaries estimated the median income for Trump supporters to be $72,000. But even this lower number is almost double the median household income for African Americans, and $15,000 above the American median. Trump's white support was not confined by income. According to Edison Research, Trump won whites making less than $50,000 by 20 points, whites making between 50,000 and $100,000 by 28 points, and whites making $100,000 or more by 14 points. This bears out the profile of Trump's primary base, but more important, it shows that Trump assembled a broad white coalition that ran the gamut from Joe the Dishwasher to Joe the Plumber to Joe the Banker. So when white pundits cast the elevation of Trump as the handiwork of an inscrutable white working class, they are being much too modest, declining to claim the credit their own economic class so richly deserves.

Trump's dominance among whites across class lines is of a piece with his larger dominance across nearly every white demographic. Trump won white women (+9) and white men (+31). He won white people with college degrees (+3) and white people without them (+37). He won young whites, age 18 to 29 (+4), adult whites, age 30 to 44 (+17), middle-age whites, age 45 to 64 (+28), and senior whites, age 65 and older (+19). According to Edison Research, Trump won whites in midwestern Illinois (+11), whites in mid-Atlantic Maryland (+12), and whites in sunbelt New Mexico (+5). In no state that Edison polled did Trump's white support dip below 40 percent. Hillary Clinton broke that plane in states as diverse as Florida, Utah,

Indiana, and Kentucky. From beer track to wine track, from soccer moms to NASCAR dads, Trump's performance among whites was dominant. According to *Mother Jones,* based on preelection polling data, if you only tallied the popular vote of "white America" to derive 2016 electoral votes, Trump would defeat Clinton 389 to 81, with the remaining 68 votes either a "toss-up" or unknown.

Part of Trump's dominance among whites is that he ran as a Republican, the party that has long cultivated white voters. Trump's share of the white vote was similar to that of Mitt Romney in 2012. But unlike the others, Trump secured this support by running against his party's leadership, against accepted campaign orthodoxy, and against all notions of decency. By his sixth month in office, embroiled in scandal after scandal, a Pew poll found Trump's approval rating underwater with every single demographic group. Every demographic group, that is, except one: voters who identified as white.

The focus on one sector of Trump voters—the white working class—is puzzling, given the breadth of his white coalition. Indeed, there is a kind of theater at work in which Trump is pawned off as a product of the white working class as opposed to a product of an entire whiteness that includes the very authors doing the pawning. The motive is clear: escapism. To accept that even now, some five decades after Martin Luther King Jr. was gunned down on a Memphis balcony, the bloody heirloom remains potent—even after a black president, and, in fact, strengthened by the fact of the black president—is to accept that racism remains, as it has since 1776, at the heart of the country's political life. That acceptance frustrates the aims of the left, which would much rather be talking about the class struggles that might entice the working white masses, instead of the racist struggles that those same masses have historically been agents and beneficiaries of. Moreover, to accept that whiteness brought us Donald Trump is to accept whiteness as an existential danger to the country and the world. But if the broad and remarkable white support of Donald Trump can be reduced to the righteous anger of a noble class of smallville firemen and observant evangelicals, mocked by Brooklyn hipsters and womanist professors into voting against their interests, then the threat of racism and whiteness, the threat of the heirloom, could be dismissed. Consciences could be eased and no deeper existential reckoning would be required. This transfiguration is not novel. It is a return to form. The tightly intertwined stories of the white working class and black Americans go back to the prehistory of the United States—and the use of one as a cudgel to silence the claims of the other goes back nearly as long. Like the black working class, the white working class originates in bondage—the former in the lifelong bondage of slavery, the latter in the temporary bondage of indenture. In their early seventeenth-century primordial state, these two classes were remarkably, though not totally, free of racist enmity. But by the eighteenth century the country's master class had begun etching race into law while phasing out indentured servitude in favor of a more enduring labor solution. From these and other changes of law and economy, a bargain emerged—the descendants of indenture would enjoy the full benefits of whiteness, the most definitional benefit being that they would never sink to the level of the slave. But if the bargain protected white workers from slavery, it did not protect them from near-slave wages nor backbreaking labor to attain them, and always there lurked a fear of being degraded to the level of "black" slave labor. This early white working class "expressed soaring desires to be rid of the age-old inequalities of Europe and of any hint of slavery," writes historian David Roediger. "They also expressed the rather more pedestrian goal of simply not being mistaken for slaves, or 'negers' or 'negurs.'"

Roediger relates the experience, around 1807, of a British investor who made the mistake of asking a white maid in New England whether her "master" was home. The maid admonished the investor, not merely for implying that she had a "master" and thus was a "sarvant" but for his basic ignorance of American hierarchy. "None but negers are sarvants," the maid is reported as saying. In law and economics and then custom, a racist distinction not limited to the household emerged between the "help," "the freemen," the white workers and the "servants," the "negers," the slaves. The former was virtuous and just, worthy of citizenship, progeny of Jefferson and, later, Jackson. The other was servile and parasitic, dim-witted and loafing, the children of African savagery. But the dignity accorded to white labor was situational and dependent upon the scorn heaped upon black labor, much as the honor accorded a "virtuous lady" was then dependent upon the derision directed at a "loose woman." And like chivalrous gentlemen who claim to honor a lady while raping the "whore," planters and their apologists could claim to honor white labor while driving the enslaved.

And so southern intellectual George Fitzhugh could, in a single stroke, deplore the exploitation of white free labor while defending the exploitation of enslaved black labor. Fitzhugh attacked white capitalists as "cannibals," feeding off the labor of their fellow whites. The white workers were " 'slaves without masters;' the little fish, who were food for all the larger." Fitzhugh dismissed a "professional man" who'd "amassed a fortune" by exploiting his fellow whites:

> Whilst making his fortune, he daily exchanged about one day of his light labor for thirty days of the farmer, the gardener, the miner, the ditcher, the sewing woman, and other common working people's labor. His capital was but the accumulation of the results of their labor; for common labor creates all capital. Their labor was more necessary and useful than his, and also more honorable and respectable. The more honorable, because they were contented with their situation and their profits, and not seeking to exploitate, by exchanging one day of their labor for many of other people's. To be exploited, ought to be more creditable than to exploite.

But whereas Fitzhugh imagined white workers as devoured by capital, he imagined black workers as elevated by enslavement. The slaveholder "provided for them, with almost parental affection"—even when the loafing slave "feigned to be unfit for labor." Fitzhugh proved too explicit—going so far as to argue that white laborers might be better off if enslaved. ("If white slavery be morally wrong," he wrote, "the Bible cannot be true.") But the argument that America's original sin was not deep-seated white supremacy but rather the exploitation of white labor by white capitalists— "white slavery"—proved durable. Indeed, the panic of white slavery lives on in our politics today. Black workers suffer—if it can be called that—because it was and is our lot. But when white workers suffer, something in nature has gone awry. And so an opioid epidemic is greeted with a call for treatment and sympathy, as all epidemics should be, while a crack epidemic is greeted with a call for mandatory minimums and scorn. Op-ed columns and articles are devoted to the sympathetic plight of working class whites when their life expectancy approaches levels that, for blacks, society simply accepts as normal. White slavery is sin. Nigger slavery is natural. This dynamic serves a very real purpose—the consistent awarding of grievance and moral high ground to that class of workers who, by the bonds of whiteness, stands closest to America's master class.

This is by design. Senator and celebrated statesman John C. Calhoun saw slavery as the explicit foundation for a democratic union among whites, working or not:

> With us the two great divisions of society are not the rich and poor, but white and black; and all the former, the poor as well as the rich belong to the upper class, and are respected and treated as equals.

On the eve of secession, Jefferson Davis, the eventual president of the Confederacy, pushed the idea further, arguing that such equality between the white working class and the white oligarchs could not exist at all without black slavery:

> I say it is there true that every mechanic asumes among us the position which only a master workman holds among you. Hence it is that the mechanic in our southern States is admitted to the table of his employer, converses with him on terms of equality—not merely political equality, but an actual equality—wherever the two men come in contact. The white laborers of the South are all of them men who are employed in what you would term the higher pursuits of labor among you. It is the presence of a lower caste, those lower by their mental and physical organization, controlled by the higher intellect of the white man, that gives this superiority to the white laborer. Menial services are not there performed by the white man. We have none of our brethren sunk to the degradation of being menials. That belongs to the lower race—the descendants of Ham.

Southern intellectuals found a shade of agreement with Northern white reformers who, while not agreeing on slavery, agreed on the nature of the most tragic victim of the emerging capitalism. "I was formerly like yourself, sir, a very warm advocate of the abolition of slavery," the labor reformer George Henry Evans argued in a letter to the abolitionist Gerrit Smith. "This was before I saw that there was white slavery." Evans was a putative ally of Smith and his fellow abolitionists. But still he asserted "the landless white" as worse off than the enslaved blacks, who at least enjoyed "surety of support in sickness and old age."

The invokers of "white slavery" held that there was nothing unique in the enslavement of blacks when measured against the enslavement of all workers. What evil there was in enslavement resulted from its status as subsidiary to that broader exploitation better seen among the country's noble laboring whites. Once the broader problem of white exploitation was solved, the subsidiary problem of black exploitation could be confronted or perhaps even fade away. Abolitionists focused on slavery were dismissed as "substitutionists" who wished to trade one form of slavery for another. "If I am less troubled concerning the Slavery prevalent in Charleston or New-Orleans," wrote the reformer Horace Greeley, "It is because I see so much Slavery in New-York, which appears to claim my first efforts."

The Civil War destroyed the charge of substitutionism and rendered the "white slavery" argument ridiculous. But its operating premises—white labor as noble archetype, and black labor as something else—lived on. This was a matter of rhetoric, not fact. The noble white labor archetype did not give white workers immunity from capitalism. It could not, in itself, break monopolies, alleviate white poverty in Appalachia or the South, nor bring a decent wage to immigrant ghettos in the North. But the model for America's original identity politics was set. Black lives literally did not matter and could be cast aside altogether as the price for even incremental gains for the white masses. It was this juxtaposition that allowed Theodore Bilbo to campaign in the 1930s as someone who would "raise the same kind of hell as President [Franklin D.] Roosevelt" and endorse lynching black people to keep them from voting.

The juxtaposition between the valid and even virtuous interests of the "working class" and the invalid and pathological interests of black Americans was not merely the province of blatant white supremacists like Bilbo. Acclaimed scholar, liberal hero, and future senator Daniel Patrick Moynihan, in his time working for President Nixon, approvingly quoted Nixon's formulation of the white working class: "A new voice" was beginning to make itself felt in the country. "It is a voice that has been silent too long," claimed Nixon, alluding to working-class whites. "It is a voice of people who have not taken to the streets before, who have not indulged in violence, who have not broken the law."

Moynihan's sense of history was creationist. It had been only eighteen years since the Cicero riots, eight years since Daisy and Bill Myers had been run out of Levittown, Pennsylvania, three years since Martin Luther King Jr. had been stoned while walking through Chicago's Marquette Park. But as the myth of the virtuous white working class was made central to American identity, its sins—which were parcel to the sins of white people of every class—needed to be rendered invisible. The fact was that working-class whites had been agents of racist terrorism since at least the draft riots of 1863, and that terrorism could not be neatly separated from the racist animus found in every class of whites. Indeed, in the era of lynching, it was often the daily newspapers that served to whip up the fury of the white masses by invoking the last species of property that all white men held in common—white women. But to conceal the breadth of white racism, these racist outbursts were often disregarded or treated not as racism, but as the unfortunate side effect of legitimate grievances against capital. By focusing solely on that sympathetic laboring class, the sins of whiteness itself were, and are still being, evaded.

When David Duke, a former grand wizard of the Ku Klux Klan, shocked the country in 1990 by almost winning the Republican primary for one of Louisiana's seats in the U.S. Senate, the apologists came out once again. They elided the obvious—that Duke had appealed to the base, racist instincts of a state whose schools are, at this very moment, still desegregating—and instead decided that something else was afoot. "There is a tremendous amount of anger and frustration among working-class whites, particularly where there is an economic downturn," a researcher told the *Los Angeles Times*. "These people feel left out; they feel government is not responsive to them." By this logic, postwar America—with its booming economy and low unemployment—should have been an egalitarian utopia and not the violently segregated country it actually was.

But this was the past made present. It was not important to these commentators that a large swath of Louisiana's white population thought it was a good idea to send a white supremacist who once fronted a terrorist organization to the nation's capital. Nor was it important that blacks in Louisiana had long felt left out. What was important was the fraying of an ancient bargain, and the potential degradation of white workers to the level of "negars." "A viable left must find a way to differentiate itself strongly from such analysis," Roediger wrote.

The challenge of differentiation has largely been ignored. Instead, an imagined white working class remains central to our politics and our cultural understanding of those politics, not simply when it comes to addressing broad economic issues but also when it comes to addressing racism. At its most sympathetic, this belief holds that all Americans—regardless of race—are exploited by the structure and particulars of an unfettered capitalist economy. The key, then, is to address those broader patterns that afflict the masses of all races, and those who suffer from those patterns more than others (blacks, for instance) will benefit disproportionately from that which benefits everyone. "These days, what ails working-class and middle-class blacks and Latinos is not fundamentally different from what ails their white counterparts," wrote Senator Barack Obama in 2006:

> Downsizing, outsourcing, automation, wage stagnation, the dismantling of employer-based health-care and pension plans, and schools that fail to teach young people the skills they need to compete in a global economy.

Obama allowed that "blacks in particular have been vulnerable to these trends"—but not so much because of racism but for reasons of geography and job sector distribution. This rendition—raceless anti-racism—marks the modern left, from New Democrat Bill Clinton to socialist Bernie Sanders. With few exceptions, there is little recognition among national liberal politicians that there is something systemic and particular in the relationship between black people and their country that might require specific policy solutions.

III

In 2016, Hillary Clinton offered more rhetorical support to the existence of systemic racism than any of her modern Democratic predecessors. She had to—black voters well remembered the previous Clinton administration as well as her previous campaign. While her husband's administration had touted the rising tide theory, it did so while slashing welfare and getting "tough on crime," a phrase that stood for specific policies but also as rhetorical bait for white voters. One is tempted to excuse Hillary Clinton for having to answer for the sins of her husband. But in her 2008 campaign, Hillary Clinton evoked the old dichotomy between white workers and loafing blacks, claiming to be the representative of "hardworking Americans, white Americans." By the end of the 2008 primary campaign against Barack Obama, her advisers were hoping someone would uncover the apocryphal "whitey tape," in which an angry Michelle Obama was alleged to have used the slur. During Bill Clinton's earlier campaign for president, it was Hillary Clinton herself who had employed the "super-predator" theory of conservative William Bennett, who cast "inner-city" children of that generation as "almost completely unmoralized" and the font of "a new generation of street criminals . . . the youngest, biggest and baddest generation any society has ever known." The "baddest" generation did not become super-predators. But by 2016, they were voters who judged Hillary Clinton's newfound consciousness to be lacking.

It's worth asking why the country has not been treated to a raft of sympathetic portraits of this "forgotten" young black electorate, forsaken by a Washington bought off by Davos elites and special interests. They too toil in this new global economy. The unemployment rate for young black people (20.6 percent) in July of 2016 was double that of young white people (9.9 percent). And since the late 1970s, William Julius Wilson and other sociologists following in his wake have noted the disproportionate effect that the decline in "hardworking" manufacturing jobs has had on African American communities. And if anyone should be angered by the devastation wreaked by the financial sector and a government that declined to prosecute the perpetrators, it is African Americans—the housing crisis was one of the primary drivers in the past twenty years of the wealth gap between black families and their country. But the cultural condescension and economic anxiety of black people is not news. Toiling blacks are in their proper state; toiling whites raise the specter of white slavery.

Moreover, a narrative of long-neglected working-class black voters, injured by globalization and the financial crisis, forsaken by out-of-touch politicians, and rightfully suspicious of a return of Clintonism, does not serve to cleanse the conscience of white people for having elected Donald Trump. Long-suffering working-class whites do. And though much has been written about the distance between elites and "Real America," the existence of a trans-class, mutually dependent tribe of white people is evident.

From Joe Biden, vice president:

They're all the people I grew up with. . . . And they're not racist. They're not sexist.

To Bernie Sanders, senator and candidate for president:

I come from the white working class, and I am deeply humiliated that the Democratic Party cannot talk to the people where I came from.

To Nicholas Kristof, columnist for *The New York Times*:

> My hometown, Yamhill, Ore., a farming community, is
> Trump country, and I have many friends who voted for
> Trump. I think they're profoundly wrong, but please don't
> dismiss them as hateful bigots.

These claims of fidelity and origin are not merely elite defenses of
an aggrieved class but also a sweeping dismissal of the concerns of
those who don't share kinship with white men. "You can't eat
equality," asserts Biden—a statement worthy of someone unthreat-
ened by the loss of wages brought on by an unwanted pregnancy, a
background-check box at the bottom of a job application, or deportation of a breadwinner. Within a week of Sanders lambasting
Democrats for not speaking to "the people" where he "came from,"
he was making an example of a woman who dreamed of representing the people she came from. Confronted with a young woman
who hoped to become the second Latina senator in American history, Sanders responded with a parody of the Clinton campaign:
"It is not good enough for someone to say, 'I'm a woman! Vote for
me!' No, that's not good enough. . . . One of the struggles that
you're going to be seeing in the Democratic Party is whether we go
beyond identity politics." The upshot—attacking one specimen of
identity politics after having invoked another—was unfortunate.

But other Sanders appearances proved more alarming. On
MSNBC, Sanders attributed Trump's success, in part, to his willingness to "not be politically correct." Sanders admitted that Trump
had "said some outrageous and painful things, but I think people
are tired of the same old, same old political rhetoric." Pressed on
the definition of political correctness, Sanders gave an answer
Trump would have doubtlessly approved of. "What it means is you
have a set of talking points which have been poll-tested and focus-
group-tested," Sanders explained. "And that's what you say rather

than what's really going on. And often, what you are not allowed to say are things which offend very, very powerful people."

This was a shocking definition of "political correctness" proffered by a politician of the left. But it matched a broader defense of Trump voters. "Some people think that the people who voted for Trump are racists and sexists and homophobes and just deplorable folks," Sanders said later. "I don't agree." This is not exculpatory. Every Trump voter is most certainly not a white supremacist, just as every white person in the Jim Crow South was not a white supremacist. But every Trump voter felt it acceptable to hand the fate of the country over to one.

One can, to some extent, understand politicians embracing a self-serving identity politics. Candidates for high office, like Sanders, have to cobble together a working coalition. The white working class is seen, understandably, as a large cache of potential votes, and capturing these votes, in the near term, necessitates the eliding of uncomfortable truths. But journalists have no such excuse. In the past year, Nicholas Kristof could be found repeatedly pleading with his fellow liberals not to dismiss his old comrades in the white working class as "bigots"—even when that bigotry is evidenced in his own reporting. A visit to Tulsa, Oklahoma, found the anthropological Kristof wondering why Trump voters support a president who threatens to cut the programs they depend upon. But the problem, according to Kristof's interviewees, isn't Trump's attack on benefits so much as an attack on *their benefits*. "There's a lot of wasteful spending, so cut other places," a man tells Kristof. When Kristof pushes his subjects to identify that wasteful spending, a fascinating target is revealed—"Obama phones," a fevered conspiracy theory that turned a longstanding government program into a scheme through which the (former) president gave away free cellphones to undeserving blacks. Kristof doesn't shift his analysis based on this comment, and continues on as though it were never said, aside from a one-sentence fact-check tucked into parentheses.

Observing a Trump supporter in the act of deploying racism

does not much perturb Kristof. That is because his defenses of the innate goodness of Trump voters and of the innate goodness of the white working class are in fact defenses of neither. On the contrary, the white working class functions in the rhetoric and argument not as a real community of people so much as a tool to quiet the demands of those who want a more inclusive America.

Mark Lilla's essay "The End of Identity Liberalism" is perhaps the most profound specimen of this genre. Lilla denounces the perversion of liberalism into "a kind of moral panic about racial, gender and sexual identity," which distorted its message "and prevented it from becoming a unifying force capable of governing." Liberals have turned away from their working-class base, according to Lilla, and must look to the "pre-identity liberalism" of Bill Clinton and Franklin D. Roosevelt. You would never know from this essay that Bill Clinton was one of the most skillful identity politicians of his era— flying to see a black and lobotomized Ricky Ray Rector executed, upstaging Jesse Jackson at his own conference, signing the Defense of Marriage Act—consistently signaling his attachment to "Real America." Nor would you know that "pre-identity" liberal champion Roosevelt depended on the literally lethal identity of politics of a white supremacist "solid South." The name Barack Obama does not appear in Lilla's essay, and he never attempts to grapple, one way or the other, with the fact that it was identity politics—the possibility of a first black president—that brought a record number of black voters to the polls, winning the election for the Democratic Party, and thus enabling the deliverance of the ancient liberal goal of national health care. "Identity politics . . . is largely expressive, not persuasive," Lilla claims. "Which is why it never wins elections—but can lose them." That Trump ran and won on identity politics is beyond Lilla's powers of conception. Whatever appeals to the white working class is ennobled. What appeals to black workers, and all others outside the tribe, is dastardly identitarianism. All politics are identity politics—except the politics of white people, the politics of the blood heirloom.

White tribalism haunts even more nuanced and skilled writers. George Packer's essay "The Unconnected" is a lengthy plea for liberals to focus more on the white working class, a population that "has succumbed to the ills that used to be associated with the black urban 'underclass.'" Packer believes these ills, and the Democratic party's failure to respond to them, explain much of Trump's rise. He offers no opinion polls to weigh their views on "elites," much less their views on racism. He offers no sense of how their views and relationship to Trump differ from those of other workers and other whites.

That is likely because any empirical evaluation of the relationship between Trump and the white working class would reveal that one adjective in that phrase was doing more work than the other. In 2016, Trump enjoyed majority or plurality support among every economic branch of whites. It is true that his strongest support, among whites, came from those making $50,000 to $99,999. This would be something more than working class in many nonwhite neighborhoods, but even if one accepts that branch as the "working class," the difference in vote is revealing. Sixty-one percent of whites in this working class supported Trump. Only 24 percent of Hispanics and 11 percent of blacks did. Indeed, the plurality of all voters making under $100,000 and the majority making under $50,000 voted for the Democratic candidate. So when Packer laments the fact that "Democrats can no longer really claim to be the party of working people—not white ones, anyway," he commits a kind of category error. The real problem is that Democrats aren't the party of white people—working or otherwise. White workers are not divided by the fact of labor from other white demographics; they are divided from all other laborers by the fact of their whiteness.

Packer's essay was published before the election, and so the vote tally was not available. But it should not be surprising that a candidate making a direct appeal to racism would drive up the numbers among white voters, given that racism has long been a dividing line for the national parties, at least since the civil rights movement. Packer finds inspiration for his thesis in West Virginia—a state that remained Democratic into the 1990s before turning decisively Republican, at least at the level of presidential politics. This relatively late rightward movement evidences, to Packer, a shift "that couldn't be attributed just to the politics of race." This is likely true—the politics of race are, themselves, never attributable "just to the politics of race." The history of slavery is also about the growth of international capitalism, the history of lynching must be seen in the light of anxiety over the growing independence of women, and the civil rights movement can't be disentangled from the Cold War. Thus, to say that the rise of Donald Trump is about more than race is to make an empty statement—one that is small comfort to those who live under its boot. And the dint of racism is not hard to detect in West Virginia. In the 2008 Democratic primary in the state, 95 percent of that state's voters were white. Twenty percent of those— one in five—openly admitted that race was influencing their vote, and more than 80 percent voted for Hillary Clinton over Barack Obama. Four years later, an incumbent Obama lost in ten counties in West Virginia to Keith Russell Judd, a white felon incarcerated in a federal prison who racked up more than 40 percent of the Democratic primary vote. A simple thought experiment should be run here—can one imagine a black felon in a federal prison running in a primary against an incumbent white president doing the same?

But racism occupies a mostly passive place in Packer's essay. There's no attempt to understand why black and brown workers, victimized by the same new economy and cosmopolitan elite Packer lambastes, did not join the Trump revolution. Like Kristof, Packer is gentle with his subjects. When a white woman "exploded" and told Packer, "I want to eat what I want to eat, and for them to tell me I can't eat French fries or Coca-Cola—no way," he sees this as rebellion against "the moral superiority of elites." In fact, this elite conspiracy dates back to 1894, when the government first began advising Americans on their diets. As recently as 2003, President

George W. Bush spoke of the benefits of his HealthierUS initiative, explaining an exciting healthcare plan that "says if you exercise and eat healthy food, you will live longer." But Packer never allows himself to wonder whether the explosion he witnessed had anything to do with the fact that similar advice now came from the country's first black First Lady. Packer concludes in true tribal fashion, passively asserting that Obama has left the country "more divided and angrier than most Americans can remember," a statement that is likely true only because most Americans identify as white. Certainly the men and women forced to live in the wake of the beating of John Lewis, the lynching of Emmett Till, the firebombing of Percy Julian's home, and the assassinations of Martin Luther King Jr. and Medgar Evers, which is to say those forced to carry the weight of slavery, would disagree.

The maintenance of white honor and whiteness remains at the core of liberal American thinking. Left politics are not exempt. The triumph of Trump's campaign of bigotry presented the problematic spectacle of an American president succeeding at best in spite of his racism and possibly even because of it. Trump removed the questions of racism from the euphemistic and plausibly deniable to the realm of the overt and freely claimed. This presented the country's thinking class with a dilemma. It simply could not be that Hillary Clinton was correct when she asserted that a large group of Americans was endorsing a president because of bigotry. The implications—that systemic bigotry is still central to our politics, that the country is susceptible to that bigotry, that the salt-of-the-earth Americans whom we lionize in our culture and politics are not so different from those same Americans who grin back at us in lynching photos, that Calhoun's aim of a pan-Caucasian embrace between workers and capitalists still endures—are just too dark. Leftists would have to cope with the failure—yet again—of class unity in the face of racism. Technocrats and centrists would find no solace as their class proved just as susceptible. Incorporating all of this into an analysis of America and the path forward proved too much to ask. Instead, the response has largely been an argument aimed at emotion—the summoning of the white working class, emblem of America's hardscrabble roots, inheritor of its pioneer spirit, as a shield against the horrific and empirical evidence of trenchant bigotry.

Packer dismisses the Democratic Party as a coalition of "rising professionals and diversity." The dismissal is derived from Lawrence Summers (of all people), the economist and former Harvard president, who labels the Democratic Party little more than "a coalition of the cosmopolitan élite and diversity." The inference is that the party has forgotten how to speak on hard economic issues and prefers discussing presumably softer cultural issues like "diversity." It's worth unpacking what, precisely, falls under this rubric of "diversity"—resistance against the monstrous incarceration of legions of black men, resistance against the destruction of health providers for poor women, resistance against the effort to deport parents, resistance against a policing whose sole legitimacy is rooted in brute force, resistance against a theory of education that preaches "no excuses" to black and brown children, even as excuses are proffered for those "too big to jail." That this suite of concerns, taken together, can be dismissed by both Summers and a brilliant journalist like Packer as "diversity" simply evidences the safe space they enjoy. Because of their identity.

IV

When Barack Obama came into office in 2009, he believed that he could work with "sensible" conservatives by embracing aspects of their policy as his own. Instead he found that his very imprimatur made that impossible. Mitch McConnell announced that the GOP's primary goal was not to find common ground but to make Obama a "one-term president." A healthcare plan derived from a Republican governor and pioneered by a conservative think tank was suddenly rendered as socialism and, not coincidentally, a form of reparations when proposed by Obama. The first black president found that he was personally toxic to the GOP base. An entire political party was organized around the explicit aim of negating Obama. It was thought by Obama and others that this toxicity was the result of a relentless assault waged by Fox News and right-wing talk radio. Trump's genius was understanding that it was something more, that it was a hunger for revanche so strong that a political novice and accused rapist could topple the leadership of one major party and throttle the presumed favorite of another.

"I could stand in the middle of Fifth Avenue and shoot somebody and I wouldn't lose any voters," Trump once bragged. This statement should be met with only a modicum of doubt. Trump mocked the disabled, bragged of sexual assault, endured multiple accusations of sexual assault, fired an FBI director, sent his minions to mislead the public about his motives, personally exposed that lie by boldly stating his aim to scuttle an investigation into his possible collusion with a foreign power, then bragged about that same obstruction in the White House to representatives of that same foreign power. It is utterly impossible to conjure a black facsimile of Donald Trump—to imagine Obama, say, implicating an opponent's father in the assassination of an American president or comparing his physical endowment with that of another candidate and successfully capturing the presidency. Trump, more than any other politician, understood the valence of the bloody heirloom and the great power in not being a nigger.

But the power is ultimately suicidal. Trump evidences this too. In a recent *New Yorker* article, a former Russian military officer pointed out that Russian interference in the election could only succeed where "necessary conditions" and an "existing background" were present. In America that "existing background" was a persistent racism and the "necessary condition" was the symbolic threat of a black president. The two related factors hobbled America's ability to safeguard its electoral system. As late as July 2016, a majority of the Republican Party doubted that Barack Obama was born in the United States, which is to say they did not view him as a legitimate president. The party's politicians acted accordingly, famously refusing his Supreme Court nominee a hearing, and then most fatefully refusing to work with the administration to defend the country against the Russian attack. Before the election, Obama found no takers among Republicans for a bipartisan response, and Obama himself, underestimating Trump and thus underestimating the power of whiteness, believed the Republican nominee too objectionable to actually win. In this Obama was, tragically, wrong. And so the most powerful country in the world has handed over all of its affairs—the prosperity of an entire economy, the security of some 300 million citizens, the purity of its water, the viability of its air, the safety of its food, the future of its vast system of education, the soundness of its national highways, airways, and railways, the apocalyptic potential of its nuclear arsenal—to a carnival barker who introduced the phrase "grab 'em by the pussy" into the national lexicon. It is as if the white tribe united in demonstration to say, "If a black man can be president, then any white man—no matter how fallen—can be president." And in that perverse way the democratic dreams of Jefferson and Jackson were fulfilled.

The American tragedy now being wrought is larger than most imagine and will not end with Trump. In recent times, whiteness as an overt political tactic has been restrained by a kind of cordiality that held that its overt invocation would scare off "moderate" whites. This has proved to be only half-true at best. Trump's legacy will be exposing the patina of decency for what it is and revealing just how much a demagogue can get away with. It does not take much to imagine another politician, wiser in the ways of Washington, schooled in the methodology of governance, now liberated from the pretense of anti-racist civility, doing a much more effective job than Trump.

It has long been an axiom among certain black writers and thinkers that whiteness endangers the bodies of black people in the immediate sense, but the larger threat was to white people them-selves, the shared country, and even the whole world. There is an impulse to blanch at this sort of grandiosity. When Du Bois claims that slavery was "singularly disastrous for modern civilization" or Baldwin claims that whites "have brought humanity to the edge of oblivion . . . because they think they are white," the instinct is to claim exaggeration. But there really is no other way to read the presidency of Donald Trump. The first white president in Ameri-can history is also its most dangerous president—and made more dangerous still by the fact that those charged with analyzing him cannot name his essential nature, because they too are implicated in it.

But not damned by it. There is nothing done in the service of whiteness that places it beyond the boundaries of human behavior and history. Indeed, what makes the epoch of Indian killing and African slavery, of "war capitalism," as Sven Beckert dubs it, so frightening is how easily its basic actions cohere with all we know of human greed and the temptations of power. There is something terrible in being able to imagine oneself as the plunderer, some-thing discomfiting in knowing that moral high ground is neither biological nor divine. This understanding does not require a flight of fantasy. Americans, too, belong to a class—one responsible for and intrinsically tied to a history of torture, bombings, and coups d'état carried out in our name. And Trump has only heaped more upon that burden. In the global context, perhaps, we Americans are all white.

Still there was nothing inevitable about Donald Trump's elec-tion, and while great damage has been done by his election, at the time of this writing it is not yet the end of history. What is needed now is a resistance intolerant of self-exoneration, set against blind-ing itself to evil—even in the service of warring against other evils. One must be able to name the bad bargain that whiteness strikes with its disciples—and still be able to say that it is this bargain, not a mass hypnosis, that has held through boom and bust.

And there can be no conflict between the naming of whiteness and the naming of the degradation brought about by an unrestrained capitalism, by the privileging of greed and the legal encouragement to hoarding and more elegant plunder. I have never seen a contradiction between calling for reparations and calling for a living wage, on calling for legitimate law enforcement and single-payer health care. They are related—but cannot stand in for one another. I see the fight against sexism, racism, poverty, and even war finding their union not in synonymity but in their ultimate goal—a world more humane.

ACKNOWLEDGMENTS

THIS BOOK WAS MADE POSSIBLE BY
The Atlantic, which, from fact check to paycheck,
supported me through these eight years.

ABOUT THE TYPE

This book was set in Bembo, a typeface based on an old-style Roman face that was used for Cardinal Pietro Bembo's tract *De Aetna* in 1495. Bembo was cut by Francesco Griffo (1450–1518) in the early sixteenth century for Italian Renaissance printer and publisher Aldus Manutius (1449–1515). The Lanston Monotype Company of Philadelphia brought the well-proportioned letterforms of Bembo to the United States in the 1930s.

FROM NATIONAL BOOK
AWARD-WINNING AUTHOR

TA·NEHISI COATES

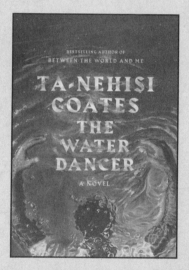

A bracingly original vision of slavery and freedom,
The Water Dancer is the story of young Hiram Walker,
whose struggle to master his mysterious magical gift, solve
the riddle of his past, and reunite with the people he loves
will take him from Virginia's proud plantations to desperate
guerrilla cells in the wilderness, from utopian movements in
the North to the hidden path to true freedom.

ONE WORLD

A ONE WORLD HARDCOVER AND EBOOK
OneWorldLit.com | RandomHouseBooks.com